The 100
Most Important Events
in Christian History

The 100
Most Important Events
in Christian History

A. Kenneth Curtis
J. Stephen Lang
Randy Petersen

Fleming H. Revell
A Division of Baker Book House Co
Grand Rapids, Michigan 49516

© 1991 by Christian History Institute

Published by Fleming H. Revell
a division of Baker Book House Company
P.O. Box 6287, Grand Rapids, MI 49516-6287

New paperback edition published 1998

Eighth printing, September 2001

Previously published under the title *Dates with Destiny*

Printed in the United States of America

Library of Congress Cataloging-in-Publication Data

Curtis, A. Kenneth.
    [Dates with destiny]
    The 100 most important events in Christian history / A. Kenneth Curtis, J. Stephen Lang, Randy Petersen.—New pbk. ed.
       p.   cm.
    Originally published: Dates with destiny. c1991.
    Includes index.
    ISBN 0-8007-5644-4 (paper)
    1. Church history. 2. Church history—Chronology. I. Lang, J. Stephen. II. Petersen, Randy.
III. Title.
BR148.C77 1998
270'.02'02—dc21

    97-35333

Unless otherwise indicated, Scripture quotations are from the King James Version of the Bible.

Scripture quotations identified NIV are from the HOLY BIBLE, NEW INTERNATIONAL VERSION®. NIV®. Copyright © 1973, 1978, 1984 by International Bible Society. Used by permission of Zondervan Publishing House. All rights reserved.

Scripture quotations identified RSV are from the Revised Standard Version of the Bible, copyright 1946, 1952, 1971 by the Division of Christian Education of the National Council of the Churches of Christ in the USA. Used by permission.

For current information about all releases from Baker Book House, visit our web site:
http://www.bakerbooks.com

Preface

What are the ten most important things that have happened in your life in the past five years? Now ask your father, daughter, wife or husband, or any two close friends to answer the same question in regard to you. You will quickly see how capable we are of attaching different significance to events even among those who live in the closest intimacy and proximity.

Right at the start let us admit that no one has the final word on what are the most important dates in the history of the church. Indeed, God's list would probably differ significantly from any we could make.

We have not intended to set ourselves up as the authoritative arbiters of what finally counts in the life of the church over the centuries. Instead we have attempted to give an overview of events in the perplexing history of the people of God that will provide the nonhistorian and nonspecialist with a convenient look at major contours and catalysts that have shaped Christianity.

Many Christians today want to know more about the roots of their faith and how many of the teachings and practices of their churches came into existence. But few have the time or inclination to take on a multi-volume academic work. This kind of book should help in serving that interest. Non-Christians will find this a handy reference to acquaint themselves with major people, movements, meanings, and events in the long history of Christianity.

We started our consideration of church history after (or at least outside of) the events recorded in the New Testament. Obviously, the Resurrection, the conversion of Paul, the Council of Jerusalem, and so on are important dates in church history, but where does one stop? We judged it best, therefore, to select only events not recorded in the New Testament.

Rather than rank the events in any kind of order of importance, we have presented them in chronological order, to give a kind of tour through the centuries.

Some worthy selections were left out because we felt that we could incorporate them into another. For example, while a survey that we did included both the posting of Luther's Ninety-five Theses and the Diet of Worms, we have included only the former to encompass both.

Other events were included not only for their immediate significance but what they led to or how things might have been greatly different had they not happened. For example, the Synod of Whitby will not go down as one of the great councils of the church, but it is of tremendous importance that the English church chose to unite with Rome at that time. History could have been vastly different had they taken the other alternative.

We also introduced several entries that may seem contrived and artificial. The world did not change, nor did the church, on the birth dates of Bach and Handel, but not to include the contribution of great music to the life of worship would be defective indeed. Therefore, several entries are included primarily for their symbolic value.

We avoided inclusions from the last two decades, because, although we saw some attractive alternatives, we are too close to those events to have the necessary perspective.

Some may accuse us of weighting our choices in favor of the West, males, Protestants, and evangelicals. This is partly unavoidable but no doubt also reflective of our bias.

But, as noted above, we make no claims to finality in this list and from the beginning have expected brisk response from readers who will want to challenge us on possibilities that they think must be included and others they think could have been omitted. So we invite readers to write and let us know what you think and detail your reasons. If response warrants we will issue a second volume of "more important dates in church history." Those of you who just want advance word about a second volume are also invited to write. Write to Ken Curtis, Christian History Institute, Box 540, Worcester, PA 19490, or FAX to 215-584-4610.

When I was editor of *Christian History* magazine, we wrote to our subscribers and asked them to tell us what dates they thought should be on the list. We then collated and tabulated these and sent the list back out to subscribers, asking them to check off the selections they agreed with, cross out the ones they disagreed with, and add others that were not on our list. Their replies generated a new list. A survey was also sent to all of the members of the American Society of Church History, a group of professional church historians. The selections included in this book took the above surveys into view, but I must take responsibility for the final choices.

All along in these choices, we have been fully aware that some of the most important things are hardest to identify and quantify. We are like the treasurer in the temple, who in all probability would have missed the importance of the "widow's mite." Jesus made it clear that love was the foremost distinguishing mark of His followers. He also spoke most approvingly of simple things like the cup of water given in His name. Many of the entries reflect these basic qualities of Christianity, and others most surely do not. Most of what is of eternal importance will not be known until that day when the judge of us all shows us what is *really* the wheat and the chaff.

KEN CURTIS

Dates With Destiny

These are the dates we identified as some of the most important ones in church history.

Year	Event
64	The Fire in Rome
70	Titus Destroys Jerusalem
C. 150	Justin Martyr Writes His *Apology*
C. 156	The Martyrdom of Polycarp
177	Irenaeus Becomes Bishop of Lyons
C. 196	Tertullian Begins to Write Christian Books
C. 205	Origen Begins Writing
251	Cyprian Writes *On the Unity of the Church*
270	Anthony Begins His Life as a Hermit
312	The Conversion of Constantine
325	The Council of Nicea
367	Athanasius's Letter Recognizes the New Testament Canon
385	Bishop Ambrose Defies the Empress
387	Conversion of Augustine
398	John Chrysostom Becomes Bishop of Constantinople
405	Jerome Completes the Vulgate
432	Patrick Goes as Missionary to Ireland
451	The Council of Chalcedon
529	Benedict of Nursia Establishes His Monastic Order
563	Columba Goes as a Missionary to Scotland
590	Gregory I Becomes Pope
664	Synod of Whitby
716	Boniface Sets Out as Missionary
731	The Venerable Bede Completes His *Ecclesiastical History of the English Nation*
732	The Battle of Tours
800	Charlemagne Crowned Emperor
863	Cyril and Methodius Evangelize Slavs
909	Monastery Established at Cluny
988	Conversion of Vladimir, Prince of Russia
1054	The East-West Schism
1093	Anselm Becomes Archbishop of Canterbury
1095	Pope Urban II Launches the First Crusade
1115	Bernard Founds the Monastery at Clairvaux

C. 1150   Universities of Paris and Oxford Founded
    1173   Peter Waldo Founds the Waldensians
    1206   Francis of Assisi Renounces Wealth
    1215   The Fourth Lateran Council
    1273   Thomas Aquinas Completes Work on *Summa Theologica*
    1321   Dante Completes *The Divine Comedy*
    1378   Catherine of Siena Goes to Rome to Heal the Great Schism
C. 1380   Wycliffe Oversees English Bible Translation
    1415   John Hus Burned at the Stake
    1456   Johann Gutenberg Produces the First Printed Bible
    1478   Establishment of the Spanish Inquisition
    1498   Savonarola Executed
    1512   Michelangelo Completes the Sistine Chapel Ceiling
    1517   Martin Luther Posts His Ninety-five Theses
    1523   Zwingli Leads Swiss Reformation
    1525   Anabaptist Movement Begins
    1534   Henry VIII's Act of Supremacy
    1536   John Calvin Publishes *The Institutes of the Christian Religion*
    1540   The Pope Approves the Jesuits
    1545   Opening of the Council of Trent
    1549   Cranmer Produces the Book of Common Prayer
    1559   John Knox Returns to Scotland to Lead Reformation
    1572   Saint Bartholomew's Day Massacre
1608–1609   John Smyth Baptizes the First Baptists
    1611   Publication of the King James Bible
    1620   Pilgrims Sign the Mayflower Compact
    1628   Comenius Driven From His Homeland
    1646   The Westminster Confession of Faith
    1648   George Fox Founds the Society of Friends
    1662   Rembrandt Completes the *Return of the Prodigal Son*
    1675   Philip Jacob Spener Publishes *Pia Desideria*
    1678   John Bunyan's *The Pilgrim's Progress* Published
    1685   The Births of Johann Sebastian Bach and George Frederic Handel
    1707   Publication of Isaac Watt's *Hymns and Spiritual Songs*
    1727   Awakening at Herrnhut Launches Moravian Brethren
    1735   Great Awakening Under Jonathan Edwards
    1738   John Wesley's Conversion
    1780   Robert Raikes Begins Sunday Schools
    1793   William Carey Sails for India
    1807   The British Parliament Votes to Abolish the Slave Trade
    1811   The Campbells Begin the Disciples of Christ

1812   Adoniram and Ann Judson Sail for India

1816   Richard Allen Founds African Methodist Episcopal Church

1817   Elizabeth Fry Begins Ministry to Women in Prison

1830   Charles G. Finney's Urban Revivals Begin

C. 1830   John Nelson Darby Helps Start Plymouth Brethren

1833   John Keble's Sermon "National Apostasy" Initiates the Oxford Movement

1854   Hudson Taylor Arrives in China

1854   Søren Kierkegaard Publishes Attacks on Christendom

1854   Charles Haddon Spurgeon Becomes Pastor in London

1855   Dwight L. Moody's Conversion

1857   David Livingstone Publishes *Missionary Travels*

1865   William Booth Founds the Salvation Army

1870   Pope Pius IX Proclaims the Doctrine of Papal Infallibility

1886   Student Volunteer Movement Begins

1906   Azusa Street Revival Launches Pentecostalism

1910–1915   Publication of *The Fundamentals* Launches Fundamentalist Movement

1919   Karl Barth's *Commentary on Romans* Is Published

1921   First Christian Radio Broadcast

1934   Cameron Townsend Begins Summer Institute of Linguistics

1945   Dietrich Bonhoeffer Executed by Nazis

1948   World Council of Churches Is Formed

1949   Billy Graham's Los Angeles Crusade

1960   Beginnings of the Modern Charismatic Renewal

1962   Second Vatican Council Begins

1963   Martin Luther King, Jr., Leads March on Washington

1966–1976   Chinese Church Grows Despite Cultural Revolution

The 100
Most Important Events
in Christian History

64
The Fire in Rome

Nero at the burning of Rome.

Without the Roman Empire, Christianity might never have spread so successfully. You could say the empire was a tinderbox awaiting the spark of Christian faith.

The empire's unifying elements aided in the expansion of the Gospel: Roman roads made travel easier than it had ever been before; throughout the realm, people spoke Greek; and the mighty Roman army kept peace. As a result of the increased mobility, pockets of migrant craftsmen settled for a time in a major city—Rome, Corinth, Athens, or Alexandria—then moved on to another.

Christianity stepped into an open climate, religiously. In a sort of "new age" movement many people had begun to embrace eastern religions—the worship of Isis, Dionysus, Mithras, Cybele, and others. Worshipers searched for new beliefs, but some of these religions had been declared illegal, because they were suspected of offensive rituals. Other faiths were officially recognized—like Judaism, which had enjoyed a protected position since the days of Julius Caesar, though its monotheism and biblical revelation set it apart from the other ways of worship.

Taking full advantage of the situation, Christian missionaries traveled throughout the empire. In the Jewish synagogues, craftsmen's quarters, and tenements, they shared their message and won converts. Soon all the major cities, including the imperial capital, had churches.

Rome, center of the empire, drew people like a magnet. Paul had wanted to visit the city (Romans 1:10–12), and by the time he wrote his letter to the Roman church, he could greet many Christians there by name (Romans 16:3–15)—perhaps because he had met them on his travels.

When Paul arrived in Rome, he did

so in chains. The Book of Acts closes with the apostle under rather loose house arrest, receiving guests and teaching them.

Tradition tells us that Peter, too, spent time with the Roman church. Though we have no definite numbers on it, we can guess that under the leadership of these two men the church grew strong, including nobles and soldiers as well as craftsmen and servants.

For three decades the Roman officials perceived Christianity as a branch of Judaism—a legal religion—and had little interest in persecuting the new Jewish "sect." But many Jews, scandalized by the new faith, went on the attack, even trying to draft Rome into the conflict.

Roman obliviousness to the situation may be shown in the report of the Roman historian Tacitus. In one of the tenements of Rome he reports a disturbance among the Jews at the instigation of a certain "Chrestus." Tacitus could have misheard; the people were probably arguing about *Christos,* that is, Christ.

By A.D. 64, some Roman officials had begun to realize that Christianity differed significantly from Judaism. The Jews rejected the Christians, and more and more others saw Christianity as an illegal religion. Even before Rome's fatal fire, public opinion may have begun to turn against the fledgling faith. Though the Romans eagerly accepted new gods, Christianity was not willing to share honors with any other faith. As Christians challenged the deep-set polytheism of Rome, the empire struck back.

On July 19 a fire broke out in a working-class section of Rome. For seven days it raged, consuming block after block of crowded tenements. Ten of the fourteen wards were destroyed, and many people died.

Legend has it that Emperor Nero "fiddled" while Rome burned. Many of his contemporaries thought Nero was responsible for the fire. When the city was rebuilt, at great public expense, Nero seized a substantial hunk of land for himself and built his Golden Palace on the site. The fire may have been a quick way to achieve urban renewal.

Deflecting the blame from himself, the emperor established a convenient scapegoat—the Christians. *They* had set the fire, he charged. As a result, Nero vowed to hunt them down and have them killed.

The first wave of Roman persecution lasted from shortly after the fire until Nero's death in 68. With barbaric bloodthirstiness, he had Christians crucified and set afire. Their bodies lined the Roman roads, providing torchlight. Christians dressed in animal skins were mauled by dogs in the arena. According to tradition, both Peter and Paul became martyrs in Nero's persecution; Paul was beheaded, and Peter was crucified upside-down.

But persecution occurred sporadically and remained localized. An emperor might heat up the persecution for ten years or so, but a time of peace would follow, only to be abruptly broken when a local governor lashed out at the Christians in his area—with Rome's blessing. This pattern lasted for two and a half centuries.

Tertullian, a second-century Christian writer, said, "Blood of the martyrs is the seed of the Church." Amazingly, each time persecution erupted, there were more Christians to persecute. In his first letter, Peter had encouraged Christians to endure suffering, confident of the ultimate victory and rule that would be established in Christ (1 Peter 5:8–11). The growth of the church under such pressure in part proved his words.

70
Titus Destroys Jerusalem

At the Roman Forum, in Rome, the Arch of Titus celebrates his victory in Jerusalem.

Gessius Florus loved money and hated Jews. As Roman procurator, he ruled Judea, caring little for their religious sensibilities. When tax revenues were low, he seized silver from the Temple. In 66, as the uproar against him grew, he sent troops into Jerusalem to crucify and massacre some of the Jews. Florus's action sparked the explosion of a rebellion that had been sizzling for some time.

For the previous century, Rome had not handled the Jews very well. First Rome had propped up the hated usurper Herod the Great. For all the beautiful public buildings he erected, Herod could not buy his way into the people's hearts.

Herod's son and successor, Archelaus, was so bad that the people cried to Rome for relief. Rome obliged by sending a series of governors—Pontius Pilate, Felix, Festus, and Florus. These and others had the unenviable task of keeping the peace in a volatile land.

The Jews' independent streak had never died. They looked back with fondness to the days of the Maccabees, when they had thrown off the yoke of their Syrian overlords. Now their own petty divisions and the awesome rise of Rome had put them back under the thumb of foreigners.

The heartbeat of revolution had continued during Herod's rule. Zealots and Pharisees, each in their own way, looked for change to occur. Messianic fervor ran high. When Jesus warned that people would say, "Here is the Christ—or there!" He wasn't kidding. That was the spirit of the age.

At Masada (a virtually impregnable hunk of rock that looked out over the Dead Sea, where Herod had built a palace and the Romans had erected a fortress), the Jewish revolt would have its beginning—and its bitter end.

Inspired by the atrocities of Florus, some crazy Zealots decided to attack the fortress. Amazingly they won,

slaughtering the Roman army encamped there.

In Jerusalem, the Temple captain declared open rebellion against Rome by stopping the daily sacrifices for Caesar. Soon all Jerusalem was in an uproar, expelling or killing the Roman troops. Judea revolted, then Galilee. For a brief time it looked as if the Jews might pull an upset.

Cestius Gallus, the Roman governor of the region, marched from Syria with 20,000 soldiers. He besieged Jerusalem for six months and failed, leaving behind 6,000 dead Roman soldiers and a fair amount of weaponry that the Jewish defenders picked up and used.

Emperor Nero sent Vespasian, a decorated general, to quell the revolt. Vespasian nibbled away at the rebels' strength, putting down the opposition in Galilee, then Transjordan, then Idumea. Then he circled in on Jerusalem.

But before the coup de grace, Vespasian was called back to Rome. Nero had died. A leadership struggle concluded with the eastern armies calling for Vespasian to be emperor. In one of his first imperial acts, he appointed his son, Titus, to conduct the Jewish War.

The tide had turned for Jerusalem, now isolated from the rest of the nation. Factions within the city fought over defense strategies. As the siege wore on, people were dying from starvation and plague. The high priest's wife, who once basked in luxury, scavenged for crumbs in the city streets.

Meanwhile the Romans employed new war machines to hurl boulders against the city walls. Battering rams assaulted the fortifications. Jewish defenders fought all day and struggled to rebuild the walls at night. Eventually the Romans broke through the outer wall, then the second wall, finally the third wall. Still the Jews fought, scurrying to the Temple as their last line of defense.

That was the end for the valiant Jewish defenders—and for the Temple. The Jewish historian Josephus said that Titus wanted to preserve the Temple, but his soldiers were so angry at their resilient opponents that they burned it.

The fall of Jerusalem essentially ended the revolt. Jews were slaughtered or captured and sold as slaves. The Zealot band who had taken Masada stayed there for three years. When the Romans finally built their siege ramp and invaded the mountain fortress, they found the defenders dead. They had committed suicide to avoid being captured by foreigners.

The Jewish revolt marked the end of the Jewish state, at least until modern times.

The destruction of Herod's Temple signified a change in the Jews' worship. When the Babylonians had destroyed Solomon's Temple, in 586 B.C., the Jews had established synagogues, where they could study God's law. The destruction of Herod's Temple ended the Jewish sacrificial system and forced them to rely on the synagogue, which increased in importance.

Where were the Christians during the Jewish revolt? Remembering Christ's warning (Luke 21:20–24), when they saw armies surrounding Jerusalem, they fled. They refused to take up arms against the Romans and escaped to Pella, in Transjordan.

Once the Jewish nation and its Temple had been destroyed, the Christians could no longer rely on the empire's protection of Judaism. There was nowhere to hide from Roman persecution.

Circa 150 Justin Martyr Writes His Apology

The young philosopher walked along the seashore, his mind active, always active, seeking new truths. He had studied the teachings of the Stoics, of Aristotle, and of Pythagoras—now he was following Plato's system. Plato had promised a vision of God to those who delved deeply enough into truth. That is what Justin the philosopher wanted.

As he walked, he came across an elderly Christian man. Justin was struck by his dignity and humility. The man quoted from Jewish prophecies, showing that the Christian way was indeed true; Jesus was the true expression of God.

That was Justin's turning point. Poring over those prophetic writings, reading the Gospels and letters of Paul, he became a devoted Christian. For the remaining thirty or so years of his life, he traveled, evangelized, and wrote. He played a crucial role in the church's developing theology, in its understanding of itself, and the image it presented to the world.

Almost from the start, the church functioned in two worlds—Jewish and Gentile. The Book of Acts depicts the slow and sometimes painful opening of the bud of Christianity onto the Gentile world. Peter and Stephen preach to Jewish hearers, and Paul speaks to Athenian philosophers and Roman governors.

In many respects Justin's life paralleled Paul's. The apostle was a Jew born in a Gentile area (Tarsus); Justin was a Gentile born in a Jewish area (ancient Shechem). Both were well-educated and used the gift of argument to convince Jew and Gentile of the truth of Christ. In Rome each was martyred for his faith.

During the reigns of first-century emperors like Nero and Domitian, the church had focused on surviving, continuing its tradition, and showing Christ-like love. Outsiders saw Christianity as a primitive sect, an offshoot of Judaism noted for its strange teachings and practices.

By the middle of the second century, under the reasonable rule of emperors like Trajan, Antoninus Pius, and Marcus Aurelius, the church had a new concern: explaining itself to the world in convincing terms. Justin became one of the first Christian *apologists,* those who explained the faith as a reasonable system. Along with later writers such as Origen and Tertullian, he interpreted Christianity in terms familiar to the educated Greeks and Romans of his day.

Justin's greatest work, the *Apology,* was addressed to Emperor Antoninus Pius (in Greek the title is *Apologia,* a word that refers to the logic upon which one's beliefs are based). As Justin explained or defended his faith, he contended that it was wrong for the Roman authorities to persecute Christians. Rather, they should join forces with Christians in exposing the falsehood of the pagan systems.

For Justin, all truth was God's truth. The great Greek philosophers had been inspired by God, to some extent, but had remained blind to the fullness of the truth of Christ. So Justin borrowed freely from Greek thought, explaining Christ as its fulfillment. He seized on John's principle of Christ as *Logos,* the Word. God the Father was holy and separated from evil humanity—Justin could agree with Plato on this. But through Christ, His Logos, God could reach out to human beings. As the Logos of God, Christ was part of God's essence, though separate, as a flame lit from a flame. (Thus Justin's thought was instrumental in the church's developing awareness of the Trinity and the Incarnation.)

Yet Justin had a Jewish stream of thought along with his Greek leanings. He was fascinated by fulfilled prophecy. Maybe this went back to his encounter with the old man by the sea. But he saw that Hebrew prophecy confirmed the unique identity of Jesus Christ. Like Paul, Justin did not abandon the Jews in his move toward the Greeks. In Justin's other major work, *Dialogues with Trypho,* he writes to a Jewish acquaintance, presenting Christ as the fulfillment of the Hebrew tradition.

Besides his writing, Justin traveled extensively, always arguing for the faith. He met Trypho in Ephesus. In Rome, he encountered the Gnostic leader Marcion. On one trip to Rome, he alienated a man called Crescens the Cynic. When Justin returned to Rome in about 165, Crescens denounced him to the authorities. Justin was arrested, tortured, and beheaded, along with six other believers.

He had once written: "You can kill us, but cannot do us any real harm." The apologist carried that conviction to his death. In so doing, he won the name he would wear throughout history: Justin *Martyr.*

Circa 156 The Martyrdom of Polycarp

Polycarp.

The heat was on. The Smyrna police hunted for Polycarp, the revered bishop of that city. Already they had put other Christians to death in the arena; now a mob cried for the leader.

Polycarp had left the city and was hiding out at the farm of some friends. As the soldiers moved in, he fled to another farm. Though the aged churchman felt no fear of death and had wanted to stay in the city, his friends had urged him to hide, perhaps fearing that his death would demoralize the church. If so, they were quite wrong.

When the police reached the first farm, they tortured a slave boy to learn Polycarp's whereabouts. Then they rushed, fully armed, to apprehend the bishop. Though Polycarp had time to escape, he refused. "God's will be done," he resolved. Instead, he welcomed his captors as guests, offered them food and asked for an hour alone to pray. He took two hours.

Some of the captors seemed sorry to be arresting such a nice old man. On the way back to Smyrna, the police chief tried to reason with Polycarp: "What harm is there in saying, 'Lord Caesar' and offering incense?"

Polycarp announced calmly that he would not do it.

The Roman authorities had developed the idea that the spirit (or genius) of the emperor (Caesar) was divine. Most Romans, with their pantheon of gods, had no problem doing homage to the emperor, too; they saw it as a matter of national loyalty. But Christians knew this was idolatry.

Because the Christians refused to worship the emperor or the other gods of Rome and worshiped Christ quietly and secretly in homes, most people thought they had no faith. "Away with the atheists!" cried the people of Smyrna as they hunted down the Christians. Because they only knew that Christians didn't participate in the many pagan festivals or perform the usual sacrifices, the crowd attacked this unpatriotic, impious group.

So Polycarp entered an arena filled with an angry mob. The Roman proconsul seemed to respect the bishop's old age. Pilate-like, he wanted to avoid an ugly scene, if possible. If only Polycarp would perform the sacrifice, everyone could go home.

"Have respect for your age, old man," the proconsul pleaded. "Swear by the fortune of Caesar. Change your mind. Say, 'Away with the atheists!' "

The proconsul obviously intended for Polycarp to save his own life by dissociating himself from those "atheistic" Christians. But Polycarp just gazed up at the jeering crowd, gestured toward them, and said, "Away with the atheists!"

The proconsul tried again: "Take the oath, and I shall release you. Curse Christ!"

The bishop stood firm. "Eighty-six years have I served him, and he never did me any wrong. How can I blaspheme my king who has saved me?"

Tradition has it that Polycarp had studied with the Apostle John. If so, he was probably the last living link with the apostolic church. About forty years earlier, when Polycarp began his ministry as bishop, the church father Ignatius had written him a special epistle. Polycarp had written an epistle of his own to the Philippians. Though it is not especially brilliant or original, it passes on the truths he had learned from his teachers. Polycarp didn't exegete Old Testament texts, as later Christian scholars would, but he quoted the apostles and other church leaders to exhort the Philippians.

About a year before his martyrdom, Polycarp had traveled to Rome to patch up differences with the Roman bishop over the date of Easter. One story says he debated there with the heretic Marcion, whom he called "the firstborn of Satan." His presentation of apostolic teaching is said to have converted several of Marcion's followers.

That was Polycarp's role: the faithful witness. Later leaders would come up with creative approaches to changing situations, but Polycarp's era required only faithfulness. He was faithful unto death.

In the arena, the exchange continued between the bishop and the proconsul. At one point, Polycarp chided his inquisitor: "If you . . . pretend that you do not know who I am, listen plainly: I am a Christian. If you want to learn the teaching of Christianity, set a day and give me a hearing."

The proconsul threatened to throw him to the wild beasts. "Call them," said Polycarp. "If this were a change from the bad to the good, I would consider it, but not a change from the better to the worse."

Threatened with fire, Polycarp countered, "Your fire burns for an hour and goes out, but the fire of the coming judgment is eternal."

Finally, it was announced that Polycarp would not recant. The people of Smyrna cried, "This is the teacher of Asia, the father of the Christians, the destroyer of our gods, who teaches many not to sacrifice or to worship!"

The proconsul ordered the bishop to be burned alive. He was tied to the stake and the fire was set. But according to an eyewitness account, his body was not consumed. "He was in the middle, not as burning flesh, but as bread baking or as gold and silver refined in a furnace. And we smelled such a sweet aroma as the breath of incense or some other precious spice." When an executioner stabbed him, the blood poured out and quenched the fire.

This account was distributed to congregations throughout the empire. The church treasured such reports and began to celebrate the lives and deaths of its martyrs, even collecting their bones and other relics. On February 23 of each year they commemorated Polycarp's "birthday" into heavenly realms.

Over the next century and a half, as hundreds of other martyrs faithfully went to their deaths, many were buoyed up by the account of the faithful witness of the bishop of Smyrna.

177
Irenaeus Becomes Bishop of Lyons

Even in heresy there is "nothing new under the sun" (Ecclesiastes 1:9 NIV) The false teachings that spring up in and around the church remain much the same.

Instead of turning to Christ's atoning works, many have sought to save themselves by discovering some secret knowledge. In the early church, it appeared in a group of heresies called Gnosticism (*gnosis* is a Greek word meaning "knowledge").

Before the founding of the church, some form of Gnosticism apparently existed. When John wrote his first epistle, he struck a blow at this false teaching. Yet it still had a following in the second century.

We know little about Irenaeus, the man who opposed Gnosticism in the latter part of the second century. He was probably born in Asia Minor in about 125. Active trading between Asia Minor and Gaul had allowed Christians to bring their faith to Gaul, where they had established a vigorous church in the chief city, Lyons.

While he served as an elder in Lyons,

Irenaeus lived up to his name, which means "peaceful," by traveling to Rome to ask the bishop there to extend leniency to the Montanists in Asia Minor. During this mission, persecution arose in Lyons, and the bishop there was martyred.

Irenaeus became bishop in his place and found that Gnosticism had gained converts in Gaul. It had spread easily because the Gnostics used Christian terms—though they gave them radically different interpretations. The fusion of Christian terms with concepts from Greek philosophy and Asian religion appealed to those who wanted to believe they could save themselves without depending on the grace of the Almighty Father.

Irenaeus studied the forms of Gnosticism. Though they varied greatly, they commonly taught that the physical world was evil; that the world was created and is governed by angelic powers, not God; that God is distant and not really connected with this world; that salvation can be attained by learning special secret teachings; that spiritual persons (*pneumatikoi*)—that is, the Gnostics themselves—are superior to regular Christians (*psychikoi*). Gnostic teachers supported these ideas with the Gnostic Gospels—volumes that usually bore an apostle's name and portrayed Jesus teaching Gnostic doctrines.

When the bishop of Lyons had learned about this heresy, he wrote *Against Heresies,* an enormous work in which he sought to unveil the foolishness of the "Gnosis Falsely So Called."

Drawing on Old and New Testaments, he showed that a loving God created the world, which became corrupted through human's sin. Adam, the innocent first man, became sinful by yielding to temptation. But his fall has been undone—recapitulated—by the work of the second innocent man, Christ, the new Adam. The body is not evil, and at the last day believers' bodies and souls will be raised; they will live with God forever.

Irenaeus understood that Gnosticism appealed to the human desire to know something others didn't know. Of the Gnostics he wrote, "As soon as a man has been won over to their way of salvation, he becomes so puffed up with conceit and self-importance that he struts about with the air of a rooster." But Christians should humbly accept God's grace, not become involved in intellectual exercises that lead to vanity.

All his life Irenaeus had happily recalled his acquaintance with Polycarp, who had personally known the Apostle John, so perhaps it's not surprising that Irenaeus appealed to the authority of the apostles when he disproved the claims of Gnosticism. The bishop pointed out that the apostles had taught in public, keeping nothing secret. Throughout the empire, the churches agreed on certain teachings that came from Christ's apostles, and these alone formed the foundation of belief. By declaring the apostles' successors, the bishops, guardians of the faith, Irenaeus enhanced the respect paid to bishops.

In *Against Heresies* Irenaeus set forth the standard for the church's theology: All the truth we need is embodied in the Bible. He also proved himself the greatest theologian since the Apostle Paul. His widely circulated argument dealt a deadly blow to Gnosticism in his age.

Circa 196 Tertullian Begins to Write Christian Books

Painting of Tertullian.

"**B**lood of the martyrs is the seed of the Church."

"It is certain because it is impossible."

"What has Athens to do with Jerusalem?"

Such tart epigrams are typical of the works of Quintus Septimius Florens Tertullianus—or Tertullian. A native of Carthage, he had been reared in a cultured pagan household and trained in the literary classics, speech making, and the law. About 196, when he turned his powerful intellect to Christian topics, he changed the face of thinking and literature in the Western church.

Up to this point, most Christian writers had used Greek—a flexible, subtle language, perfect for philosophizing and hair splitting. And often the Greek-speaking Christians carried this bent for philosophy into their faith.

Though the African Tertullian knew Greek, he preferred writing in Latin, and his works reflect the Latin-speaking Romans' practical, morals-oriented streak. This influential lawyer drew many other writers to his favorite language.

While Greek Christians squabbled over the divinity of Christ and His relation to the Father, Tertullian sought to unify the faith and clarify the orthodox position. So he laid down a helpful formula that we still use today: God is one substance, consisting of three persons.

As he anticipated what became the doctrine of the Trinity, Tertullian drew his terminology not from the philosophers, but from Roman law courts. The Latin *substantia* did not mean "material," but "property rights." God's *substantia* is His "turf," so to speak. *Persona* did not mean "person" as we use the word; it referred to a party in a legal action. Used that way, it is conceivable that three *personae* could share one *substantia*. Three persons (Father, Son, and Spirit) share one substance (the divine sovereignty).

Though Tertullian asked, "What has Athens [philosophy] to do with Jerusalem [the church]?" the Stoic philosophy, which was popular during his age, influenced him. Some say that the idea of original sin passed from Stoicism, to Tertullian, to the Western church. Tertullian seems to have thought that the soul was in some way material: As a body is formed by conception, so is a soul. Adam's sin is passed on like a genetic trait.

The Western church took hold of this idea, but it did not pass into the East (which took a more optimistic view of human nature).

About 206 Tertullian left the church to join the Montanist sect, a group of "puritans," who reacted against what they perceived as lax morals among Christians. They expected the Second Coming to occur soon and emphasized the immediate leadership of the Holy Spirit, not the ordained clergy.

Though Tertullian had begun by emphasizing the idea of apostolic succession—the passing on of the apostles' power and authority to bishops— he became disturbed by the bishops' claim that they had the power to pardon sins. This would lead to moral laxity, he believed, and the bishops presumed too much in claiming it. After all, he reasoned, weren't *all* believers priests? Was this a church of saints who administered themselves or a rabble of saints and sinners administered by a professional "class," the clergy?

Tertullian was swimming against the tide. For more than twelve hundred years the clergy would have a special place. Not until Martin Luther challenged the church would an emphasis on "the priesthood of all believers" be recaptured.

Circa 205 Origen Begins Writing

Origen, from a stained-glass window in Winter Park Presbyterian Church, Florida.

In its earliest days, Christianity had been criticized as a religion of the poor and uneducated, and indeed many of the faithful had come from the lower classes. As Paul had written, in the church there were "not many wise men after the flesh, not many mighty, not many noble" (1 Corinthians 1:26).

By the third century, however, the greatest scholar of the age was a Christian. Heathens, heretics, and Christians admired Origen, and his immense learning and scholarship would have an important influence on future Christian scholarship.

Origen was born in Alexandria, about 185, of devout Christian parents. In about 201 his father, Leonidas, was imprisoned during the persecution of Septimus Severus. Origen wrote to his father in prison and encouraged him not to deny Christ for the sake of his family. Though Origen wanted to turn himself in to the authorities and suffer martyrdom with his father, his mother hid his clothes and kept him from such zealous foolishness.

After Leonidas's martyrdom, his property was confiscated, and his widow was left with seven children. Origen set about supporting them by teaching Greek literature and copying manuscripts. Since many of the older scholars had fled Alexandria at the time of the persecution, the Christian catechetical school had a great need for teachers. At eighteen Origen became president of the school and embarked on his long career of teaching, studying, and writing.

He lived an ascetic life, spending much of the night in study and prayer and sleeping on the bare floor, whenever he did sleep. Following Jesus' command, he only had one coat and no shoes. He even followed Matthew 19:12 literally and castrated himself as a defense against all fleshly temptations. Origen's strongest desire was to be a faithful man of the church and to bring honor to the name of Christ.

A tremendously prolific writer, Origen was able to keep seven secretaries busy with his dictations. He produced over 2,000 works, including commentaries on almost every book of the Bible and hundreds of homilies. His *Hexapla* was a feat of textual criticism. In it he tried to find the best Greek rendering of the Old Testament, and in six parallel columns displayed the Hebrew Old Testament, a Greek transliteration, three Greek translations, and the Septuagint. *Against Celsus* was a major apologetic work defending Christianity from pagan attacks. *On First Principles* was the first attempt at a systematic theology; here Origen carefully examined the Christian beliefs concerning God, Christ, the Holy Spirit, creation, the soul, free will, salvation, and the Scriptures.

Origen was largely responsible for establishing the allegorical interpretation of Scripture that was to dominate the Middle Ages. In every text he believed there were three levels of meaning: the literal sense; the moral sense, which was to edify the soul; and the allegorical or spiritual sense, which was the hidden meaning important to the Christian faith. Origen himself neglected the literal or historical-grammatical meaning of the text and emphasized the deeper, allegorical meaning.

Origen tried to relate Christianity to the science and philosophy of his day. He believed Greek philosophy was a preparation for understanding Scripture and used the analogy, later adopted by Augustine, of Christians "spoiling the Egyptians" when they used the wealth of pagan learning in their Christian cause (Exodus 12:35–36).

In accepting the teachings of Greek philosophy, Origen adopted many Platonic ideas alien to orthodox Christianity. Behind most of his errors was the Greek assumption that matter and the material world are implicitly evil. He believed in the preexistence of the soul before birth and taught that man's position in the world was due to his conduct in a preexistent state. He denied the material resurrection and toyed with the idea that eventually God would provide salvation for all men and angels. Since God could not create the material world without coming in contact with base matter, the Father eternally generated the Son, who created the eternal world. When the Son died on the cross, it was only Jesus' humanity that died as a ransom-payment to the devil for the world.

For errors such as these Bishop Demetrius of Alexandria called a council that excommunicated Origen from the church. Though the Roman and Western church accepted the excommunication, the church in Palestine and much of the East did not. They still sought out Origen for his learning, wisdom, and scholarship.

During the Decian persecution, Origen was imprisoned, tortured, and sentenced to the stake. Only the death of the emperor prevented that sentence from being carried out. Broken in health from the ordeal, Origen died about 251. He had done more than anyone else to promote the cause of Christian scholarship and make the church respected in the eyes of the world. Later fathers in both the Eastern and Western church would feel his influence. The diversity of his thought and writings easily gained for him the reputation as the father of orthodoxy as well as the father of heresy.

251
Cyprian Writes *On the Unity of the Church*

What relationship exists between the people of the church and their leaders? How can the church discipline members? These are questions the church must deal with in any age.

During the middle of the third century, the answers to these questions were promoted by Cyprian, a one-time wealthy, cultured pagan born around 200. When he became a Christian, he forsook his former life-style, gave his goods and money to the poor, and took a vow of chastity. Of his conversion he wrote, "A second birth created me a new man by means of the Spirit breathed from heaven."

A former teacher of rhetoric and a renowned orator, the eloquent and devout Cyprian rose through the ranks of the church, becoming bishop of Carthage about 248.

Though he had training in the Greek and Roman classics, Cyprian was no theologian. Unlike Tertullian, whom he admired, Cyprian was a practical man who cared little for the theological disputes of his day. He simply wanted unity in the church. In a church with little unity, he sought to bind Christians together through the authority of bishops.

Roman emperor Decius had persecuted the Christians, and some had denied their faith. Decius hadn't sought to make martyrs, because he knew martyrdom simply brought Christianity more attention. Instead, he tortured Christians, hoping they would say, "Caesar is Lord." Those who did were known as the "lapsed."

The Christians who stood fast, the "confessors," often took a dim view of the lapsed. So a council of bishops set up strict rules concerning readmitting lapsed believers to the church. In the face of this discipline, a priest named Novatus started a rival church that offered easy admittance to the lapsed.

Though Cyprian had not suffered for his faith, he couldn't abide the division. He believed sincere believers should do penance, to prove their faith. Penance involved a period of sincere sorrowing, after which the person could be readmitted to the Lord's Supper. Once the penitent had "done his time," he appeared before the congregation in sackcloth and ashes, and the bishops pronounced forgiveness. Cyprian perceived this as a graded system—the more serious the sin, the more penance the person had to do. His idea caught on and became one of the most powerful—and sometimes abused—methods of church discipline.

In 251 Cyprian called a council at Carthage and read *On the Unity of the Church,* his landmark work that had a profound influence on church history. The church, he said, is a divine institution, the Bride of Christ, and there can only be one Bride. Only in the church can people have salvation; outside it is darkness and confusion. Beyond the church, sacraments and pastors—even the Bible—have no significance. An individual cannot live the Christian life through direct contact with God; he needs the church. Since Christ established the church on Peter, the Rock, Cyprian said all bishops were in some sense successors of Peter—and as such, should be obeyed. Though he did not declare that the bishop of Rome was above the others, Cyprian saw that bishopric as special because of Peter's connection with the city.

Cyprian's statements like "Outside the church there is no salvation" and "He cannot have God for his Father who has not the church for his mother" encouraged people to give bishops a place of great importance. A bishop could determine church membership, so in effect he had the power to say, "You are saved. You are not saved." Instead of relying on the Spirit working through the church at large, Cyprian implied that the Spirit worked through the bishops.

The bishops, of course, gained power through an acceptance of these ideas. Cyprian also promoted the idea that the mass was a sacrifice of Christ's body and blood. Since the priests, functioning on behalf of Christ, offered up the sacrifice anew at every worship service, this also increased their power.

Cyprian would die under the persecution of Emperor Valerian. Because he refused to sacrifice to pagan gods, the bishop of Carthage was beheaded in 258.

The church in Cyprian's time, filled with disunity, held onto his ideas. The bishop could not have foreseen the consequences of the means he devised to hold the church together. In the Middle Ages, some incredibly greedy, immoral men would hold the office of bishop, using it to their own ends, rather than to care for spiritual matters. The hierarchical structure that created "unity" also caused a massive clergy-laity rift.

270 Anthony Begins His Life as a Hermit

Saint Anthony Leaving His Monastery. Painting by Sassetta.

One of the key founders of monastic communities had no notion of founding anything—he was simply concerned for his own spiritual condition and spent much of his life alone.

Anthony was born in Egypt, probably about 250, to well-to-do parents who died when he was about twenty and left him all their possessions. A sermon text, Jesus' command to the rich young ruler, "If you would be perfect, go and sell all you have," changed the young man's life. The words seemed directed to him, and Anthony took them literally. He gave his lands to his fellow villagers, sold his other property, and donated the money to the poor. He put himself under the care of an elderly Christian who taught him the joys of self-denial. Anthony lived on one meal a day of bread and water and slept on the bare ground.

With the conversion of Emperor Constantine in 312, the church's situation changed drastically. Christians lost their position as a persecuted minority and became members of a respectable religion with official sponsorship. As masses of people began to pour into the church, however, it became less easy to distinguish those with a real commitment to Christ from those who wanted a part of this popular religion. Faith became easy, and sincerity suffered.

Zealous Christians of this age often chose to fight back against the compromising of their faith by withdrawing from the world. Anthony sought to do that by living in a tomb. According to his biographer, Athanasius, for about twelve years Anthony was besieged by demons who took the shapes of various strange beasts and sometimes struck him, on occasion leaving him nearly dead. They were trying to call Anthony back to a world of sensuous pleasures, but Anthony always emerged triumphant.

To withdraw even farther from the world, Anthony moved to an abandoned fort, where he lived for twenty years without seeing a human face. His food was thrown to him over the wall. But people heard of his amazing self-denial and battles with demons. Some admirers set up crude homes near the fort, and he reluctantly became their spiritual adviser, giving them guidance on fasting, prayer, and works of charity. Anthony certainly provided a role model in self-denial.

The hermit could never totally detach himself from the world. In 311 Maximian, one of the last pagan emperors, persecuted Christians, and Anthony left his home, willing to die for his faith. Instead he ended up ministering to Christians condemned to work in the imperial mines. That experience convinced him that living the Christian life could be as saintly as dying for it. Again, in 350, he left home to defend orthodoxy against the Arian heresy, which had by no means been squelched by the Council of Nicea (325). Many people, including Emperor Constantine, sought the hermit's spiritual advice.

Anthony died at the age of 105, to the end apparently still vigorous in mind and body. He insisted on being buried secretly, so no cult would develop around his grave.

But a cult following grew up nonetheless. Athanasius—the influential theologian who played an important role in the Council of Nicea—wrote an extremely popular *Life of Anthony,* in which he portrayed Anthony as the ideal monk, who could work miracles and discern between good and evil spirits. Before long, the idea that a real spiritual warrior became a monk and denied himself took hold within the church.

The practice of communities of monks living together was begun by Pachomius, a young companion of Anthony's. Like the ruggedly individualistic Anthony, most of his followers were also hermits. For better or for worse, Anthony communicated the idea that a truly religious person withdraws from the world, abstaining from marriage, family, and worldly pleasures.

Not until the Reformation would anyone seriously challenge that idea.

312
The Conversion of Constantine

Bust of the Emperor Constantine.

It was October, 312. A young general who had the allegiance of all the Roman troops from Britain and Gaul was marching toward Rome to challenge Maxentius, another claimant to the imperial throne.

As the story goes, General Constan-tine looked up and saw a cross of light in the sky. An inscription read, "In this conquer." The superstitious soldier was already beginning to reject the Roman deities in favor of a single god. His father had worshiped a supreme sun-god. Could this be a favorable omen from that god on the eve of battle?

Later, Christ appeared to Constantine in a dream, bearing the same sign, a cross with the top bent over, resembling the Greek letters *chi* and *rho,* the first two letters of *Christos.* The general was instructed to mark this sign on his soldiers' shields. He did.

As promised, Constantine won the battle.

It was one of several decisive moments in a quarter century of violent change. If you had left Rome in A.D. 305, to spend twenty years in the desert, you would have returned expecting to find Christianity dead or facing the final deathblows of persecution. Instead, Christianity had become the favored religion of the empire.

After Diocletian, one of the most brilliant Roman emperors, had taken power in 284, he began a massive reorganization that would shape up the military, the economy, and the civil service. For quite a while, he left the Christians alone.

One of Diocletian's brainstorms was the restructuring of imperial power. He divided the empire into East and West; each side would have an emperor and a vice-emperor (or caesar). Each emperor would serve twenty years, and then the Caesars would take over for twenty years, and so on. In 286, Diocletian appointed Maximian as emperor of the West, while he himself continued to rule the East. The caesars were Constantius Chlorus (father of Constantine) in the west and Galerius in the east.

Galerius was strongly anti-Christian. (He reportedly blamed the loss of one battle on a Christian soldier who crossed himself.) When the Eastern emperor took anti-Christian positions, he probably did so at Galerius' instigation. It was all part of the reorganization of the empire—so the logic went: Rome had a uniform currency, a uniform political system, it should have a uniform religion. Christians were in the way.

Beginning in 298, Christians were rooted out of the army and civil service. In 303, the Great Persecution started. Authorities planned a crackdown on Christians to begin at the Feast of Terminalia, February 23. Churches were razed, Scriptures seized, and services prohibited. At first there was no bloodshed, but Galerius soon changed that. When Diocletian and Maximian resigned (according to schedule), in 305, Galerius unleashed a fiercer persecution. Constantius, who ruled in the West, was generally lenient. But horror stories from the East are plentiful. Continuing through 310, the persecution took the lives of many Christian martyrs.

But Galerius was unable to crush the church. Strangely, on his deathbed, he changed his mind. In another great moment, April 30, 311, the vicious emperor gave up the fight against Christianity, issuing the Edict of Toleration. Always a politician, he insisted that he had done everything for the good of the empire, but that "great numbers" of Christians "held to their determination." So now it was best to allow them to meet freely, as long as they were orderly about it. Further, he declared, "It will be their duty to pray to their god for our good estate." Rome needed all the help it could get. Galerius died six days later.

But Diocletian's grand scheme was falling apart. When Constantius died in 306, his son Constantine was proclaimed ruler by his loyal soldiers. But Maximian tried to come out of retirement and rule the West again, along with his son, Maxentius (who eventually forced Maximian—his own father—out of power). Meanwhile Galerius appointed a favorite general of his, Licinius, as the Western emperor. Each of these would-be emperors claimed a slice of the western territory. They would have to fight it out. Shrewdly, Constantine forged an alliance with Licinius and fought against Maxentius, and at the battle of Milvian Bridge, Constantine prevailed.

At that point, Constantine and Licinius forged a delicate balance of power. Constantine was eager to thank Christ for his victory, so he moved to secure freedom and status for the church. In 313, he and Licinius officially issued the Edict of Milan, granting religious freedom within the empire. "Our purpose," it said, "is to grant both to the Christians and to all others full authority to follow whatever worship each man has desired."

Constantine immediately took an imperial interest in the church, restoring property, granting money, ruling in the Donatist controversy, and calling church councils in Arles and Nicea. He was also jockeying for power over Licinius, whom he finally ousted in 324.

Thus the church passed from persecution to privilege. In an amazingly short time, its prospects changed completely. After centuries as a counter-culture movement, the church had to learn how to deal with power. It did not do everything well. Constantine's own dynamic presence shaped the church of the fourth century and thereafter. He was a master of power and politics; and the church learned to use those tools.

Was Constantine's vision authentic, or was he just an opportunist, using Christianity for his own ends? Only God knows the soul. Though in many ways he failed to reflect his faith, the emperor certainly took an active interest in the Christianity that he professed, often at personal risk.

God certainly used Constantine to make things happen for the church; the emperor affirmed and secured official toleration of the faith. But in doing so, he followed in the footsteps of the beaten, broken Galerius who had granted it earlier. Thus the battle against Roman persecution had in a sense been won, not at the Milvian Bridge, but in the arenas, as Christians went bravely to their deaths.

325
The Council of Nicea

Council of Nicea.

Though Tertullian had provided the church with the formula that God is one substance, consisting in three persons, he had by no means given the world a complete understanding of the Trinity. Indeed, this doctrine has puzzled the greatest theologians.

Early in the fourth century a pastor of Alexandria, Egypt—Arius—called himself a Christian. But Arius also accepted Greek theology, which taught that God is unique and unknowable. According to such thought, He is so radically different that He cannot share His substance with anything: Only God can be God. In his book *Thalia* Arius proclaimed that Jesus was divine, but not God. Only God the Father, Arius said, could be immortal, so the Son had to be a created being. He was *like* the Father, but not truly God.

Many former pagans felt comfortable with Arius's views, because they could preserve the familiar idea of an unknowable God and see Jesus as a kind of divine superhero, not much different from the divine-human heroes of Greek mythology.

An eloquent preacher, Arius knew how to make the most of this appeal and even put some of his propositions into jingles, which the common folk sang. *Why would anyone make a fuss about Arius's ideas?* many wondered. But Arius's bishop, Alexander, saw that in order to save sinful humanity Jesus *had* to be truly God. Alexander had Arius condemned by the synod, but the popular pastor had many supporters. Soon riots erupted in Alexandria over this ticklish theological contest and other clergymen began to take sides.

Once the riots had erupted, Emperor Constantine could not afford to see the debate as "just a religious issue." This "religious issue" threatened the security of his empire. To deal with the problem, Constantine called an empirewide council at the city of Nicea, in Asia Minor.

Dressed in jewel-encrusted, multicolored robes, Constantine opened the council. He told the more than three hundred bishops attending that they must resolve the issue. Division in the church, he said, was worse than war, because it involved eternal souls.

The emperor let the bishops debate. Called before them, Arius plainly proclaimed that the Son of God was a created being, and unlike the Father, He was capable of change.

The assembly denounced and condemned Arius's view—but they needed to go beyond that. Making their own view plain required a creed.

So they formulated some statements about God the Father and God the Son. In it they described the Son as "true God from true God, begotten not made, of one substance with the father."

That "of one substance" was critical. The Greek word they used was *homoousios*. *Homo* meant "same"; *ousios* meant "substance." The Arian party wanted to add one more letter to that word: *Homoiousios* meant "of like [similar] substance."

All but two bishops signed the statement of faith. Those two and Arius were exiled. Constantine seemed pleased with the results of his work, but it did not last.

Though Arius was temporarily out of the picture, his theology would remain for decades. A deacon of Alexandria, Athanasius, became one of Arianism's most capable foes. In 328 Athanasius became bishop of Alexandria and continued the fight within that flock.

But the battle was hotly waged throughout the Eastern church until another council, held in Constantinople in 381, reaffirmed the Council of Nicea. Even so, traces of Arius's thoughts have remained within the church.

The Council of Nicea both began to settle a theological issue and set precedents for church and state. In later years, when thorny issues arose in the church, it would consult the collective wisdom of its bishops. Constantine had also begun the practice of uniting an empire and church in decision making; it would have many baneful consequences in the centuries to come.

367 Athanasius's Letter Recognizes the New Testament Canon

How can a Christian be certain what books should appear in the New Testament?

When Paul mentioned Scripture to Timothy ("All Scripture is inspired . . ." [2 Timothy 3:16 RSV]), he referred to the Old Testament, but even within the pages of the New Testament, we have indications that Christians had begun to regard the Gospels and Paul's epistles as somehow special. Peter wrote that Paul's epistles are sometimes "hard to understand." Nevertheless, Paul's wisdom was God given, and Peter chided the "ignorant and unstable" who distort Paul's words as they distort *other* Scriptures (2 Peter 3:16 RSV). Obviously Peter had begun to realize that Christians had some edifying writings other than the Old Testament works.

The Jews had established that some books—what we call the Old Testament—were clearly inspired by God, while others were not. As they faced heresies Christians also began to feel the need to distinguish between those truly inspired writings and the questionable ones.

Two major criteria used by the church to identify the canon (*canon* is the Greek word for "standard") were *apostolic origin* and *the use of the writing in the churches.*

When it considered apostolic origin, the church included Paul among the apostles. Although Paul had not walked with Christ, he had met Him on the road to Damascus, and his widespread missionary activity—testified to by the Book of Acts—made him the very model of an apostle.

Each Gospel had to be attached to an apostle. Thus Mark's Gospel, which was associated with Peter, and Luke's, which was associated with Paul, took a place in the canon. After the death of the apostles, Christians valued the books' witness, even if they did not bear an apostle's name.

Concerning the use of the writing in churches, the guideline seemed to be, "If many churches use this and it continues to edify them, it must be inspired." Though that standard shows a rather pragmatic approach, logic lay behind it. Something inspired by God will no doubt inspire many worshipers. A writing that was not inspired would eventually fall out of use.

Unhappily, these standards alone could not settle the books of the canon. Many blatantly heretical writings carried the name of an apostle. In addition, some churches used writings others did not care to use.

By the end of the second century, the four Gospels, Acts, and Paul's epistles were highly valued almost everywhere. Though no "official" list existed, churches had a growing tendency to turn to these as having spiritual authority. Influential bishops such as Ignatius, Clement of Rome, and Polycarp had helped these writings achieve wide acceptance. Yet much dispute remained over Hebrews, James, 2 Peter, 2 and 3 John, Jude, and Revelation.

Heresy has a way of making orthodox Christians clarify their position. As far as we know, the first attempt at a canon was made by the heretic Marcion, who included only ten of Paul's thirteen epistles and a heavily edited Gospel of Luke. Later heretical groups would cherish their own special "secret books," usually ones that had an apostle's name attached to them.

One early orthodox list, compiled around the year 200, was the Muratorian Canon of the church of Rome. It included most of our present-day New Testament, but added the Revelation of Peter and the Wisdom of Solomon. Later listings would omit one book and leave in another, but they remained quite similar. Works such as the Shepherd of Hermas, the *Didache,* and the Letter of Barnabas were highly regarded, though many felt reluctant to view them as inspired Scripture.

In 367 the influential, highly orthodox bishop of Alexandria, Athanasius, wrote his widely circulated Easter Letter. In it he named the twenty-seven books we now include in our New Testament. Hoping to guard his flock from error, Athanasius stated that no other books could be regarded as Christian Scripture, though he allowed that some, like the *Didache,* might be useful for private devotions.

Athanasius's list did not settle the matter. The Council of Carthage in 397 confirmed his list, but the Western churches were slow to settle on a canon. Wrangling continued over the questionable books, though eventually all accepted Revelation.

In the end Athanasius's list received general acceptance, and churches throughout the world since have not seriously deviated from his wisdom.

385
Bishop Ambrose Defies the Empress

Ambrose, bishop of Milan, refuses Emperor Theodosius entrance into the church after his pagan excesses in Constantinople.

In Milan, soldiers surrounded the cathedral. Bishop Ambrose had been ordered by Empress Justina to relinquish control of the building, but he hadn't moved. The emperor's Germanic bodyguard added muscle to her command. Not only did they have a different loyalty, the Germans were also probably Arian, while the bishop held to the orthodox teachings of the Council of Nicea.

Many expected a massacre of the worshipers huddled inside the cathedral, but onlookers heard the sound of psalms wafting through the air. Imperial force had been met with imperturbable faith.

The man on whom this conflict centered—Bishop Ambrose—was one of the strongest leaders the church had known, the son of a high-ranking official in Constantine's government. Young Ambrose had been groomed to follow in his father's footsteps. When he finished his studies in the law, he had been named governor of the territory surrounding Milan. Many regarded him as a just and highly capable leader.

While Ambrose held the position of governor, an Arian, Auxentius, was bishop of Milan. The bishop died in 374, and a riot broke out as the church tried to select a successor. In his governmental role, Ambrose had moved in to quell the strife.

Someone had begun to shout, "Ambrose for bishop!" Others took up the cheer.

The only problem was, Ambrose hadn't been baptized. Though he had believed in Christ for a long time, he remained a catechumen. No matter. The popular acclaim swept him through baptism and several intermediate offices, and eight days later he was consecrated as the new bishop of Milan.

Arianism lost its power. The last Eastern emperor to champion that cause, Valens, died in 378. Gratian, emperor in the West, appointed General Theodosius to rule the eastern half of the empire from Constantinople. In 380, the two emperors issued an edict declaring Nicene Christianity as the religion of the realm. This effectively put down the Arian sect, except in the hinterlands, among the Goths, and among some members of the imperial family.

Ambrose took his new job as bishop very seriously. He studied Scripture and the church Fathers voraciously, and he began to preach each Sunday. He had always been a fine orator, and now his speaking had even greater depth. One of his contemporaries, Basil of Caesarea, described Ambrose as "a man eminent for intellect, illustrious lineage, prominence in life, and power of speech, an object of admiration to all in this world."

One of his admirers was a speech writer named Augustine. This young Carthaginian had dabbled in Manichaeism and had been coddled by the pagans of Rome. He had been sent to Milan as a teacher and rhetorician for the teenage emperor Valentinian II. In those days, the emperor's power was based in Milan, while the Senate still held sway in Rome. The Senators generally still embraced the old Roman pagan ways, while the emperors were Christian. It is quite possible that Augustine was sent by the pagans in the Senate to help influence the boy emperor.

For political reasons, Augustine became a catechumen in the Christian church. In the process, he came in contact with Ambrose and was impressed with the bishop's humility and power. Later, through the witness of one of Ambrose's aides, Augustine was converted (see the next chapter for more about Augustine).

Ambrose was also known as a hymn writer. Even in the fourth century music in worship raised controversy. Critics feared that Ambrose's musical experiments would set off a craze of hymn singing. In any case, it was no surprise that singing was heard from Milan's besieged cathedral on that day in 385. It is very possible that one of the singers was Monica, Augustine's devout mother.

But another woman created the conflict on that day. Justina was the mother of Emperor Valentinian, Gratian's successor as ruler of the western Roman Empire. She was the power behind his throne. An Arian, she wanted to claim Ambrose's cathedral and another church building in Milan for use by Arian congregations. Ambrose refused. She sent the soldiers. The stage was set for a bloodbath.

But then the troops dispersed. No one knows why. Some think Ambrose may have managed to get a message out to Theodosius, the ardent non-Arian who ruled the East. Perhaps a message to Valentinian, threatening the wrath of Theodosius, caused the boy to quash his mother's plans. Or maybe Justina was just bluffing to begin with. In any case, Ambrose stood up to the imperial court and won.

Later Ambrose stood up to an emperor—this time Theodosius himself. The emperor had overreacted to a disturbance in Thessalonica, sending an army to massacre its citizens. Ambrose considered this a heinous deed and excommunicated Theodosius until the emperor did proper penance. It is a testimony both to Ambrose's courage and Theodosius's humility that the emperor returned to the cathedral in sackcloth and knelt before the bishop, seeking forgiveness.

Once the church had faced the persecution of emperors. With Ambrose a different kind of pattern began to develop between the church and state.

387 Conversion of Augustine

The oldest known portrait of Augustine from a fresco on a wall in the Lateran Palace.

"**L**ord, make me chaste, but not yet," prayed a sensual intellectual who was flirting with Christianity—and a lot of other things as well. Once he had surrendered himself to God, that man would have no trouble being chaste and would become one of the most influential authors the church has known.

This complex man was Aurelius Augustinus, better known as Augustine. Born in 354, in Tagaste, he had a devout Christian mother named Monica. His pagan father, Patricius, was a Roman official.

Because they saw their son's brilliance, Monica and Patricius arranged the best schooling for him. He studied rhetoric in Carthage and was stimulated by reading Latin authors such as Cicero. Convinced by his studies that truth was life's goal, at first he rejected Christianity because he saw it as a religion for the simple-minded.

While still in his teens, Augustine took a concubine, who bore him a son. For the rest of his life, Augustine would look back on his days in Carthage with loathing. In his *Confessions* he commented, "I came to Carthage, where a cauldron of unholy loves was sizzling and crackling around me."

The restless young man tried Manichaeism, which taught that the world was a battleground for light and dark, flesh and spirit. But Manichaeism couldn't satisfy his desire for the ultimate truth. Neither could Neoplatonism.

Hounded by his own spiritual dissatisfaction, Augustine moved from Carthage to Rome to Milan, teaching rhetoric. In Milan he met Bishop Ambrose and learned that not all Christians were simple-minded; this man was brilliant.

In 387, as Augustine sat in a garden in Milan, he heard a child's singsong voice say, "Take it and read; take it and read." Augustine read what was nearby: Paul's Letter to the Romans. As he read Romans 13:13, 14, Paul's words about clothing ourselves with the Lord Jesus instead of gratifying our sinful desires took hold, and Augustine believed. Later he wrote, "It was as though the light of faith flooded into my heart and all the darkness of doubt was dispelled."

Though Augustine could have been happy leading a quiet monastic life, his reputation as a brilliant Christian spread. In 391 he was pressured into being ordained a priest. In 395 he became bishop of the North African city of Hippo.

Every controversy of his day involved Bishop Augustine. A group called the Donatists felt great concern for having a moral clergy. Under the persecution of Emperor Diocletian, some clergy had given copies of the Scriptures to their persecutors, to be burned. Later, some of these "hander-overs," as they were called, were reinstated as clergy. The Donatists refused to accept these "traitors" and set up a rival church. Thousands of Donatists lived in Augustine's see.

Augustine denied the need for a rival church. Though there may be some less than holy persons in the church, he said, the church is one. The sacraments, which Augustine defined as visible signs of an invisible grace, are not effective because of the priest's righteousness, but because God's grace operates through them. Augustine's view prevailed, and Donatism lost momentum.

Pelagius, a British teacher, spread the heresy that man's work in choosing God was essential. Though God's grace played a role, it was not everything. Pelagius didn't quite teach that man could save himself, but he denied that sin was inherited from Adam.

Augustine countered that no one could choose good unless God led him to it. In fact, God had predestined the elect, His redeemed ones, and nothing man could do would change that eternal decree. In 431, a year after Augustine's death, the Council of Ephesus officially condemned Pelagianism.

Not only did Augustine challenge heresy, he wrote of his own spiritual quest in his *Confessions,* which is probably the first real spiritual autobiography. The famous words "Our hearts are restless until they rest in You" come from its opening paragraph.

Because Augustine's teaching has become so basic to Christianity, we don't realize how original he was in his day. His thoughts have trickled down to both Catholic and Protestant theologians. Luther and Calvin constantly quoted him; they liked his emphasis on God's grace and man's inability to save himself.

Augustine wrote hundreds of treatises, letters, and commentaries. His classic work *On the Trinity* is probably the best-known work on that subject. However, his most important work was

City of God, a monumental work written in response to the fall of Rome to the Visigoths. Some people blamed the Christians, arguing that Rome fell because its people had neglected the native gods. So Augustine responded by defending and explaining God's plan and working in history. Since Cain and Abel, he said, there have been two cities in the world: the City of God (the faithful) and the City of Man (pagan society). Though they intertwine, God will see that the City of God, the church, will endure through eternity.

Though Augustine wrote at the end of the ancient world, his thoughts would dominate scholars of the Middle Ages and last into the Reformation.

398
John Chrysostom Becomes Bishop of Constantinople

A tax revolt first brought John Chrysostom to public attention. He was a pastor in Antioch in 387, when Emperor Theodosius imposed a new tax.

The people of Antioch were incensed. In protest, they rioted, attacking imperial officials and defacing statues of Theodosius and his family. Order was soon restored, and the people waited to be punished.

Flavian, the bishop of Antioch, hurried to the capital, Constantinople, to beg the emperor for clemency. Theodosius had been known to send armies to massacre citizens who gave him a hard time. While the bishop and a team of monks pleaded with the emperor, John tried to calm the crowds. In a series of twenty sermons *(Homilies on the Statues),* he inspired, rebuked, and challenged the crowds. It was prophetic preaching at its finest. The bishop returned with news of amnesty, and John urged the people to change their lives for the better.

This would not be the last time John would face a hot political situation. He did so with courage, faithfulness, and perhaps a bit of arrogance.

Maybe he had learned that from his mother. His father was a military officer who died shortly after John was born. Anthusa was just twenty and quite beautiful, yet she spurned her many suitors in order to rear John and his sister in the best way possible. She came from a well-to-do family and was able to provide John with an excellent education, including studies in rhetoric with the famous pagan teacher Libanius. John also studied law, but was drawn more and more to the ascetic life. Shortly after his mother died, he entered a monastery.

In 381, John returned to his hometown of Antioch and was ordained a deacon. The bishop noticed his communication skills and made him a pastor and chief preacher at one of the Antioch assemblies. In this capacity he faced the tax revolt. During ensuing years he continued to gain respect for his preaching skills. That's how he won the nickname *Chrysostom,* Greek for "golden mouth."

Following the Antioch school of theology, John took a more literal approach to the Bible (as opposed to the Alexandrian school's more allegorical interpretation). He also emphasized the full humanity of Jesus in a time when others were ignoring it. Chrysostom preached lengthy series of messages on Genesis, Matthew, John, and Romans, most of which we still have. He also wrote commentaries.

In 397, the bishopric of Constantinople was open. This was a prestigious appointment, in the capital itself. Emperor Arcadius selected the Golden Orator John. He might have been sorry later.

John was so popular in Antioch that he practically had to be kidnapped to get him to Constantinople. But he was consecrated as bishop in the capital city in 398. Officiating at the consecration was Bishop Theophilus of Alexandria.

Largely for political reasons, Theophilus caused great problems for John. He wanted John to be subservient to him and may have envied the following the new bishop gained through his preaching skills. Theophilus also opposed the theology of Origen, which John borrowed from heavily. In his bold way, John probably did little to appease Bishop Theophilus.

John tried to minister to the large Gothic community in the city, welcoming them but not approving the Arian heresy that many of them held. He also preached strongly against sin where he saw it—and he saw it among his own clergy. Priests were dabbling in immorality, and he wanted it to stop. He also preached against the suggestive dress of the women of Constantinople. Whether or not he meant it that way, the Empress Eudoxia took his words as a personal affront.

As far as Theophilus was concerned, the last straw was when John welcomed four monks who had been disciplined in Alexandria (they were adherents of Origen's theology). The Alexandrian bishop traveled to Constantinople and gathered John's enemies. At an estate called the Oak, in 403, they held a synod that condemned John's teaching and banished him from the church.

But Eudoxia was superstitious. Some accident, perhaps an earthquake, occurred at the palace shortly after the synod, and the empress was scared. She immediately got the emperor to rescind the synod's decisions. John was brought back—for about a year. Undaunted, he continued to speak his mind— especially when a statue of Eudoxia was set up next to the cathedral.

The empress struck back. Imperial soldiers broke up an Easter service, and some of John's supporters were slain. John was sent into exile, to a dismal place near Armenia, called Cucusus.

Pope Innocent I protested his treatment, to no avail. The Eastern emperor had his way. Even in exile, John continued to correspond with his followers, directing the affairs of the church. So the emperor decided to send him even farther away.

That was how John died, traveling to a more remote exile in 407. Over the next few decades, Pope Innocent managed to clear John's name, forcing Bishop Theophilus and others to include John on lists of people for whom the church prayed.

John left a legacy of good preaching. He advanced the Antioch style of literal Bible exposition, and he was one of the first church leaders (along with Ambrose) to stand courageously before rulers and announce, "Thus says the Lord. . . ." At critical times in church history, others would do the same.

405 Jerome Completes the Vulgate

Saint Jerome Reading, by Giovanni Bellini.

From the beginning the church has accepted the necessity for Bible translation. Though the common Greek of the New Testament was widely understood in the Roman Empire, not everyone knew the language, and the church had the goal of reaching everyone with the Gospel.

Early translations appeared in various languages, notably Latin (which in time became the language of the empire), Syriac, and Coptic. Though we may admire the zeal of the first translators, alas, they did not always show a good command of Greek.

From 366 to 385 Damasus was bishop of Rome. Though Rome's bishopric was held in great esteem, it had not yet achieved power beyond the other bishoprics, and Damasus liked power. He wanted to free Western Christianity from the dominance of the East. Greek had long been the accepted language of the church, but Damasus wanted the Western church to become clearly Latin. One way he could accomplish this was to have the Bible translated into Latin.

Damasus's secretary was named Eusebius Hieronymus Sophronius, though he is better known to the church as Jerome. He was trained in Latin and Greek classics, and Jerome berated himself for his fondness for secular authors. To chastise himself he practiced a life of renunciation and withdrew to Syria to study Hebrew. By the time he entered Damasus's service, Jerome had become one of the greatest living scholars.

So Damasus suggested that his secretary produce a new Latin translation of the Bible, one that would throw out the inaccuracies of older translations. Damasus sought uniformity. Just as he had standardized the worship service of the churches under his authority, he wanted a standardized set of Scriptures.

Jerome began his work in 382. When Damasus died in 384, Jerome apparently nursed a desire to take the bishop's position in Rome. Partly in bitterness at not being chosen and partly out of a desire to rid himself of distractions, Jerome moved from Rome to the Holy Land, settling in Bethlehem. In 405 he finished this translation. But it had not been his only task. During those twenty-three years, he also churned out commentaries and other writings and served as spiritual counselor for some wealthy—and very devout—widows. He became involved in every theological battle of his day, contributing eloquent—and often caustic—letters that are still dramatic reading.

Jerome had begun his translation by working from the Septuagint, the Greek version of the Old Testament. But soon he established a precedent for all good Old Testament translators: Work from the original Hebrew. In his quest for accuracy, Jerome consulted many Jewish rabbis.

Jerome had been struck by the fact that the Jewish Scriptures did not include the books we call the Apocrypha. Because they had been included in the Septuagint, Jerome was compelled to include them in his translation, but he made his opinion clear: These were *liber ecclesiastici* ("church books"), not *liber canonici* ("canonical books"); though the Apocryphal books could be used for edification, they could not establish doctrine. Hundreds of years later, the leaders of the Reformation would go one step farther and not include them at all in the Protestant Bible.

The divine library, as Jerome called the Bible, was finally available in a well-written, accurate version, in the language commonly used in the Western churches. It became known as the *Vulgate* (from the Latin *vulgus,* "common"). Jerome's enormous influence caused all serious scholars of the Middle Ages to highly regard his translation. Martin Luther, who knew Hebrew and Greek, quoted from the Vulgate throughout his life.

Because Jerome's work had the church's seal of approval, other translators had a hard time following him. Until the Reformation, only a few translations were made into common European languages, and even then, instead of working from the Greek New Testament, translators returned to the Vulgate.

Ironically, the translation of the Bible into a language every Western church could use probably caused the church to have a worship service and Bible no layman could understand. Jerome's translation gave Latin the impetus Damasus had sought, but the Vulgate became so sacrosanct that eventually translating the Bible into common tongues was prohibited.

432 Patrick Goes as Missionary to Ireland

Landing of Patrick on his first missionary visit to Ireland in A.D. 432.

An ex-slave who was not even born in Ireland would become that nation's most effective Christian witness.

Somewhere around 390, Patrick was born in Roman Britain, the son of Christian parents. Though previously the boy had not taken his faith too seriously, at sixteen, when he was captured, enslaved, and sent to work as a swineherd on a farm in northern Ireland, he began to pray ardently. Escaping from his slavery, Patrick traveled two hundred miles on foot to the coast. There a ship carrying a cargo of hounds took him on as a dog tender. He traveled to France and on to a Mediterranean monastery.

When he returned to his homeland, Patrick dreamed of Irish children begging him to bring the Gospel to them, "We beseech you to come and walk among us once more." Because he felt he had an inadequate understanding of the faith, he returned to France to study in a monastery. Around 432 he returned to Ireland.

A few years earlier the British monk Palladius had attempted to convert the Irish, with little success. Patrick's years in slavery among the Irish seem to have prepared him to be a man of courage who understood this people and how to preach to them.

Legend clouds much of Patrick's life, and many villages tell of his ministry there. We know that the missionary converted most of the Irish to Christianity, establishing around 300 churches and baptizing around 120,000 people. Though Patrick contended with hostile chieftains and the Druids— keepers of the old paganism—"the common people heard him gladly." Not a single martyr was part of the conversion of this contentious tribal people.

Using the nature that they had once worshiped, Patrick described the Trinity by comparing it to the shamrock. The Irish understanding that Patrick acted for God, when he drove out false religion and established the truth, can be seen in the legend that he expelled the snakes from Ireland.

After thirty years of selfless ministry, Patrick died around 460. He has left us a few short writings, including the notable hymn "I bind unto myself today" (known as "Patrick's Breastplate").

Many years later, when missionaries from the Western church came to Ireland, they discovered a thriving Irish faith. The priests and monks of Ireland were notable scholars and missionaries, and the church had had a profound effect on the common people. The clergy lived simple, devoted lives, often in rough circumstances. Though their monasteries were unpretentious stone structures, learning and art (for example, the exquisite Book of Kells) showed the monks' amazingly vital piety. Indeed, that piety reached the rest of Europe as they took the Word abroad.

The church in Ireland had developed outside the hierarchical system of Rome, because Patrick evangelized the nation without relying on the established church. The Irish church was organized around monasteries, which reflected the nation's tribal system. Lacking the desire to establish church bureaucracies, Irish abbots encouraged their monks in the "real business" of the church—preaching, studying, and ministering to the poor.

Ireland did not really become Catholic until the 1100s, when the pope gave the English king, Henry II, sovereignty over Ireland. The Catholic Church, admiring the way Patrick had converted the Irish, made him a saint.

451
The Council of Chalcedon

Though the Council of Nicea had proclaimed that Jesus was fully God, the church had yet to understand His human nature. How did the humanity and Godhead interrelate in the Son?

The answer would come through one of the most heated power plays in the church.

As the church grew in power, the premier cities of the empire grew in theological influence. (As a result, their archbishops were called patriarchs.) Alexandria and Rome generally tended to side together on issues, against Antioch and Constantinople. The combination of politics and theology was especially potent.

The Alexandrian school of thought showed its Greek influence. Many people in Alexandria had a Greek philosophical background. Theologically, they believed Jesus had been fully human, but they tended to emphasize Christ the divine Word (*Logos*) more than the human Jesus. Taken to an extreme, this tended to swallow the humanness of Jesus in His divinity. One of Alexandria's primary supporters, Apollinarius, had fought heatedly against heresies such as Arianism and Manichaeism. But when he claimed that at the Incarnation the divine *Logos* replaced the human soul, so that Christ's humanness was only bodily, he slipped into error. In 381 the second ecumenical council condemned his teaching.

The Antiochene school tended to focus on the human Jesus. Though Jesus was divine, they said His humanity was complete and normal.

When Nestorius, patriarch of Constantinople, became involved in a dispute over the veneration of Mary, he attacked Apollinarius's position. To him, the idea that Mary had been the "bearer of God" smacked of Apollinarius's views. Cyril, patriarch of Alexandria, desiring to sway power away from Constantinople, accused the patriarch of saying that Jesus was two separate natures in one body.

In 431, at the third ecumenical council, in Ephesus, the scheming Cyril had Nestorius deposed before he and his supporters could arrive. When the missing churchmen arrived, under the leadership of John, patriarch of Antioch, they condemned Cyril and his followers. Pressured, Emperor Theodosius, who had called the council, exiled Nestorius.

Add to this volatile situation a clergyman who carried the Alexandrian emphasis to heretical lengths. Eutyches, the head of a monastery near Constantinople, taught a view that came to be called Monophysitism (from *mono,* "one," and *physis,* "nature"). It said that Christ's nature is lost in the divine, "as a drop of honey, which falls into the sea, dissolves in it."

Patriarch Flavian of Constantinople condemned Eutyches as a heretic, but Patriarch Dioscurus of Alexandria upheld him. At Dioscurus's request, Theodosius summoned another council, which met at Ephesus in 449. It ruled that Eutyches was no heretic, but many churches declared the council invalid. Pope Leo labeled it the "robber synod," and today it is not considered a valid ecumenical council.

Leo asked the emperor to summon yet another council, one that would represent the church at large. It gathered at Chalcedon, near Constantinople, in 451, and drew nearly four hundred bishops, more than any previous one. Dioscurus had always been a rather sinister character. Now he was excommunicated for his deeds at the "robber synod."

Pope Leo's *Tome,* a statement about Christ's nature, was read at the Council of Chalcedon. The bishops incorporated his teaching into the statement of faith that is called the Chalcedonian Definition. In it Christ is "acknowledged in two natures, without confusion, without change, without division, without separation . . . the characteristic property of each nature being preserved, and coming together to form one person." This condemned the distinctive views of Apollinarius and Eutyches and those ascribed to Nestorius.

Chalcedon was the first council in which the pope played a major role. Increasingly the focus of battle would be between Rome and Constantinople.

Chalcedon would be the last council both East and West would regard as official, in terms of defining correct teachings. It was also the last in which all regions were represented and able to agree on key issues.

Though Chalcedon could not solve the problem of how Jesus was both God and man, it built fences, defining certain incorrect interpretations. The council said, "However this occurred, we know it did not occur in these ways."

529
Benedict of Nursia Establishes His Monastic Order

Once Christianity became acceptable, under Constantine, it was hard to distinguish between those who followed Christ because it was the popular thing to do and those of real faith. As a result, many zealous Christians sought to separate themselves from the masses by withdrawing from them.

Hermits, such as Anthony, became famous for feats of self-denial. Seeking holiness, they practiced going without food or sleep; standing for hours, while praying; and even living atop pillars. Those who had tired of a compromising church laden with sin felt an attraction to the bizarre behaviors that seemed to prove the hermits' dedication to God.

About 320 Pachomius had begun communal monasticism. Aware that the tendency toward self-denial could get out of hand and even degenerate into spiritual rivalry, Pachomius worked to regulate the ascetic lifestyle, allowing for a simple, self-denying life that did not go too far. Others, such as Basil the Great (330–379) and the Irish Christians, also founded monastic communities.

But Benedict of Nursia became the real force behind European monasticism. He was born into an upper-class Italian family, and as a young man he went to Rome to study. But Rome, which had the reputation of being one of the most Christian cities on earth, struck him as immoral and frivolous. Disgusted, Benedict left and became a hermit.

He gained a reputation for spirituality, and families brought their sons to him, for training in the Christian life. Rather reluctantly the hermit agreed to become abbot of a monastic group. When he proved a strict disciplinarian, however, their enthusiasm for Benedict faded—one monk even went so far as to attempt to poison him. Fearing for his life, Benedict hid in a cave and then left the region. Yet his troubles taught him an important lesson: Discipline is good, but allow for the frailties of human nature.

Around 529, Benedict moved to Monte Cassino, where he destroyed a pagan temple that was still in use and built a monastery.

Had Benedict simply given the church a monastery, he might not be so well remembered. The rule he wrote to govern it was by far more important than the buildings. Benedict envisioned the monastery as a self-contained, self-supporting community that had its own fields and workshops. He wanted to create a "spiritual fortress," to ensure the monks wouldn't have to go elsewhere for life's necessities. Within the confines of the monastic community, monks wove their own cloth, grew their own food, and made their own furniture. Wandering outside the monastery walls was seen as a great spiritual danger.

As Benedict had already seen, some would-be monks had a shallow commitment. So he provided for a one-year novitiate, a time for the monk to decide that this was what he truly wanted. Only after that test year would he take the three vows that forever cut him off from the world: The vow of *poverty* required that he surrender all personal goods to the community; with the *chastity* vow he renounced all sexual relations; in the vow of *obedience* he promised always to obey the monastery's leaders.

Worship played a large role in monastic life. The Benedictine Rule provided for seven services each day, including a vigil service, at about 2:00

A.M., which was considered especially important. Each service took about twenty minutes and largely consisted of reciting Psalms.

In addition to public worship, the monks took part in individual devotions—reading the Bible, meditating, and praying. Though many have accused monastic communities of withdrawing from the world, they prayed for those outside their walls.

"Idleness is the enemy of the soul," declared the rule. So every monk had to take part in manual labor, including kitchen work.

Though this life of work, prayer, and worship may sound tedious, it was an attempt to create an ordered life without going to extremes.

Benedict also sought to make the holy life available to ordinary human beings. In the rule, he wrote, "If we seem to be severe, do not get frightened and run away. The entrance to the path of salvation must be narrow. But as you progress along the life of faith, the heart expands and speeds with love's sweetness along the pathway of God's commandments."

In a crude, unstable era, Benedictine monasticism provided the religiously sensitive with a haven. Though Western Europe had become nominally Christian, much of the populace still behaved like pagans. Benedict offered a quiet, purposeful, and noble life that was unavailable outside the cloister. Many may not sympathize with such withdrawal, but it is certainly understandable why some would seek peace in the midst of a coarse world.

Benedict gave monasticism a permanent place in Western Europe—for good or ill. His rule has guided monastic communities for centuries and is still in effect today.

563
Columba Goes as a Missionary to Scotland

Embarkation of Columba for Scotland.

An Irishman evangelized Scotland.

The man was named *Columba,* which means "dove," and he came from a family of Christians. He was born in 521, in the north of Ireland—today's County Donegal. After attending monastic schools, he became noted for his learning and piety, and he would help establish several monasteries in Ireland.

On more than one occasion, it is said, Columba had had disputes with his clan's chieftain, Diamait. Though he was a Christian, Columba had a hasty temper that got him into trouble. This time he seems to have caused a battle in which 3,000 men died. He had not intended to cause such harm, but for his own safety and to do penance for his error, he left Ireland, planning to convert the same number of souls as those whose deaths he had caused. Some sources claim he also agreed never to return to his homeland.

With twelve companions, in 563, Columba courageously took to the seas in a *currach,* the hide-covered vessel popular in Ireland. They set forth for Iona, a western Scottish island. When they arrived, the thirteen men erected humble dwellings and a plank church, which they used as a base for their missionary efforts with the Picts, the neighboring Scottish tribe.

Columba called on Brude, the chief in Inverness, but Brude wanted nothing to do with missionaries. According to the story, he bolted his gates against them. When Columba made the sign of the cross, and the gates flew open, the awestruck chieftain willingly listened to their message.

They received some opposition from the pagan priests, the Druids, but before long the Christians had success-

fully evangelized Scotland and northern England.

Columba continued to travel, but he also became abbot of a large monastery on Iona. After his death, the abbots there would retain his power, becoming the highest-ranking church officials in Scotland.

Evangelists spread out from Iona, creating new monasteries in Europe, and each looked to Iona for guidance. As a result, Iona became known for its learning, piety, and evangelism. The Vikings repeatedly ravaged the community, but it continued. Forty-six Scottish kings are buried there, along with the first abbot, though Columba's remains were several times disturbed by the Viking invasions.

As with other monasteries, at the Reformation, Iona was torn down. In 1900 a Scottish duke granted the lands to the Church of Scotland. Thirty-eight years later a community of clergy and laymen was formed on the island, and it now receives the support of thousands of associate members worldwide.

A devoted scholar, Columba copied books and wrote his own. By preserving the importance of learning, he influenced the monks of the Dark Ages, who kept copying manuscripts as literacy generally declined in Europe.

Many historians have noted the great influence Christianity has had on Scotland. As its first great evangelizer, Columba may be counted as one of the witnesses that led to so many preachers, missionaries, and writers who have come from a tiny land.

590
Gregory I
Becomes Pope

Pope Gregory I ("the Great").

Though no longer capital of an empire, Rome still had prestige. After all, the ancient city had connections with the Apostles Peter and Paul.

For many years the bishops of Rome had attempted to increase their power. Slowly theirs had achieved a favored position over the other sees, and the bishop of Rome had become the pope.

Yet the man who would do the most to bolster the authority and power of the papacy did not do so for political gain. A humble monk who did not seek high office, he rose to the papacy over his own objections.

Gregory was born in 540 to a noble Roman family with a history of political service. He became prefect of Rome—the highest civil office. Yet he did not feel cut out for public life and resigned, divvying up his estates for the founding of monasteries and joining one himself. A few years later, he would become an abbot.

His piety—and no doubt his background as a skillful administrator—attracted attention. In 590, when the pope died, the Romans unanimously asked Gregory to become his successor. Though Gregory refused, the public will prevailed.

As a former statesman, the new pope brought his powers of ruling to his office. When the Lombards threatened Rome, Gregory appealed to the emperor at Constantinople for help. When none came, the bishop of Rome mustered troops, negotiated treaties, and did all required to bring peace. Gregory's independent actions proved to the emperor's exarch (his representative, who was in Ravenna) that Gregory was quite able to keep order in Rome. These political moves would become some of the first steps in dividing the Christians of the Eastern and Western empires.

But Gregory did not really have political ambitions. His interests were spiritual. Greatly concerned about pastoral care, he insisted that the clergy see themselves as shepherds and servants of the flock. He referred to himself as the "servant of the servants of God," and his *Pastoral Rule,* an amazingly insightful study of people's spiritual trials and how the clergy should deal with them, became a kind of ministerial textbook for the Middle Ages.

Gregory's *Dialogues* was an early attempt at *hagiography,* "writing about the saints," which emphasized the fantastic and miraculous, turning the saints into sort of superheroes. During his papacy, veneration of the body parts, clothing, and so on of saints was encouraged; it would become a major feature of medieval piety. For centuries no church could be established without the relic of a saint to be placed in it.

Though Gregory did not claim to be a theologian, some of his beliefs became essentials in Catholic theology. He believed in purgatory and taught that masses celebrated in behalf of the dead could relieve their pains there. In addition he helped popularize the teachings of Dionysius the Areopagite, who had written about different categories of angels. After Gregory, these ideas would become widely accepted.

Though he may not have originated the Gregorian chant, Gregory was interested in church music, and the plainsong chant owes much to his influence.

In addition, Gregory authorized an evangelization mission to Kent, under Augustine, the missionary who would later become the first Archbishop of Canterbury. Though Christianity had already reached Britain, in sending the mission under Augustine, he extended the power of Rome to those isles. A Christianity that looked to Rome for leadership was definitely taking shape.

The bishop of Constantinople claimed the title Ecumenical ("global" or "universal") Patriarch. Gregory both refused to accept his use of that title and rejected it for himself. Yet everything he did showed that Gregory saw himself as chief pastor of the worldwide church.

Within fourteen years Gregory achieved so much that later generations named him Gregory the Great. Perhaps he became great because he was a humble man.

664
Synod of Whitby

Synod of Whitby.

Two Christianities existed in England. One was Celtic, strongly monastic, contemplative, and mission minded. The other was Roman, well-organized, and firmly tied to the rest of Christendom.

Columba's mission to Iona had resulted in an outgoing community of Celtic-style Christians who aggressively evangelized the Angles and Saxons. Shortly before Columba died, Pope Gregory sent Augustine and over thirty other monks to England, to evangelize and to bring the Celtic church into conformity with the Roman church. Augustine's moderate success centered on Kent and Essex. In 627, Paulinus of York established the Roman church in Northumbria, but his efforts soon fell apart when a heathen king came to power. When the church was reestablished there, it was Celtic.

Yet in the early 600s, there was a great deal of cross-pollination going on. The two traditions were not vastly different. The major distinction between them was the date on which they celebrated Easter. Though their monks also shaved their heads differently, and there were minor ceremonial discrepancies, it was largely a question of power. Would the pope rule over the English church, appointing bishops to lead the people? The Celtic tradition gave great power to the abbots, who functioned rather independently.

Because of their independence, the Celtic monasteries were prone to abuses. In the medieval feudal system, it was advantageous to set up sham monasteries, to avoid subservience to secular landlords. Such monasteries enjoyed economic independence but lacked spiritual motives. Though the Celtic church was largely known for its spiritual devotion, abuses like these may have swayed some believers toward the more stringent Roman policies.

The matter was brought to a head by Oswy, the new king of Northumbria, in 664. He followed the Celtic tradition, but his wife was of the Roman tradition. So he would be celebrating Easter when the queen was fasting for Lent, and that simply would not do. He summoned an assembly at Whitby, where the renowned Abbess Hilda ruled the monastery. There the king heard arguments from Cedd and Colman, on the Celtic side, and from Wilfrid and James the Deacon, on the Roman. These were all devout churchmen. Cedd, an abbot, had founded monasteries. Colman and Wilfrid were bishops. Wilfrid had even served as a missionary in Friesland. And James had carried on Paulinus's work in Northumbria, during difficult times.

They argued about Easter. The Celtic leaders quoted from Columba. The Roman leaders cited Saint Peter. Smiling, the king announced that he would rather follow Peter, since he was the keeper of heaven's keys. The Roman way prevailed.

Some historians argue that the decision proved to be wise. The English church got the best of both worlds. The Celtic spirit was still very much alive, but it needed the Roman organization to focus it. Others rue the missed opportunity for a separate major, vital Christian tradition.

In the immediate wake of Whitby, things turned sour. A plague hit England about the time that the Archbishop of Canterbury died. For five years the church struggled without leadership. Then Theodore of Tarsus arrived to take the position. Wisely, he bolstered the church leadership, appointing bishops and priests from both Celtic and Roman traditions.

The next century was a golden age of art and scholarship in Britain as the Roman and Celtic styles complemented each other. Much of this was destroyed by the Viking invasions, but numerous stone crosses remain, carved in both Celtic and Roman styles, symbolizing the interdependence of these two traditions.

716
Boniface Sets Out as Missionary

Statue of Boniface, missionary to the Germans, in the marketplace at Fulda, the town in which he was buried.

Almost like Elijah, on Mount Carmel, Boniface, the Saxon missionary from England, stood against paganism, deep in the heart of Germany. He had an ax in his hand. Before him was the huge Thundering Tree, a local landmark that the pagan peoples said was sacred to the thunder god, Donar. Even some who had been converted to Christianity through Boniface's preaching secretly worshiped at this tree.

Boldly, Boniface denounced this false worship. As a representative of the true God of the Christians, he would destroy this evil shrine. He struck the "sacred" tree with the ax, and amazingly the Thundering Tree thundered to the ground.

So goes the legend. Whether or not the details are true, it fairly depicts Boniface's boldness, his faith, and his unrelenting challenge to false religion.

Born to Christian parents in Wessex in 680, he was originally named Winfred. He was trained in a Benedictine monastery and ordained at age thirty. He had obvious gifts of learning and leadership and could have stayed in England, studying, teaching, and perhaps running a monastery. But his heart burned for others who were not yet in the Christian fold. Thousands of his fellow Saxons in the Low Countries and in Germany needed to hear the Gospel.

In 716, Winfred set out for Frisia, where English missionaries had labored for several decades. The Frisian king, Radbod, opposed Christianity. The pressure was too great, and Winfred returned to England, his first mission a failure.

His fellow Benedictines asked him to serve as abbot of their monastery. After the harrowing experiences in Frisia, he may have felt tempted. But Winfred's vision was still outward. He traveled to Rome in 718 and there received a missionary commission from the pope. He was to go farther onto the continent, beyond the Rhine, and establish the Roman church among the German peoples.

Much of Germany had been exposed to Christianity of one sort or another, but no strong church existed there. In the fourth century, the German tribes had latched onto Arianism and mingled it with their own superstitions. More recently, Celtic missionaries had won some converts, but they had not followed up with a viable church organization. The pope was eager for the church to establish a presence there.

Winfred went first to Thuringia, to revive a weakened church there. Then, hearing that his old foe Radbod had died, he returned to Frisia. The papal authorization may have given Winfred more clout with local rulers. He worked there for three years and moved southeastward to Hesse.

He returned to Rome in 723 and was consecrated as a bishop. It was then he received his new name—*Boniface*. He was also given a letter of introduction to Charles Martel, king of the Franks. Charles's military prowess was renowned (he would later turn back the Muslims at Tours). His patronage was a great support for Boniface.

Returning to Hesse, Boniface continued his efforts at tearing down paganism and building up the church. This was when he supposedly felled the sacred tree. Perhaps the fear of Charles Martel kept the citizens from felling Boniface. Still, the upshot of the legend was that Christianity became the new force to be reckoned with in Germany. If the German gods couldn't even keep their tree standing, they had little to offer compared with Boniface's God.

Boniface attracted numerous missionaries from England—monks and nuns who were eager to serve with him. With their help, he set up a sturdy church organization throughout the region.

Ironically, his protector, Charles Martel, was frustrating attempts at church reform among the Franks. Charles kept the church there under his thumb, seizing its land and selling church offices. Only after he died, in 741, could Boniface overhaul the Frankish church.

In 747, Boniface journeyed once again to Rome, where he was named archbishop of Mainz and spiritual leader of all Germany. Yet as he passed the age of seventy, he was eager to settle unfinished business. Resigning his archbishopric in 753, he went back to Frisia, where he had started his missionary work. There, he reclaimed some of his earlier converts who had lapsed into paganism, and he moved out again—to unreached areas.

On Pentecost Sunday, 755, at Dackum, along the Borne River, he planned an open-air service of preaching and confirmation of new believers. As he stood by the river, preparing for the service, a band of pagan hoodlums rushed upon him. Others in his party prepared to fight them off, but Boniface shouted, "Cease, my children, from conflict. . . . Fear not those who kill the body but cannot kill the immortal soul. . . . Receive with constancy this momentary blow of death, that you may live and reign with Christ forever." It is said that he died with the Gospels in his hands.

Critics say that Boniface was merely an organization man, that most of his "mission work" was largely political, fostering allegiance to the Roman church in an area where it had been weak. And it is true that he helped lay the foundation for the Holy Roman Empire and the politics of the medieval papacy. Because of Boniface, Germany was a stronghold of the Roman church up to the Reformation.

But few can question Boniface's personal devotion, his courage, or his faithful service. As historian Kenneth Scott Latourette has written, "Few, if any, Christian missionaries have more accurately presented by their conduct the ideals of the faith they have sought to propagate. Humble, in spite of the temptations which came with high ecclesiastical position; above the breath of scandal; a man of prayer and self-reliance; courageous, self-sacrificing; and with a passion for righteousness— Boniface was one of the outstanding exemplars of the Christian life."

731
The Venerable Bede Completes His *Ecclesiastical History of the English Nation*

The Venerable Bede, English historian.

In an age not noted for its scholarship, Bede stands out like a beacon. The fact that he was called the Venerable Bede testifies to his great learning and the esteem in which he was held.

Though political confusion had effectively destroyed much culture, the monasteries remained medieval centers of education. There boys learned their letters, the scribes copied ancient manuscripts, and learned men like Bede pored over texts. The monks kept the wisdom of ancient Greece and Rome alive, along with the works of the church Fathers. Life went on at an unhurried pace between monastic walls.

Not only was he one of the most brilliant scholars of this age, Bede was also very devout. In a very brief autobiography, he tells of his birth on the lands of the Wearmouth and Jarrow monastery, in northern England, in the year 635. At seven he came under the tutelage of the abbot there and spent the remainder of his life at the monastery, never venturing far afield.

Although the usual minimum age for ordination to the deaconate was twenty-five, Bede received it at nineteen, doubtless a recommendation of his piety. At thirty he became a priest and spent the rest of his life writing Bible commentaries and other religious works. His biography seems more a catalog of his books than one of his deeds.

Bede's great gift to the church, *Historia Ecclesiastica Gentis Anglorum (Ecclesiastical History of the English Nation)*, traced the history of England from the days of Julius Caesar to his own. Though in many ways it was an all-purpose history, the chief focus of the book was the Christianization of England and the way paganism gradually gave way to the new religion.

Bede's book abounded in stories of valiant missionaries and pagan chieftains who finally saw the light of truth, yet the author retained a healthy skepticism. Naturally, in a prescientific age, he could have included almost any story, and few would have disputed his report. But Bede, concerned for historical truth, carefully cites his sources by referring to some reliable witness. Though Bede had no trouble believing in miracles, he wanted *real* ones, not simply pious legends.

What a history he tells! Julius Caesar and Claudius, Pope Gregory and the missionary Augustine, and the invading tribes of Angles, Saxons, and Jutes all populate its pages. Through it we know wonderful stories, such as that of Gregory the Great, who saw fair-haired slave boys for sale in Rome and was so struck by their beauty that he never forgot his desire to evangelize their homeland. We also read of the pagan King Edwin, whose advisor told a parable comparing life to a sparrow flitting through a banquet hall and exiting into darkness. He then advised the king to convert to Christianity, since it gave some hope of a life beyond the "brief flit in the banqueting hall."

Bede's history contains some quaint passages like this, "No snake can exist there [in Ireland]; for although often brought over from Britain, as soon as the ship nears land, they breathe the scent of its airs, and die. In fact, almost everything on this isle confers immunity to poison." But even secular historians don't doubt Bede's carefulness as a reporter, because they continue to find his facts correct in almost every detail.

Prior to the *Historia Ecclesiastica Gentis Anglorum,* the various tribes of England had their own histories, mostly in the form of pagan poetry, frequently recited by bards. But Bede presented history through the lens of Christianity, as a diverse group of tribes became one nation with a single religion.

Instead of valiant warrior heroes like Beowulf, Bede's heroes are saints, people dependent on God's grace. He, along with other medieval historians, gave history a new framework: It was to be as accurate as possible; it was to inspire.

Without Bede, many of these stories would have passed away with the age. To this venerable monk the English can give thanks for a consciousness of their identity as a nation and their place as a Christian country.

732
The Battle of Tours

Charles Martel at the Battle of Tours.

If it weren't for Charles Martel, we might all be speaking Arabic and kneeling toward Mecca five times a day. At Tours, Charles Martel and his Frankish army turned back the massive juggernaut of Muslim forces that had swept across North Africa and into Europe. The Battle of Tours saved the day for Western civilization.

The rapid rise of Islam is one of the most incredible movements in history.

In 622, the followers of Muhammad were a persecuted band of visionaries huddled in Mecca. One hundred years later, they controlled not only Arabia, but all of North Africa, Palestine, Persia, Spain, parts of India—and they were threatening France and Constantinople.

How did they do it? Conversion, diplomacy, and a fiercely dedicated fighting force. It might also be said that the fallen Roman Empire had left the territory ripe for the picking.

Muhammad's religion developed in Mecca, one of two major Arabian cities. It was vehemently monotheistic and legalistic, but fairly simple. Muhammad claimed to have received his system from God (Allah) and said he was Allah's designated prophet. The citizens of Mecca opposed Muhammad's new teachings and made life rough for his followers. So in 622 the prophet took his band and fled to Medina (Arabia's other major city). This flight (hegira) marks the start of the Muslim calendar and the beginning of their incredible expansion.

Arabia at the time was a diverse collection of nomadic tribes that were always warring against each other. Islam brought unity—not only in religion, but law, economics, and politics as well. When Muhammad died (632), there was infighting among several would-be successors. But still the faith expanded.

By 636, the Muslims controlled Syria and Palestine. They took Alexandria in 642, Mesopotamia in 646. Carthage fell in 697, as the Muslims swept across North Africa, winning territory that re-

mains in Muslim hands to this day. In 711, they crossed the Strait of Gibraltar and entered Spain. They quickly solidified control of the Iberian Peninsula and eventually moved beyond the Pyrenees. In the meantime, Muslims had entered the Punjab area of India and were knocking at the door of Constantinople.

Constantinople was the capital of the Byzantine Empire, all that remained of the once-proud Roman Empire. Centuries earlier, the Roman Empire had divided into East and West, and the Western empire quickly fell to various Germanic tribes—Vandals, Ostrogoths, and Franks. The only power Rome held now was in the church, but this was growing. Through missionaries such as Augustine in England and Boniface in Germany, Rome was gaining spiritual allegiance in its old political territories.

The Muslim threat combined religion and political power. Islam not only overthrew political authorities, it converted people and offered them (or forced on them) a new religious system.

Charles Martel was ruler of the Franks, one of the Germanic tribes that had overrun the Western empire. The Franks had invaded Gaul in 355 and had officially converted to Roman Christianity under the reign of Clovis I (481–511). Like previous Frankish rulers, Charles sought to use the church to his advantage. He was quite happy to support Roman missionaries among the other Germanic tribes—this might advance Frankish power in Germany. However, he was also quick to corrupt the Frankish church for his own profit. Though he may have saved the Roman church from ruin at Tours, he no doubt fought to protect the territory of the Franks.

The Muslim general Abd-er-Rahman led his troops northward, well into Frankish territory. Charles Martel (*Martel* means "the Hammer") met him between Tours and Poitiers and beat him back. In a series of strenuous battles, the Franks pushed the Muslims back into Spain, ending the Muslim advance on Europe.

Certainly the successful defense of Constantinople in 718 was equally important in containing the Muslim conquest. But for those who trace their heritage to Western Europe, the Battle of Tours was crucial. If the Muslims had won, they might have fallen back later; they might have spread themselves too thin. But almost as incredible as their rapid expansion is the way the Muslims have held onto the bulk of the territory they gained. Twelve and a half centuries later, they remain a formidable force in the world, and the lands they hold remain largely resistant to Christian witness.

800 Charlemagne Crowned Emperor

Visit of Charlemagne to the pope.

Should church and state be one?

In the ancient world, every state had its own gods—and the Roman emperor had been one of them. No one separated religion from politics. When Constantine converted and brought Christianity to the empire as its favored religion, that connection found its way into the church.

Even after the empire fell, many people clung to the idea that there *should* be a Christian empire. But who would lead? Was the spiritual leader, the pope, to rule, or would authority lie in the hands of a king? Through the Middle Ages leaders would seek the answers to these questions.

By the middle of the eighth century the papacy had become powerful, yet it still had not achieved the goal of restoring order to the Western world. In 754 a forged document, the Donation of Constantine, would attempt to keep alive the idea of a Roman empire. According to the Donation, the Roman emperor Constantine had moved to Constantinople to allow the pope control of the West. Constantine had purportedly bequeathed that part of the empire to the bishop of Rome.

Following the ideas in the Donation of Constantine, the Frankish king Pepin III, son of Charles Martel, decided to take Ravenna from the Lombards and give it to the pope. In 756 the Donation of Pepin conferred the Papal States on him.

Though the pope had gained his own territory, he never achieved direct imperial control. That would lie in the hands of Pepin's son, Charles the Great—or Charlemagne.

In 771, when Charlemagne took his throne, he began three decades of conquering. He pushed the borders of his kingdom east, and in the end he controlled Burgundy, much of Italy, Alamania, Bavaria, and Thurginia. To the north he had power over Saxony and Frisia. East of these he created territories with a special military organization, called marches. They stretched from the Baltic Sea to the Adriatic. For the first time, a large part of Europe had a stable leadership.

Until Christmas Day, 800, Charlemagne held the title *king*. On that holiday Pope Leo II crowned him emperor, and again it seemed that Western Europe had an emperor to follow in Constantine's footsteps.

Certainly Charlemagne took seriously the idea that he had become the Christian emperor, for all his official dispatches began "Charles, by the will of God, Roman Emperor."

The new emperor was an imposing man—tall, strong, a great horseman, and a fearless and sometimes cruel fighter. He presented Europe with a powerful but benevolent father figure.

Charlemagne by no means wished to lose any of his power. The emperor in Constantinople presented no problem, for he had officially recognized Charlemagne's rights. But those under him or the pope might seek to strip Charlemagne of some authority. Because his was a vast realm, Charlemagne appointed a pair of officials known as the *missi dominici*. These men traveled the empire to check on local officials. Even the pope could not hide from their watchful eyes, and the *missi* held sway over church and state.

Though he was barely literate, Charlemagne held learning in high esteem; under his peaceful rule an awakening of art and scholarship, known as the Carolingian Renaissance, took place. The emperor sponsored a palace school at Aachen. Alcuin, a brilliant Anglo-Saxon scholar, was master there; he exhorted his students "The years go by like running water. Waste not the teachable days in idleness!" Alcuin wrote textbooks on grammar, spelling, rhetoric, and logic: he also wrote biblical commentaries and took the side of orthodoxy in many theological debates.

Not only did Aachen's school stimulate learning through the empire, Charles decreed that every monastery should have a school for teaching "all those who with God's help are able to learn."

The Carolingian Renaissance preserved many writings of the ancient world. As monks made copies of ancient Latin works—some of them beautifully illuminated—monasteries became "culture banks." In many cases, without the labors of these monks, ancient works would have been lost to us.

In an age of confusion and warfare, Charlemagne's rule provided political stability and culture. He insured that the West would retain its ancient cultural legacy, that Christianity would be spread in his empire, and that the clergy would preach on the basic elements of the faith. He also gave the pope his protection.

However, Charlemagne saw no reason to give the pope his power. Was he not a Christian emperor whose ultimate loyalty was to God? In fact, this formidable figure submitted to no one but Him.

When Charlemagne died in 814, his empire began to gradually disintegrate. It was divided among his three sons, and slowly the pope gained more and more power.

But Charlemagne had bequeathed the West an alluring vision: A Christian king with supreme authority throughout his domain. For hundreds of years popes and kings would seek such control over their own territories—and others'. It was an idea that would take a long time to die.

863 Cyril and Methodius Evangelize Slavs

Centuries before Michelangelo or chalk talks, an artistic missionary painted a picture of the Last Judgment on a wall—and won a king to Christ.

As the story goes, the artist was Methodius, who was also a monk and a missionary; the monarch was King Boris of Bulgaria. Methodius, with his brother, Cyril, had a noteworthy career. Among their exploits, they brought Christian faith to the Slavs—and in the process did much to transform and preserve the Slavic culture. The church that later produced Hus, Comenius, and many of the followers caught up in Zinzendorf's spiritual revolution started with these two Greek brothers from Thessalonica.

Both were dedicated churchmen.

Methodius, the older, was the abbot of a Greek monastery. Cyril (then known as Constantine), a philosophy professor at Constantinople, had already been on a mission to the Arabs. In 860 they joined forces to evangelize the Khazar tribe, northeast of the Black Sea.

East-West tensions were already strong as Rome vied with Constantinople for religious and political control of border territories. When Rostislav, the ruler of the Great Moravian State (one such border territory), grew worried about the Western encroachment of the Franks and Germans on his Slavic people, he turned east. He appealed to the emperor in Constantinople, Michael III, to send help—and missionaries. Thus the call came to Cyril and Methodius.

Arriving in 863, the brothers quickly learned the native language and began translating Scripture and the church liturgy into Slavonic. Cyril invented a new alphabet based on Greek letters. (This became the foundation for the Russian alphabet. "Cyrillic" is still used by some today.)

Centuries before Wycliffe, Hus, or Luther, the idea of worshiping in any language other than Latin or Greek shocked many. The German archbishop of Salzburg raised a fuss, probably motivated by politics more than by piety. The Roman church could not sit idly by while this Moravian territory on its doorstep was being easternized. Cyril and Methodius went to Rome in 868 to argue their case for indigenous worship. Pope Adrian II agreed with Cyril and Methodius, authorizing the Slavic

liturgy. The two became Roman monks. Cyril died the next year, but Methodius returned to Moravia as a bishop. Even though he was the official papal legate, the German clergy arrested and jailed him for three years. The succeeding pope, John VIII, intervened on his behalf and ratified the Slavic church's independence. But Methodius continued to face opposition from German clergy until his death in 885.

Shortly afterward, the Latin liturgy replaced the Slavic, and the church in this area declined. But a fiercely independent strain of Christian faith had been spawned. Despite their problems, Cyril and Methodius had established a Christian tradition in Moravia and neighboring countries that has nurtured and extended the faith throughout the world.

---

909 Monastery Established at Cluny

The church was hurting in the ninth and tenth centuries. Political struggles had torn Europe apart. Church leaders were grabbing for land and power, practicing violence and deceit, and indulging in wanton behavior—just like the secular warlords.

Then William the Pious, Duke of Aquitaine, set up a monastery at Cluny. It would be an independent society, free from the power struggles of the empire, under the protection of the pope. The monastery would follow the rule laid out by Benedict of Nursia in the 500s—poverty, chastity, and obedience. Benedict's rule had been applauded. Luminaries like Gregory the Great and Charlemagne had promoted it, and it was briefly enforced empirewide in the ninth century. But it had never really taken root until now, at Cluny.

A series of capable leaders made Cluny work: Berno, Odo, Majolus, Odilo, Hugh. Under their guidance new monasteries grew up in France, Italy, and Germany, "daughter houses" to Cluny. Existing monasteries came to Cluny for help. In a feudal age, Cluny became the center of a spiritual fiefdom. It accrued power far beyond its original ideal. But the time was right for a reform movement, and Cluny carried the flag. It was the site of the largest church building in Western Christendom, until Saint Peter's was built in Rome. By A.D. 1100, Cluny may have led as many as 2,000 monasteries.

This monastic movement had a reforming effect on the church. The monks exemplified and promoted Christian behavior. The priesthood was improved as devout Cluniac monks became bishops and even popes. Cluny stood resolutely against simony—the buying of priestly offices—and Nicolaitanism—the taking of concubines or wives by priests.

But Cluny also managed to rub a few rough edges off secular society. The knightly class began to develop a Christian chivalry. Cluny's promotion of a "Truce of God"—which stated that warring was illegal from Thursday night to Monday morning—somewhat limited petty wars between noblemen, though the ban apparently did not apply to battles with infidels. Since Pope Urban II had been prior at Cluny, its influence may be somewhat responsible for the First Crusade.

Cluny's power reached its peak under Abbot Hugh (1049–1109). Under Peter the Venerable (serving 1122–1156) things began to decline. Power may have lured Cluny from the simplicity of Benedict. The Cistercian order of Bernard would later renew the church's spiritual momentum.

988
Conversion of Vladimir, Prince of Russia

The conversion of a fun-loving pagan ruler effectively brought Christianity to Russia.

Though Christianity had already penetrated Russia by the early part of the tenth century, it did not become generally accepted. In 957 Olga, the widowed princess of Kiev, had been baptized. She asked German King Otto I to send missionaries to her country; but they must have had little success, for the pagan religions lived on.

Vladimir, Olga's grandson, was among those pagans. He built a number of pagan temples, made a name for himself with his cruelty and treachery, had 800 concubines and five wives, and when he wasn't fighting a war, he hunted and feasted. You hardly would have picked him out as the man to spread Christianity to his people.

Like most rulers, Vladimir wanted to keep his people contented. He saw that he might do this by uniting them in one religion. So reportedly he sent out men to examine each of the major religions. Neither Islam nor Judaism, with their dietary restrictions, appealed to the prince, so he had to choose between Roman Christianity and the Eastern church.

After attending worship in the Church of Holy Wisdom, in Constantinople, Vladimir's men reported: "We do not know whether we were in heaven or on earth, for surely there is no such splendor or beauty anywhere upon earth. We cannot describe it to you. Only we know that God dwells there among men and that their service surpasses the worship of all other places. We cannot forget that beauty."

According to the story, because of that beauty, Vladimir chose Orthodoxy. True, it was the religion of his nation's most powerful, wealthiest, and most civilized neighbor: the Byzantine Empire. Offered Anna, the sister of the Byzantine Emperor Basil, as his bride, Vladimir accepted, further consolidating his position with his neighbor.

In 988 Vladimir was baptized, and a year later he married Anna, but neither act was a sign that he submitted to the Byzantine Empire.

Vladimir's choice made it clear that the Russian church would focus on worship. Eastern Orthodoxy has always had an aesthetic appeal. The name of the prince's chosen religion, *Pravoslavie,* meant "true worship" or "right glory." To the Russian mind, Christianity meant liturgy.

After Vladimir's baptism, without too much difficulty, the people put aside the old religions. Though Russia would not become a Christian nation overnight, things began to change. At first the mass conversions did not run deep, but with the help of monks—always a prime force in Eastern Orthodoxy—the new religion began to make its influence felt.

Thanks to Methodius and Cyril, Russia had a Christian liturgy in its own language—Slavonic. In the beautiful churches built by Vladimir and his successors, the people could participate in a beautiful liturgy in their own tongue.

Vladimir's conversion clearly affected his life-style. When he married Anna, he put away his five former wives. He destroyed idols, protected the poor, established schools and churches, and lived at peace with neighboring nations. On his deathbed he gave all his possessions to the poor. The Greek church eventually canonized him.

1054
The East-West Schism

For many years the churches in the East and West had been growing apart. What had once been a single church slowly separated into two distinct identities.

Many nit-picking differences added heat to the conflict. The East used Greek as its language; the West used Latin, thanks to the Vulgate and Western theologians who wrote in that language. Forms of worship differed: the bread used in communion, the date for Lent, and how mass was celebrated. In the East clergy could marry, and they wore beards. Western priests could not marry and were clean shaven.

Theologies also differed. The East felt uncomfortable with the West's doctrine of purgatory. The West used the Latin word *filioque,* "and from the Son," in the Nicene Creed, after the clause about the Holy Spirit, which says the Spirit "proceeds from the Father." To the East, that addition was heretical.

Differences that had existed for centuries exploded because of two strong-willed men. In 1043, Michael Cerularius became patriarch of Constantinople. In 1049 Leo IX became pope. Leo wanted Michael—and through him, the Eastern church—to submit to Rome. The pope sent representatives to Constantinople; Michael refused to meet them. So the representatives excommunicated Michael on behalf of the pope. The patriarch responded by excommunicating the representatives.

By each declaring that the other was not a true Christian, the two bishops created a *schism.* But they alone had not caused the split. The combatants had a history of differences behind them. The schism was the final act that acknowledged that.

As the creed said, both sides believed in "one holy, catholic, and apostolic church." In 1089 Pope Urban tried to

heal the breach by revoking the patriarch's excommunication; he also promoted the First Crusade as a means of
reuniting East and West. It didn't
work.

Later centuries saw attempts to re-
unite the churches, but none were successful. The short-lived "reunion" of
1204 increased the hostility. In 1453,
when the Muslim Turks took over Constantinople, some Eastern Christians
claimed they preferred the Muslims to
Catholics. A united Christendom
seemed impossible.

Though the differences between the
two churches may seem less than essential, at the heart it was a matter of
power. In an age that saw bishops' authority as a key to the stability of the
church, no two could claim the same
authority. When East and West failed
to agree, they would go their separate
ways.

1093
Anselm Becomes Archbishop of Canterbury

One of England's greatest theologians
was born in Italy and squabbled with
two kings.

Anselm was born in the Italian Alps
around 1033. He rejected his father's
desire that he enter politics and wandered around Europe for several years.
Like many bright, young, and restless
men of his day, he joined a monastery.
At Bec, in Normandy, under a remarkable teacher named Lanfranc, Anselm
would begin a noteworthy career.

In 1066 William of Normandy con-
quered England. During the years that
followed, the new king brought many
Norman teachers and clergy across to
England. Among them was Lanfranc,
who became archbishop of Canterbury
in 1070. Anselm took his mentor's place
as abbot of Bec.

In 1093, William II, son of the con-
queror, made Anselm archbishop of
Canterbury, but it was not a move that
improved church-state relations. The
headstrong, aggressive king coveted
the right to appoint clergy in the realm.
Anselm, a humble man who wanted to
protect the church, its lands, and its

funds from the clutches of greedy kings, refused to accept that. For a time the archbishop lived in exile in Italy. William confiscated all the church funds going to Canterbury.

When William died, his brother, Henry I, succeeded him. Though he asked Anselm to return, the battles between church and state did not end. Henry was as bad as his brother, and Anselm again went into exile.

During his time in England, Anselm proved himself a compassionate shepherd and an able administrator. Exiled to the continent, he proved himself a great theologian, for it was then that he did his greatest writing.

In *Cur Deus Homo (Why Did God Become Man?)* Anselm put forth a theory about how Christ's death on the cross reconciles men to God. God, Anselm said, is Lord of the cosmos, a Being whose honor is offended by man's sin. Though He wishes to forgive man, in order to maintain moral order in the universe, He cannot simply "overlook" sin. Some satisfaction must be made, something equal to the offense. Since sin is man's, satisfaction must be made by man; yet man cannot offer adequate satisfaction. So God became man, and the one who offers satisfaction is both God and man: Christ.

Anselm's idea has become known as the Satisfaction Theory of the atonement and is still probably the best-known theological explanation of Christ's atoning work. It has biblical sources such as "God was reconciling the world to himself in Christ, not counting men's sins against them . . ." (2 Corinthians 5:19 NIV).

Anselm was one of the "schoolmen" or Scholastics, Christian scholars who tried to put logic at the service of faith. Though Anselm knew the Bible well, he was willing to test the power of human logic and would even set aside faith based on the Bible to try to prove doctrines. But faith was always foundational. In his work *Proslogium,* which was originally titled *Fides Quaerens Intellectum (Faith Seeking Understanding),* Anselm made the famous statement, "I believe in order to understand." By that he meant that those who seek truth must first have faith, not the other way around. He put forward an *ontological* argument for belief in God. Briefly, he stated that human reason demands the idea of a perfect Being, therefore that Being must exist. That idea has fascinated philosophers and theologians through the ages.

1095
Pope Urban II Launches the First Crusade

Combat between Crusaders and Saracens, from a window formerly in the Church of St. Denis.

Though by the eleventh century most of Europe was nominally Christian—every child was baptized; a church hierarchy existed that placed each believer under pastoral care; marriages took place in the church; and dying people received the last rites of the church—Europe did not seem much like the kingdom of God. Constant conflict existed between Christian princes, and the wars of land-hungry nobles caused common folk hardship.

In 1088 a Frenchman, Urban II, became pope. His papacy was marked by dispute with German King Henry IV—a fruitless continuation of Gregory VII's policies of reform. The new pope did not ardently wish to continue this battle. Instead, he wanted to draw all Christendom together. When Emperor Alexis of Constantinople appealed to the pope for help against the Muslim Turks, Urban saw that a common enemy might help him achieve his goal.

No matter that the pope had excommunicated the patriarch of Constantinople, and Catholics and Eastern Orthodox Christians were no longer one church. Urban sought to gain control over the East, while he found a diversion for the squabbling princes of the West.

In 1095 Urban called the Council of Clermont. There he preached a stirring sermon: "A horrible tale has gone forth . . . an accursed race utterly alienated from God . . . has invaded the lands of Christians and depopulated them by the sword, plundering, and fire." He appealed, "Tear that land from the wicked race and subject it to yourselves."

"Deus vult! Deus vult! [God wills it!]" cried the people. That became the battle cry of the crusades.

As the pope's representatives traversed Europe, recruiting knights to go to Palestine, they received an enthusiastic response from the French and Italian warriors. Many were spurred on by religious goals, but doubtless others went for economic gain and the sheer adventure of recapturing the pilgrimage sites of Palestine, which had fallen into Muslim hands.

Perhaps the warriors felt virtuous, slaying a non-Christian enemy. Slaughtering the infidels who had taken over the Christian holy land might seem like an act of service to God.

To encourage the crusades, Urban and the popes who followed him emphasized the spiritual "benefits" of war against the Muslims. Taking a page from the Koran, Urban assured the warriors that by doing this penance they would enter heaven directly—or at least reduce their time in purgatory.

On their way to the holy land, the crusaders stopped in Constantinople. Their time there showed one thing: Unity between East and West remained unlikely. The emperor saw the chain-mail-clad soldiers as a threat to his throne. When the crusaders learned Alexis had made treaties with the Turks, they felt this "traitor" had negated the first part of their mission: driving the Turks from Constantinople.

Provisioned by the emperor, the army made its way south and east, capturing the cities of Antioch and Jerusalem. A bloodbath followed their victory in the Holy City. "Take no prisoners" was the tactic the crusaders used. One heartily approving observer wrote that the soldiers "rode in blood up to their bridle reins."

After setting up the Latin Kingdom of Jerusalem and electing Godfrey of Bouillon as its ruler, they moved from offense to defense. They began to build new castles, some of which still remain.

In the years to follow new half-military and half-monastic religious orders were formed. The most famous were the Knights Templars and the Knights Hospitalers. Though originally created to help crusaders, they became powerful military organizations in their own right.

The first crusade would be the most successful one. Though dramatic and colorful, these military efforts did not effectively keep the Muslims out. In 1291 the Muslim troops captured the city of Acre, effectively ending the crusades.

In many ways the crusades left a negative legacy. They harmed relations between the churches of the East and West, and the brutality of the crusaders only worked to make their enemies more fanatical. In addition, the lessons the crusaders learned in warfare became part of their strategies for future wars, waged against other Christians.

The response to Urban's call greatly enhanced the power of the papacy. He had brought together a great number of soldiers who were willing to die for their faith, a feat no prince could ignore.

The power struggle between church and state had not ended.

1115
Bernard Founds the Monastery at Clairvaux

Bust of Bernard in the parish church at Fontaines-Les-Dijon, Bernard's birthplace.

Monasticism set for itself the goals of piety and simplicity. For a while, each monastic movement effectively carried out its good intentions, but eventually laxness and worldliness took over, and a new order, with greater devotion and simplicity, would spring up.

By the late tenth century the Benedictines had fallen prey to such forces and stood in need of reform. Out of their own ranks developed the Cistercians, who sought to return to a simpler life of work and prayer.

The greatest Cistercian—a man who profoundly affected the medieval church—was Bernard, who convinced thirty monks of his order to follow him to a new monastery he wanted to found at Clairvaux. From that abbey Bernard would take his name and reach out to the Christian world. By the time he died, in 1153, he would have established over sixty-five Cistercian houses, encouraged the people in their faith, harassed kings, made popes, and preached crusades.

Seeking moral reform and personal piety, Bernard stressed the need for a personal experience of Christ and encouraged self-denial and the sublimation of all worldly loves to love for God. His emphasis led to greater general piety.

Both a theologian and inspirational writer, Bernard said that theology and Bible study should "penetrate hearts rather than explain words." Unlike the Scholastics, who emphasized rationality, Bernard focused on the need for a transformed life. He did everything in his power to silence the teachings of men such as Peter Abelard, the medieval age's quintessential doubter.

Though Bernard stood strongly for orthodoxy, he brought to medieval piety a great emphasis on Mary. He denied the doctrine of the Immaculate Conception, believing that only Christ was sinless, but later Christians would expand on his ideas and make this part of the church's belief system.

Though Bernard sought a simple life, his reputation as a saint, writer, and preacher spread far beyond his monastery's walls. He became involved in the turbulent politics of his time, even to the point of deciding between two rival claimants for the papacy. He was also a vigorous spokesman for the Second Crusade—which proved most ineffective.

At times this man who was so highly thought of was intolerant and stubborn. Always a curious mixture of the mystic and the public figure, he remained a fighter for the truth; a man who could intervene in world affairs, yet remain untainted by them. Bernard of Clairvaux passed on to others his one passionate goal: total devotion to God.

Circa **1150** Universities of Paris and Oxford Founded

What happens when you debate against your theology professor—and you win? Chances were, in the Middle Ages, you were branded as a heretic and thrown out of school. That was essentially what happened to the brilliant Peter Abelard. Partly as a result, the university was invented.

At first, higher education had taken place in monasteries and cathedral schools. But these schools began to attract teachers from outside the clergy, and such teachers often questioned the official dogma of the church.

That was the case with Abelard. He and some scholars like him went into "private practice," teaching and living off the fees of their students. Abelard himself had a varied career; he set up his own school at St. Denis, returned to teach at Notre Dame Cathedral, then taught on his own again. His fame drew students to Paris, but the church was never sure it could trust him. Eventually, a group of such teachers, expelled from the Notre Dame cloisters, set up shop on the left bank of the Seine.

There is some debate as to whether Bologna or Paris had the first "university." In Bologna, the teacher Irnerius set up a law school in 1088, which was granted a charter by Emperor Frederick Barbarossa in 1159. But the name *university* comes from Paris. In medieval times, all trades were well organized. So the teachers and students along the Seine organized a guild of sorts, the *Universitas Societas Magistrorum et Scholarium* ("Universal Society of Teachers and Students"), under the authority of a chancellor. This chancellor, loosely responsible to the bishop of Paris, had the task of granting licenses to teach.

In 1200, Philip II of France granted the "university" official status. As at

Bologna, teachers and students received some of the social privileges of the clergy, yet were separate from them. Pope Innocent III (who had studied in Paris) confirmed the school's status in 1208. University personnel actually went on strike in 1229–1231, due to a conflict with bishops over control of the educational process. Pope Gregory IX ended it with a promise of self-government for the school.

The University of Paris became the hub of scholarship for most of Europe, at least north of the Alps. Thus there developed four "nations" of study, grouping teachers and students of similar background: French, English/German, Norman, Picardian (Low Countries). Foreign students also needed housing, which was provided along national lines. This established the framework for "colleges" within universities. Paris also developed four fields of study: arts, medicine, law, and theology.

In 1167, even before the University of Paris had official status, Henry II prohibited English students from studying in Paris. A *Studium Generale* was established in Oxford. It was officially organized, under a chancellor, in 1215.

The thirteenth century was a heyday for scholarship. Paris, Oxford, and Bologna became centers of theology, philosophy, and science. These events established educational traditions that have lasted to the present day.

The universities became incubators for the Renaissance and the Reformation.

1173
Peter Waldo Founds the Waldensians

Before the Reformation, some groups of Christians objected to the path the Catholic Church was taking. One of these was the Waldensians, founded by a French merchant who was discontented with the medieval church.

One day Peter Waldo heard a wandering troubadour sing about a wealthy youth who left his family and returned home, years later, dressed as a beggar and so emaciated that his family failed to recognize him. Only at his death did he reveal his true identity. He had lived among the poor and faced death gladly, happy to meet the God who smiled on the poor.

Deeply moved by the story, Waldo acted quickly, setting aside an adequate income for his wife and placing his two daughters in a convent. The rest of his estate he gave to the poor. He enlisted two priests to translate the Bible into French and began to memorize long passages. Then he went out to teach the common folk about Christ.

Though monks and nuns had preached and taught about poverty and self-denial—often despite their own inability to keep their vows—the church saw this as something only they needed to practice. Few seemed to expect the average person to live a deeply religious life.

Waldo and his followers—who referred to themselves as the Poor Men of Lyons—believed Jesus wanted His teachings put into practice by all. Going out two by two, the Waldensians visited the marketplaces, teaching the New Testament to the common people.

The contrast between the church and these preachers was apparent to the archbishop of Lyons. He ordered them to stop. Waldo quoted the Apostle Peter, "We must obey God rather than men!" (Acts 5:29 NIV). Though the archbishop excommunicated Waldo, that did not stop him or the movement that bore his name. The Waldensians appealed to Pope Alexander II. Though he was caught up in the Third Lateran Council (1179), these men who went about "two by two, barefoot, clad in woolen garments, owning nothing, holding all things in common like the Apostles," impressed the pope. Because they were mere laymen, however, he could not allow them to preach without a bishop's approval—something they were not likely to receive.

Remembering the words in Acts, Waldo and his followers continued to preach, eventually drawing down excommunication on themselves, by Pope Lucius III, in 1184.

The Waldensians were not teaching heresy, despite the claims the church made against them. They were orthodox, but because they existed outside the structure of the church, Waldo's followers could not gain the approval of the church hierarchy. To the medieval churchman, anything that stood outside the church courted heresy.

Many French and Italian Christians, discouraged with the worldly church, turned to the Waldensians, who taught the priesthood of all believers. They rejected relics, pilgrimages, paraphernalia such as holy water and clergy vestments, saints' days and other feast days, and purgatory. Communion was not an every-Sunday affair, and the Waldensian preachers spoke to the people and read the Bible to them in their own language.

In 1207 Pope Innocent III offered to receive the Waldensians back if they would submit to the Catholic Church authorities. Many did return—but others didn't, and in 1214 the pope condemned them as heretics and called for their suppression. The Inquisition did its best to stamp them out.

Despite all this, the Waldensians continued. They spread throughout Europe, and when the Reformation came, they were warmly embraced by most Protestants. Today they consider themselves Protestants. The Waldensians are a living reminder that, despite the dark moments in the history of the church, new corrective movements always seem to arise from within.

1206
Francis of Assisi Renounces Wealth

Portrait of Francis by Cimabue found on the walls of the lower church in the basilica of San Francesco, in Assisi.

At the turn of the thirteenth century, the future looked bright for young Francis Bernardone. The son of a wealthy cloth merchant in Assisi, Italy, Francis could look forward to a life of chivalry and affluence.

Assisi was warring with the neighboring town of Perugia, so Francis rode out to battle, resplendent in his knight's armor and plumed helmet, a lance at his side. Captured in battle, he was held as a prisoner of war in Perugia for a year. Shortly after his release, he became very ill. These experiences made him question the value of his inherited wealth.

Once, while riding, he saw a leper by the road. Francis had previously been nauseated by such beggars, and he began to gallop past him, but this man was different. This leper had the face of Christ. Overcome with a sense of spiritual devotion, Francis jumped down from his horse and kissed the beggar. He gave the man money and, placing him behind him on his own horse, took him to his destination.

This impulse to care for the needy grew within Francis, though his father scoffed at him. In 1206, Francis left home, renouncing his father's wealth; his father disowned him. The young man dedicated himself to a life of poverty. Any bit of food or clothing he would give to those who needed it. He became a beggar himself, unabashedly asking alms of the "haves" in order to share with the "have-nots."

Francis began to preach in deserted chapels near Assisi. His simple gospel of love and service generated a faithful following. For those willing to join him in renouncing wealth, he drafted a set of rules for living, the ground rules of the Franciscan Order. He and eleven companions journeyed to Rome to receive papal approval for their order.

By 1218, there were at least 3,000 followers of Francis. He had touched a nerve. The church had amassed power and wealth. In Italian society the rich had gotten richer, with the church's blessing, while the poor were left to starve. But Francis offered a new way of humility, untainted by greed. Many devout ones followed his example. Many more, who were unwilling to make those sacrifices themselves, admired the poor preachers and supported them with alms.

Centuries later, Martin Luther would severely criticize the Franciscan tradition because of its emphasis on good works—salvation comes by faith alone, he would say. But in many ways these two reformers fought the same foe: a church that cared mainly about preserving its own status and had forgotten the simple teaching of Scripture.

At the height of his fame, in October, 1226, Francis died. Two years later he was canonized. His last words were "I have done my duty; may Christ now teach you yours."

1215
The Fourth Lateran Council

Pope Innocent III called the Fourth Lateran Council.

The pope who ruled from 1198–1216, Innocent III, created the most powerful papacy in medieval history. This hard-driving, gifted man sought to bring order and discipline to the church. He reformed and centralized the church's administration and became involved in the political affairs of his day.

Innocent wanted the papacy to control both the affairs of church and state.

Where previous popes had called themselves the "Vicar of Peter," Innocent claimed the right to be "Vicar of Christ." Claiming to be Christ's representative on earth, he said the pope was "a mediator between God and man, below God but beyond man." With vigor he took on the tasks of his office, whether it was excommunicating unruly princes or driving out heretics.

In 1215, at the Fourth Lateran Council, the church adopted many of Innocent's ideas. In three day-long sessions, they set forth hundreds of decrees.

Because Innocent felt concern that every baptized Christian should display some semblance of Christianity, the council ruled that annually every person must make confession to a priest and take communion.

With the Fourth Lateran Council the doctrine of transubstantiation officially became part of the church. Unofficially, the idea that the communion bread and wine were actually the body and blood of Christ had circulated for many years. The church saw taking communion as a critical part of salvation; being denied it, as in excommunication, was dangerous to the soul. By having access to the very body and blood of Christ, the priest played a vital role in the church's authority. Excommunication had great power because it denied one access to Christ Himself.

Aware of the ignorance of many priests, Innocent encouraged the council to decree that every cathedral should have a theological teacher. In this way someone would provide the priests with instruction.

In concert with Innocent's high view of the authority of the pope, his belief that there was only one true church, a repository of spiritual truth, created a more powerful papacy. Disagreeing with the church no longer could be a matter of taste; the heretic endangered both his own soul and others'. The council provided for the state to punish heretics and confiscate their property. Those authorities unwilling to remove a heretic would face excommunication, and those who cooperated with the church would receive complete forgiveness.

Once again the church faced the question of secular appointment of church authorities. It denied the right of secular rulers to appoint bishops in their realms. The pope alone could make or break bishops, according to the council. Innocent had already refused to accept the archbishop of Canterbury appointed by England's King John. To force John to obey, the pope had excommunicated him; in the face of losing his throne, the stubborn king eventually submitted.

The council also declared that Jews were required to wear special identifying badges. Christians were forbidden to have any commerce with them. In time this would lead to Jewish ghettos.

In these and other decrees Innocent created an institution that, until the Reformation, would have a dominant influence in Europe.

1273
Thomas Aquinas Completes Work on *Summa Theologica*

Thomas Aquinas submitting his office to the pope (by Taddeo di Bartolo).

The man whose theological system would become the guide of his church was called "the Dumb Ox" by his fellow students at Cologne. Though the name might have suited his heavy, slow body

and serious mien, it by no means reflected the mental agility that lay beneath.

The Middle Ages' greatest theologian, Thomas Aquinas, was born in 1225 to a wealthy, noble family. By five he had a reputation for piety, and his parents sent him to an abbey school; at fourteen he went to the University of Naples, where Thomas became so impressed by his Dominican teacher that he decided to become a Dominican monk, too.

Thomas's family spent much effort trying to change his mind, even going to the length of kidnapping him, tempting him, and confining him for a year, but in the end they gave in. Thomas went to Paris to study under Albertus Magnus, who then took him on to Paris.

In this age, non-Christian philosophers stirred the minds of Christian thinkers. The works of Aristotle, the Muslim Averroës, and the Jew Maimonides had been translated into Latin. Scholars became fascinated by these philosophers who explained the entire universe without referring to New Testament Scriptures.

Continuing the tradition of scholasticism, Thomas tried to reconcile the seemingly separate streams of philosophy and theology. He distinguished between the two, which he labeled reason and revelation, yet emphasized that they did not necessarily contradict each other. Both are fountains of knowledge, he said: both come from God, but, "In sacred theology, all things are treated from the standpoint of God."

Thomas understood the limitations

of reason. It is only based on sensory knowledge, and while it can lead us to believe in God, he said, only revelation can show forth the Triune God of the Bible. Revelation alone can fully reveal man's origins and destiny. By using revelation and logical deductions based upon it, man can construct a theology that explains himself and his universe.

The complex arguments of the *Summa Theologica* show Thomas Aquinas's ability to do intricate reasoning. At first he received opposition: Many in the church did not approve of the scholastics' emphasis on reason. But before long, this and his other works, such as the *Summa Contra Gentiles,* which had once caused argument, became a prominent part of church doctrine. When Catholicism marshaled its forces against the rise of Protestantism, at the Council of Trent, it used Aquinas's works.

Though he became one of the church's foremost theologians, teachers, and preachers, Aquinas remained humble. Three months before his death in 1274, he announced that a heavenly vision had shown him clearly that his theologizing was only "so much straw." He gave up theological writing, and the *Summa Theologica* was never actually completed.

1321
Dante Completes *The Divine Comedy*

In one of the finest epics ever written, a man takes a journey through hell, purgatory, and heaven—a pilgrimage from sin to salvation. The story of that journey had immeasurable influence upon his own language—Italian—and upon readers for the following centuries.

This work, Dante Alighieri's *The Divine Comedy,* is a protracted allegorical poem divided into three parts: the "Inferno" follows Dante through the nine concentric circles of the pit of hell with, as his guide, the Roman poet Virgil; the "Purgatory" describes their journey up a nine-tiered mountain upon which the saved souls work off their sins before entering paradise; the final book, the "Paradise," tells of his journey with Beatrice (the woman he idolized all his life) and Bernard of Clairvaux through the nine concentric circles of heaven, where he meets the saints of God.

The poem is perfectly orthodox theologically—though Dante placed the pope then in power in hell. It also reflects clearly the beliefs of his age. Here, in concrete forms, we see a sample of the medieval beliefs.

Dante deeply admired Greek and Latin classics and was much influenced by Thomas Aquinas. Like Aquinas, he believed in the value of reason, yet accepted that the ultimate goal was life with God. Virgil represents the best human efforts to live a virtuous, civilized life. Though he has a special place there, he is still in hell. Beatrice and Bernard represent the life of grace.

The Divine Comedy vividly portrays the eternal reward of heretics and saints, of kings and common people. Yet, despite its differences with modern theologies, the deeper meaning beneath the figures there can speak as vividly to the soul as to the imagination.

In the end, Dante sees the throngs of heaven arranged like petals of a rose. His imagination is stretched beyond its capacities, and he ends by paying tribute to "that Love that moves the sun and other stars."

1378
Catherine of Siena Goes to Rome to Heal the Great Schism

From a tableau at Siena.

Who would have guessed that a girl born in 1347, the last of twenty-three children in a deeply religious family of Siena, would become the guide and supporter of popes?

Even as a young child Catherine showed great devotion, and she vowed to be the bride of Christ. For three years she lived apart from the world, but about the time the Black Death swept across Europe, Catherine reentered the world and ministered to the dying; some people believed she even healed sufferers. She also visited prisoners, converting some of those condemned to death.

Meanwhile, Catherine wrote many letters, giving spiritual council to everyone from common folk right up to the pope. These epistles gave her a reputation as a peacemaker, for she showed a remarkable ability to reconcile people to each other.

One of the greatest needs for reconciliation in this century lay with the papacy. For years the French had dominated the papacy—so much so that the pope had moved to Avignon, in France. Though this pleased the French, no one else liked the idea, and for years the popes had considered returning to Rome.

Like many devout people of her time, Catherine believed the pope should be in Rome, where he would not face the prospect of French domination. She encouraged Pope Gregory XI to return when she visited him in Avignon in 1376. He moved there but died soon after.

The cardinals elected Urban VI pope. When they quickly grew dissatisfied with him, however, they elected a Frenchman, Clement VII, who returned to Avignon. The Great Schism had begun—a situation that lasted thirty-nine years. What a scandal, having two popes, each of whom claimed the title Vicar of Christ! Both had a college of cardinals, and when their pope died, each college would replace him with a man who suited them.

Some nations supported one pope, some the other. It seemed to be a standoff. Catherine sided with the Roman pope and wrote stinging letters to the French cardinals for their election. In 1378 she went to Rome, hoping to heal the breach. She rallied the people around Urban, but took him to task for some of his unwise actions. Instead of feeling offended, he admired this devout woman and sought her counsel.

For a while the turbulent city became peaceful, but when Catherine died, two years later, the Great Schism remained.

Though Catherine's last mission may have failed, *she* was no failure. In an age when popes had become incredibly wealthy and powerful, she proved that one humble woman could make a great difference. Neither her sex nor her undistinguished beginnings proved a handicap.

Her influence extends down through the ages. Her *Dialogue* is famous for its emphasis on each individual's need to respond to an "inner call" from God.

Catherine's combination of mystical devotion and active Christian service appeals to both Catholics and Protestants.

Circa 1380 Wycliffe Oversees English Bible Translation

John Wycliffe sending out "poor preachers," or Lollards, from Lutterworth Church.

"**A** tall thin figure, covered with a long, light gown of black color . . . the head, adorned with a full flowing beard, exhibiting features keen and sharply cut; the eye clear and penetrating; the lips firmly closed in token of resolution."

So stood John Wycliffe before the bishop of London in 1377, answering charges of heresy. His friend and supporter, John of Gaunt, duke of Lancaster, strode arrogantly into the church. A discussion as to whether Wycliffe should stand or sit became an argu-

ment. It turned into a brawl. John of Gaunt fled for his life. One can imagine Wycliffe himself being whisked away by friends. Such was his life. Wycliffe was bold and outspoken in theology and scholarship. But when it came to politics, he was caught in the middle of other people's battles.

John Wycliffe was the leading scholar of his time. Throughout England, people respected his wisdom. University education was still a rather new phenomenon, and Wycliffe may be largely responsible for the early reputation of Oxford, where he studied and taught.

His life, however, was marked by controversy. He had a dangerous habit of saying what he thought. When his studies led him to question official Catholic teachings, he said so. He questioned the church's right to temporal power and wealth. He questioned the sale of indulgences—letters that were commonly believed to pardon sin—and church offices, the superstitious worship of saints and relics, and the pope's authority. He even questioned the official view of the Eucharist (the doctrine of transubstantiation) put forth by the Fourth Lateran Council. For these and other views, he regularly defended himself before bishops and councils.

England was full of sentiment against the Roman church, even in the 1300s. Secular leadership was strong in Britain. The princes—and many commoners—resented the way the church grabbed for power and wealth. John of Gaunt often used Wycliffe's ideas and reputation in arguments with the church. In return he granted Wycliffe a certain protection from the hierarchy.

For a time Wycliffe was a popular hero. His followers, the Lollards—priests who took on apostolic poverty and taught the Scriptures to the common people—would travel England with the Gospel. But as his influence declined, Wycliffe became less and less useful to his benefactors, including Lancaster. That brawl-ridden hearing in 1377 resulted in a ban on his writings. Opposition intensified. While he himself was kept from violence, his writings were burned, and he was stripped of his position at Oxford and forbidden to disseminate his views.

This gave him time to work on his Bible translation. Everyone, Wycliffe maintained, should be allowed to read Scripture in his own language. "Forasmuch as the Bible contains Christ, that is all that is necessary for salvation, it is necessary for all men, not for priests alone," he wrote. So despite the church's disapproval, he worked together with other scholars to translate the first complete English Bible. Using a handwritten copy of the Vulgate, Wycliffe labored to make the Scriptures intelligible to his countrymen. A first edition was published. It was improved in a second edition, which was not completed until after Wycliffe's death. Yet that edition became known as "Wycliffe's Bible" and was distributed, illegally, by the Lollards.

Wycliffe suffered a stroke in church and died December 31, 1384. Thirty-one years later, the Council of Constance excommunicated him, and in 1428 his bones were exhumed, burned, and the ashes scattered on the river Swift.

No one knew how swiftly his ideas would scatter through Europe. The effect of his teachings on later leaders, such as John Hus, earned Wycliffe the name "The Morning Star of the Reformation." He himself managed to stay within the Roman church all his life, but in the hearts and minds of his hearers, the Reformation was already quietly underway.

1415
John Hus
Burned at
the Stake

"We'll cook his goose." The man of whom those words were spoken was John Hus, whose last name meant "goose" in his native language, Czech. He who spoke the words referred to the fact that Hus would be burned at the stake. But as state and church authorities condemned Hus, they lit a fire of nationalism and church reform.

In 1401, John was ordained as a

priest. He spent much of his career teaching at Charles University, in Prague, and preaching in the influential Bethlehem Chapel, not far from the university.

Although John Wycliffe's land lay far from Bohemia, his influence had spread there after English King Richard II married Anne, sister of the king of Bohemia. Anne had opened the way for Bohemians to study in England; thus the reform-minded writings of Wycliffe had trickled into Bohemia.

On the walls of Bethlehem Chapel paintings contrasted the behavior of the popes and Christ: While the pope rode a horse, Christ walked barefoot; as Jesus washed the feet of the disciples, the pope had his feet kissed. Such clerical worldliness offended Hus, and he preached and taught against it, while stressing personal piety and purity of life. By emphasizing the role of the Bible in church authority, he lifted biblical preaching to an important place within the church service.

Hus's teachings became popular with the masses and some of the aristocracy, including the queen. As his influence in the university grew to immense proportions, the popularity of Wycliffe's writings increased.

The archbishop of Prague objected to Hus's teachings. He instructed Hus to stop preaching and asked that the university burn Wycliffe's writings. When Hus refused to comply, the archbishop condemned him. Pope John XXIII (one of three popes in the Great Schism) placed Prague under interdict—an act that effectively excommunicated the

whole city, because no one there could receive the church sacraments. Hus agreed to leave Prague, to help that city, but he continued to draw crowds as he preached in churches and held open-air gatherings.

Hus had brought about this clerical opposition not only by denouncing the immoral, extravagant life-style of the clergy—including the pope—but by asserting that Christ alone is head of the church. In his book *On the Church,* he defended the authority of the clergy, yet claimed that God alone can forgive sins. No pope or bishop, added Hus, could establish doctrine contrary to the Bible, nor could any true Christian obey a clergyman's order, if it was plainly wrong.

In 1414 Hus was summoned to the Council of Constance, to defend his teachings. Holy Roman Emperor Sigismund had promised him safe conduct.

The council had already made up its mind about Hus. He was arrested as soon as he arrived. The council condemned both the teachings of Wycliffe and Hus for supporting them.

Under attack, Hus refused to deny that he had stated that when a pope or bishop is in mortal sin, he ceases to be a pope or bishop. Orally, Hus added the king to that list.

Sigismund had called the council to rectify the Great Schism—and they accomplished that. But naturally no council that restored the pope's authority would acquit a rebel who questioned his right to it.

Wasted by long imprisonment, illness, and lack of sleep, Hus still protested his innocence and refused to renounce his "errors." To the council he proclaimed, "I would not, for a chapel full of gold, recede from the truth."

On July 6, 1415, the church formally condemned Hus and handed him over to the secular authorities for immediate punishment. On the way to his place of execution, Hus passed a churchyard where a bonfire had been made of his books. Laughing, he told the bystanders not to believe the lies circulated about him. When he arrived at the place where he would be burned at the stake, the empire's marshal asked Hus to retract his views. "God is my witness," the churchman replied, "that the evidence against me is false. I have never thought nor preached except with the one intention of winning men, if possible, from their sins. Today I will gladly die."

After his death, John Hus's ashes were scattered on a river.

Instead of harming his prestige, Hus's courageous death increased it. Fired by a combination of religious and national fervor, his followers rebeled against the Catholic Church and their German-dominated empire. They effectively overthrew both. Despite all efforts of the popes to stamp out this movement, it survived as an independent church, the *Unitas Fratrum,* "Unity of the Brethren."

1456 Johann Gutenberg Produces the First Printed Bible

Gutenberg examines pages from printing press.

During the Middle Ages, few people owned Bibles or books of any kind. Monks copied texts by hand, on papyrus sheets or parchment made of animal skins. The cost of both materials and the copyists' time lay far beyond the average man's resources—even assuming the book he might want was available.

Not many people could read their own language, and many books—the Bible included—were available only in Latin, a language even fewer understood. The average person relied on the local priest and pictures or statues in the church for information on the Bible. Often the local priest had little or no training in Latin, and his knowledge of the Bible was quite minimal. Though scholars debated Scripture and wrote commentaries, their thoughts had a hard time trickling down to the average Christian.

One of the great changes of the fifteenth century had a heavy impact on this state of affairs. In the 1440s Johann Gutenberg experimented with movable pieces of metal type. By setting books in lead type, he could make many copies, at a fraction of the cost of a hand-copied text.

In 1456 Gutenberg—or a group of which he was a part—printed 200 copies of Jerome's Vulgate Bible. The common man could not yet understand God's Word, but it was the first step in a mighty revolution.

For a while the printers of Mainz kept Gutenberg's techniques a trade secret, but by 1483, when Martin Luther was born, every large European country had at least one printing press. Within fifty years of Gutenberg's first printing of the Bible, printers had out-

produced centuries of monks. Books had become available in numerous languages, and literacy had increased.

Without Gutenberg's invention, perhaps the goals of the Reformation would have taken longer to be achieved. As long as only the clergy could read God's Word and compare it to church teachings, it had a limited impact on the common Christian.

With the invention of the printing press, Luther and other reformers could make God's Word available to "every plowboy and serving maid." Luther translated the Scriptures into a vigorous, readable German version that was used for centuries. No longer did a priest, pope, or council stand between the believer and his comprehension of the Bible. Though many had claimed the average man could not understand God's Word and needed it interpreted by churchmen, Germans began to do just that.

As they read, these ordinary men and women began to feel part of the Bible's dramatic world. Household training in the faith became possible. Slowly the boundary between pastor and parishioner broke down. Instead of worrying, *What will I have to confess to a priest?* the believer could ask, *Is my life in keeping with the Bible?*

With the invention of a complex printing tool, a fire was lit across Europe—one that spread both the Gospel and literacy.

1478
Establishment of the Spanish Inquisition

The horrors of the Inquisition.

In its earliest days, the church had felt concern about false beliefs—heresies—and had sought to deal with them. Often this had taken the form of theological give and take and the separation of heretical bodies from the church. But the fledgling church could not enforce any system of faith on those in error.

In 1184 Pope Lucius III, concerned about the beliefs of churchgoers, required all bishops to "inquire" into the faith of their flocks. A man found guilty of heresy was excommunicated—thrown out of the church. But no one physically harmed him, and if he retracted his heresy, he was restored to the church. Theoretically, the church used this instrument to lovingly correct an erring brother and protect others from his mistake.

As popular heresies—particularly the Albigensian movement in France—grew, the church took stronger measures. In the Fourth Lateran Council, Pope Innocent III provided for the state's punishing of heretics and confiscating their property. Those secular authorities who did not accommodate the church risked excommunication themselves.

But the Inquisition was not highly organized until the Synod of Toulouse, in 1229. In response to the Bible-reading Cathari—a heretical group that had included many of the Manichaean errors—and Waldensians, this synod forbade the laity to possess the Scriptures and began a systematic attack against unacceptable beliefs. Pope Gregory IX placed power to prosecute suspected heretics in the hands of the Dominican friars, who were to hold sway over orthodoxy. Subject only to the pope's authority, the Dominicans became a powerful weapon in the hierarchical arsenal.

In 1252 Pope Innocent IV authorized torture as a means of getting information and confessions in cases of heresy. He believed heresy was a "rotting limb" that had to be amputated, lest it infect the entire body. Cruelty perpetrated against heretics seemed a small price to pay for the orthodoxy of the church.

Still, the church could not shed blood, so it turned all heretics over to the state for execution—usually by burning.

Spain's rulers in the latter part of the fifteenth century, King Ferdinand and Queen Isabella, believed their country would prosper only if it was truly Christian. Because they showed great devotion to Catholicism, they received the title *Catholic Kings* from the pope. In 1478 they asked the pope to establish the Inquisition in Spain—with themselves as inquisitors.

Many Jews and Muslims in Spain had halfheartedly converted to Christianity, but fears remained that they still secretly practiced their old faiths. In 1492, the Catholic kings expelled all Jews or Muslims from their country.

Inquisitor General of Spain was Tomas de Torquemada, a Dominican friar whose name would become a byword for cruelty. Though he seemed a model Christian in his private life, self-denying and devout, this learned man carried his zeal to extremes. Under his direction, many people were brought to the stake, while others paid heavy fines or did humiliating penance.

Because the Inquisition had the power to confiscate the property of the condemned, it did not lack money to continue persecutions. In addition it sold the office of "familiar"—a person who could inform on others, while enjoying freedom from arrest.

As Protestantism took hold over Europe, in Spain it fell under the harsh hand of the Inquisition. There Protestant books were banned and even the suspicion that one was Protestant was enough to call in the inquisitors. Though few of the executed Protestants were Spanish, the pointed lesson turned many back to the Catholic Church.

As a result, Protestantism never took hold in Spain as it did elsewhere. Though Protestants faced persecution in the rest of Europe, too, it lacked the fury of the Spanish Inquisition, which lasted until the nineteenth century.

1498
Savonarola Executed

Reformer Girolamo Savonarola.

By the end of the fifteenth century the Renaissance flourished in Florence. That republic's tyrannical ruler, Lorenzo de Medici, had become patron to the arts and brought many great men there to heighten the culture of his city. But while art and literature flourished in Florence, so did corruption and greed. Medici rule had led the city into a self-centered, wealth-conscious life. The church had felt the influence, too, as the vow of poverty had little meaning in Florentine monasteries.

Into the worldly city came Girolamo Savonarola, an zealous, pious Dominican monk who took seriously his order's tradition of preaching. Though he spoke harshly against sin, prophesying the downfall of this city that called itself Christian, but only cared for its own pomp, the monk took the fancy of the Florentines. Crowds came out to hear his words.

In 1494, when France attacked them, the people of Florence came to distrust the Medicis and overthrew them in a popular revolution. Savonarola became the city's new ruler, and an amazing change occurred. People gave up the signs of their frivolous life-style— including their fine clothes and gambling devices. Bankers and traders returned what they had wrongfully taken from others. Crowds flocked to hear Savonarola's preaching. Men from good families became monks.

But Savonarola had attacked the pope, as well as the rest of the worldly clergy. Pope Alexander VI was particularly scandalous and had fathered a number of illegitimate children. In 1495, fed up with Savonarola's attacks, he ordered the Dominican to stop preaching. Savonarola obeyed, and gave himself over to study instead. A year later, apparently believing he had humbled the friar, Alexander allowed him to begin preaching again; soon the fiery monk returned to his attacks on the corruption in the church.

In 1497, the pope excommunicated Savonarola, but the people of Florence rallied behind him. One year later the pope threatened the city with interdict, unless it sent him Savonarola. Though Savonarola appealed to the rulers of several nations, asking that they call a church council to depose the pope, nothing happened.

The Florentines apparently had only experienced a superficial conversion, for when no help came they quickly turned against their leader. City government went into the hands of a hostile party, and they turned Savonarola over to two papal ambassadors, who had instructions to be certain the rebellious friar was executed. Savonarola and two of his adherents were burned in the city's great piazza.

Though many Protestants hail Savonarola as one of them, his thinking was indeed Catholic. Like many before him, however, he had a great desire to see people live as those whom Christ had called. The wealthy, worldly society he opposed could not tolerate his condemnation.

1512 Michelangelo Completes the Sistine Chapel Ceiling

Michelangelo's famous ceiling fresco, *The Creation of Man,* in the Sistine Chapel at St. Peter's, in Rome.

As one looks up at the Sistine Chapel ceiling, the larger-than-life figures seem to reach down, vividly bringing to life nine scenes from the Book of Genesis; seven Hebrew prophets; and five sybils, pagan prophetesses who supposedly foretold the Messiah's coming. In a glance one can see that this is something greatly different from the art of the medieval world.

The spiritual, but often highly stylized and unrealistic art of the Middle Ages had given way to a new realism that made greater use of perspective and knowledge of anatomy. But the new art reflected deeper changes in thought that permanently altered the Christian world.

During the fifteenth and sixteenth centuries the Renaissance had begun to take hold in Europe. The Christian poet Petrarch had unearthed ancient Latin manuscripts and popularized study of them. From this stemmed humanism, which sought to study the classics and apply their principles to life. Slowly but surely greater emphasis had begun to be placed on man, his ability to think, and his actions. Though Christianity still often had a great impact on thought, the world was slowly swinging away from a church-centered way of life.

Like many Renaissance men, Michelangelo Buonarroti achieved a wide range of knowledge. He wrote beautiful poetry and became an accomplished artist, sculptor, and architect. Under the patronage of popes Julius II, Leo X, Clement VII, and Paul III, he created magnificent paintings and sculptures that reflected the spirit of his age.

Under Julius II, Michelangelo accepted the project of painting the ceiling of the pope's private chapel, the Sistine Chapel. From 1508 to 1512 he created the magnificent frescoes of flesh-and-blood men and women, who almost seem able to take life of their own accord. The earthiness of his portrayal of biblical stories is foreign to medieval art. Despite the spiritual themes, these people seem more of this world than the next one.

In 1534, Michelangelo would return to the Sistine Chapel, to paint the altar wall. The *Last Judgment* portrays a vigorous Christ. Massive figures of the saved rise as the grief-stricken damned fall, helpless to alter their end. When Pope Paul III saw the work for the first time, stunned, he prayed, "Lord, charge me not with my sins when you come on the Day of Judgment."

Though probably best known for his paintings, Michelangelo did not consider himself primarily a painter. His first love was sculpture, in which he excelled, as shown by the magnificent young *David;* the tender *Pietà*, which portrays Mary with her sacrificed son; and the righteous, angry *Moses*.

As man became more and more the measure of things and as the Reformation challenged the authority of the Catholic Church, the influence of humanism increased. Yet it began with Christians—and most humanists remained within the faith.

1517 Martin Luther Posts His Ninety-five Theses

Martin Luther.

"**A**s soon as the coin in the coffer rings, the soul from purgatory springs." So went the jingle of Johann Tetzel, the man authorized to raise money to build a new basilica in Rome. His fund-raising gimmick—the sale of indulgences—was, quite simply, selling forgiveness. Get your dear departed loved ones out of purgatory for a fee and earn credit against your own sins.

The church was rife with corruption. Church offices were bought by wealthy nobles and used to gain more wealth and power. One such noble was Albert of Brandenburg, who borrowed money to buy himself the archbishopric of Mainz and needed a way to pay back the loan. The pope authorized the sale of indulgences in Albert's region, as long as half the money collected funded the construction of Saint Peter's Basilica, in Rome. The rest went to Albert. Everyone was happy—except for a number of devout Germans, among them Martin Luther.

Tetzel, a Dominican monk and a popular preacher, became commissioner of indulgences; he traveled from town to town, hawking their benefits: "Listen to the voices of your dear dead relatives and friends, beseeching you and saying, 'Pity us, pity us. We are in dire torment from which you can redeem us for a pittance.' Do you not wish to?"

Luther, a priest and professor at Wittenberg, strongly opposed the sale of indulgences. When Tetzel came around, Luther wrote up a list of ninety-five grievances and tacked them to the church door—which served as sort of a community bulletin board. Divine forgiveness certainly could not be bought or sold, Luther said, when God offers it freely.

Indulgences, however, were just the tip of the iceberg. Luther railed against the entire corruption of the church and pressed for a new understanding of papal and scriptural authority. Tetzel was soon out of the picture (he died in 1519), but Luther went on to lead a religious revolution that radically changed the Western world.

Luther was born in 1483 to a peasant couple in Eisleben, Germany. His father, a miner, pushed him toward the study of law, sending him to the University of Erfurt. But a narrow escape from death by lightning made young Luther change course. He entered an Augustinian monastery in 1505, becoming a priest in 1507. His superiors, recognizing his academic abilities, sent him to Wittenberg University, to earn a degree in theology.

The spiritual restlessness that harassed other great Christians through the ages fell upon Luther as well. He was deeply aware of his own sin, of God's holiness, and of his utter inability to earn God's favor. In 1510, he journeyed to Rome and was disillusioned by the kind of mechanical faith he found there. He did everything he could to be truly pious. He even climbed Pilate's stairs, where Christ supposedly walked. Luther prayed and kissed each step as he went up, but even then the doubts were brewing.

In a few years he was back at Wittenberg as a doctor of theology, teaching courses on the Bible. In 1515, he began teaching on Paul's Epistle to the Romans. Paul's words gnawed at Luther's soul.

"My situation was that, although an impeccable monk, I stood before God as a sinner troubled in conscience, and I had no confidence that my merit would assuage him," wrote Luther. "Night and day I pondered until I saw the connection between the justice of God and the statement 'the just shall live by his faith.' Then I grasped that the justice of God is that righteousness by which through grace and sheer mercy God justifies us through faith. Thereupon I felt myself to be reborn and to have gone through open doors into paradise. The whole of Scripture took on a new meaning. . . . This passage of Paul became to me a gate to heaven."

Then, more confident in his own beliefs, and with some support from colleagues, Luther was free to speak out against corruption. He had criticized indulgence selling and the worship of relics even before Tetzel came along. Tetzel merely brought the conflict to a head. Luther's Ninety-five Theses were amazingly restrained, considering the upheaval they caused. They were really merely an invitation to debate.

He got debate, first from Tetzel, later from the renowned scholar Johann Eck, who charged Luther with heresy. It seems that, at first, Luther expected the pope to agree with him about indulgence abuse. But as the controversy continued, Luther solidified his own opposition to the papacy. In 1520, the pope issued a bull (decree) condemning Luther's views, and Luther burned it. In 1521, the Diet (council) at Worms ordered Luther to retract his published views. There, as legend has it, Luther stated, "Here I stand. I can do no other. God help me. Amen."

Thereafter, Luther was excommunicated, his writings banned. For his own protection, he was kidnapped by his patron, Frederick the Wise, and hidden in Wartburg Castle. There he worked on further theological writings and a translation of the New Testament into popular German.

But the battle was just beginning. By daring to oppose the pope, Luther had set off feelings of independence in German nobles and peasants alike. Germany became a patchwork quilt, as certain nobles came out in support of Luther and others remained loyal to Rome. Reformation was brewing in Switzerland as well, led by Ulrich Zwingli. The church and the Holy Roman Empire were distracted by political struggles throughout the 1520s. By the time they got tough with the reformers, it was too late.

A meeting at Augsburg in 1530 came close to bringing the Lutheran cause back under the Roman umbrella. Luther's colleague Philip Melanchthon prepared a conciliatory statement of Lutheran views, presenting their position as being true to historic Catholicism. But the Catholic council demanded concessions that Luther would not make, and the rift became final.

In retrospect, it appears that the events of the Reformation owe a great deal to Luther's unique personality. Without his brooding self-doubt, he might never have mined the truths of Scripture as he did. Without his zeal for righteousness, he might never have posted his protest. Without his boisterousness, he might not have attracted a sizable following. He lived in a time ripe for change, and he was ideally suited to bring it about.

1523 Zwingli Leads Swiss Reformation

Ulrich Zwingli.

While the Reformation made headway in Germany, it also rose up in Switzerland, under Ulrich Zwingli. Unlike Luther, this priest had never been a monk, nor did he experience a difficult conversion. His was a slow intellectual process in which he came to understand the Scriptures and see how the Catholic Church had parted from them.

During his ten-year service as parish priest in Glarus, Switzerland, Zwingli twice acted as chaplain to some young Swiss mercenaries. What he saw turned him against the practice of young men selling their fighting services, and he spoke out against it. For Zwingli, it was only the start of a career that would span both political and religious reform.

From 1516 through 1518 he served as priest at Einsiedeln. Strongly influenced by Erasmus, Zwingli immersed himself in the great scholar's Greek New Testament. His preaching began to take on an evangelical tone.

On the first day of 1519, Zwingli became pastor at the main church in Zürich. As soon as he arrived, he announced that instead of following the prescribed texts of the lectionary, he would preach through the Gospel of Matthew. It was almost an act of defiance against the church, though he had no intention at this point of separating from Rome.

In the same year, the plague came to Zürich, and almost a third of the city's population fell victim to it. Zwingli did his best to minister to his people, until he caught the plague himself. His three-month recovery taught him life-changing lessons in dependence on God.

Zwingli continued to preach what he found in the Bible, even when it differed from the rituals and doctrines of the church. It all came to a head in 1522, when some of his parishioners defied the church's rule about eating meat during Lent—and Zwingli supported them by preaching a sermon on freedom.

Zürich's civil government made peace, but in so doing, effectively took the church into its own hands. Early the next year, they convened a public debate on the disputed matters of faith and doctrine, and Zwingli's views prevailed. On January 29, 1523, the council decreed: "That Mr. Ulrich Zwingli continue and keep on as before to proclaim the holy gospel and the pure holy scripture in accordance with his capabilities."

Over the course of two years, debates continued and reforms expanded: Priests and nuns married, Catholic images were removed from the churches, and in a final break with the Catholic Church, the mass was replaced by a simple service in which preaching was emphasized.

Not only did Zwingli face the opposition of the Catholic Church, the Anabaptists—a more radical reforming group—wanted to see reform in Zürich take place more quickly. Though many reformers agreed that they wanted a more biblical faith, they often differed on just what that meant and how to accomplish it.

In 1529, Phillip, the landgrave of Hesse, brought Luther and Zwingli together. Phillip wanted to draw the Reformed movement together militarily, politically, and spiritually. To this end, he brought the two men to Marburg. Of the fifteen doctrinal issues they discussed, Zwingli and Luther agreed on fourteen. The Eucharist was their downfall: Zwingli saw it as a "spiritual" reception of Christ's body, while Luther saw it in more concrete terms. The meeting aimed at uniting the two Protestant bodies actually resulted in a greater split.

Zwingli's reform movement took hold primarily in German-speaking Switzerland—and eventually in French-speaking Geneva, paving the way for Calvin's work there. But Zwingli still faced Catholic opposition in rural cantons, which broke out into fighting. The clergyman who had spoken out against mercenary fighting joined the Zürich troops as an armed soldier and died on October 11, 1531, at the battle of Kappel. His body was hacked to pieces and disgraced by his enemies.

It was only part of a series of religious wars that would be waged over the next hundred years.

1525 Anabaptist Movement Begins

Both the Lutheran and Swiss Reformed movements had early connections with political systems. In Luther's case, Elector Frederick the Wise protected him, and various German princes, seeking political freedom, began to support his cause. Zürich stood by Zwingli in the face of Catholic opposition.

To a group of Christians under Zwingli, replacing Rome with Zürich was not acceptable. They wanted the church to proceed quickly with reforms that would return it to a first-century ideal. Instead of focusing on church hierarchy or political systems, this more radical group sought a self-governing church ruled by the Holy Spirit.

The issue that brought on conflict was infant baptism. This dissenting group objected that the Bible showed adult baptism and wanted to make it general practice. On January 21, 1525, the Zürich council ordered their leaders to cease disputation. But the radicals only saw it as another case of political powers trying to rule their spiritual lives. That snowy evening, in a nearby village, they met and baptized one another—later they would receive the name *Anabaptist,* "rebaptizer," from their detractors.

The Anabaptists wanted to do more than reform the church—they sought to return it to the state they saw portrayed in the Scriptures. Instead of a powerful institution, they wanted a brotherhood, a family of faith, created by God, who worked in people's hearts.

The Anabaptists propounded separation of church and state, because they saw the church as something distinct from society—even a "Christian" society. They did not want political powers to compel the conscience of the believer in any way.

Nor did they favor church bureaucracies. As the first people to practice democracy in the congregation, they believed that God not only spoke through bishops and councils, but through the individual congregations.

At a time when the Muslim Turks stood at the door of Europe, the Anabaptists preached the unpopular doctrine of pacificism. Oddly enough, this precept did not carry over to the actions of many followers. The name *Anabaptist* became synonymous with "disruption." New Protestant preachers had their sermons interrupted by Anabaptists, and some of the radicals caused riots. In addition, occasions of the practice of polygamy and claims of bizarre revelations from God caused both Catholics and Protestants to believe they must rid the world of this wrongheaded group. Persecution ensued, and many Anabaptists were put to death by fire or drowning.

Yet the movement spread, especially among the lower classes. Evangelism brought new believers, and some Protestants were attracted by the Anabaptist insistence on purity and biblical preaching.

No one man tied this diverse collection of churches together, but perhaps the best-known among the Anabaptist leaders was Menno Simons (1496–1559), who gave his name to the Mennonites.

To the world the Anabaptists gave the idea of separation of church and state. In its descendants, which include the Mennonites and Brethren churches, pacifism still remains an important doctrine.

1534
Henry VIII's Act of Supremacy

Henry VIII.

Unlike the German Reformation, England's did not originally spring out of the spiritual search of one man who wanted to know God more deeply. It sprang from a combination of personal desire, political expediency, and a nation's spiritual mood.

The mood in England had been turning away from the Catholic Church.

John Colet, dean of St. Paul's, had called for reform of the clergy and a return to the study of the Bible. In Cambridge a group of scholars who affected the teachings of Luther became known as Little Germany. The alarm of the clergy at the spread of reform could not halt it.

Yet the king of England, Henry VIII, had little interest in spiritual change. In 1521 he had attacked Luther's view of the sacraments and received the title Defender of the Faith from the pope. His interests in spiritual matters were minimal.

After the death of his brother, Henry had married his sister-in-law, Catherine of Aragon. They had had no son to follow Henry on his throne. Attracted by Anne Boleyn, the king sought to rid himself of his unfruitful wife and take a more attractive one who might bear him heirs. Claiming that he should not have married his elder brother's widow and citing Leviticus 20:21 as his biblical sanction, he asked the pope for a divorce.

The pope feared angering the Holy Roman Emperor, Charles V, who was Catherine's nephew, and stalled the English king.

Impatient Henry appointed Thomas Cranmer archbishop of Canterbury, and the new archbishop granted the king a divorce. Henry quickly married Anne, and in the same year—1533— she gave birth to a child, Elizabeth.

In 1534 the English Parliament passed the Act of Supremacy, declaring, "the king's highness to be supreme head of the Church of England." That did not mean that the king intended to make radical theological changes in the church. He simply wanted a state church in which the pope had no authority. The Statute of the Six Articles, the law that brought uniformity to the new church, continued clerical celibacy, confession to priests, and private masses.

However, Henry did suppress monasteries, which had become symbols of hedonism and immorality. The king did not feel the concern of many serious Christians about this—instead he coveted the church lands. Once he had shut them down, he confiscated monastery property and put the money into the royal treasury. The lands he passed on to nobles whose loyalty he sought.

In the interests of promoting English nationalism, Henry ordered an English Bible to be installed in all churches.

Though Henry did not do so for scrupulous reasons, he had created a church that was no longer Roman Catholic. In the years to come, Henry's eldest daughter, Mary, would seek to return England to Catholicism, but it would not last. Once broken from the pope, the Church of England remained separate. Succeeding waves of Reformation in England were rapid and tumultuous. As will be seen in later chapters, they brought forth a richness and diversity of Christian expression that surely would have confounded Henry.

1536
John Calvin Publishes *The Institutes of the Christian Religion*

John Calvin, Genevan reformer and author of *The Institutes*.

"There is not one blade of grass, there is no color in this world that is not intended to make us rejoice," wrote a man often accused of generating a joyless Christianity. Those who knew him well respected his piety, but would not have been at all surprised that such delight came from his pen.

To be certain, John Calvin was very *disciplined,* and once he made up his mind, he remained firm in his course. His study of law had sharpened his gift of thinking logically, and he carried his early training into his studies of theology.

In a "sudden conversion," sometime around 1533, "God subdued and brought my heart to docility," Calvin said. Apparently he had known the writings of Luther. He broke from Catholicism, left his homeland, France, and settled in Switzerland as an exile.

In 1536 the twenty-seven-year-old Calvin published the first editions of *The Institutes of the Christian Religion,* a systematic theology that clearly defended the Reformation teachings. Impressed by Calvin's writings, Geneva's reformer Guillaume Farel persuaded him to come to help the reform. There Calvin took on a heavy work load: He pastored the church at St. Pierre, preaching three services daily; he produced commentaries on almost all the books of the Bible and wrote devotional and doctrinal pamphlets. Meanwhile, he constantly battled various ailments, including migraine headaches.

To achieve his goal of making Geneva the kingdom of God on earth, Calvin had much to do. Notorious for their lax morals, the people of that city objected when he attempted to change their life-style. Yet Calvin's influence

spread throughout Geneva. It had a powerful influence in the schools. No one could avoid his reforms, for Calvin sought to excommunicate those whose lives did not approach scriptural standards—and every citizen of Geneva had to ascribe to Calvin's confession of faith.

While some objected, others applauded the changes. The city became a magnet, attracting exiles from all Europe. John Knox called the city under Calvin "the most perfect school of Christ since the days of the apostles." Calvin's moral authority reformed Geneva. His written works—in both Latin and French—gave Protestantism a unique vigor.

In his greatest work, the *Institutes,* Calvin clearly stated the beliefs of Protestantism. In one volume the reformer dealt with the key beliefs—and he kept enlarging the book throughout his life.

It began with the Apostles Creed, taking four points: "I believe in God the Father . . . Jesus Christ . . . the Holy Spirit . . . the holy catholic church." Those became the four sections of the book. In each, not only did Calvin seek to state a theology, he sought to apply it to the Christian life.

Book III of the *Institutes,* which contains the doctrine of predestination, has received much attention. Oddly enough, though Calvin stated it, the concept was not his alone. Luther and most of the other reformers believed it. Calvin's forceful stating of the idea has led to the connection of the teaching with his name.

Calvin focused heavily on the sover-

sovereignty of God. He hated the way the Catholic Church had fallen into a salvation-by-works theology. Constantly the reformer repeated: You cannot manipulate God or put Him in your debt. He saves you; you cannot do it for yourself.

God elects to save some people, and He alone can know who is elect, the reformer taught. A moral life can show that a person is probably one of God's chosen people. But Calvin, an intensely moral and energetic man, impressed upon his followers that they needed to show their salvation by working it out. He passed on to Calvinism the need for Christians to act to transform a sinful world.

In Book IV of the *Institutes,* Calvin created a church order based upon what he saw in the Scriptures. The congregation was to elect moral men—elders—who would guide them. He also provided for pastors, doctors (teachers), and deacons.

The doctrines and Reformed policy he created would spread to Scotland, Poland, Holland, and America.

1540
The Pope Approves the Jesuits

Loyola, founder of Jesuits.

Throughout the history of the church, times of laxness had been followed by new efforts at reform and a return to spirituality. With the rise of Protestantism, the Catholic Church, confronted by its own mistakes and loss of power, began to make some changes.

The counter-reformation that resulted did not mean the Catholic Church turned to Protestant thought. But it attempted to change some of the more offensive abuses that even those within the Catholic Church objected to and it responded to the effectiveness of Protestantism in winning converts.

As in the past, a new order rose up, stressing the need for devotion and self-denial. Its founder, Ignatius of Loyola, was a Spanish soldier who had been hit in the leg by a cannonball. During his convalescence, he read a book about the lives of the saints and began a long, soul-searching process. From this he emerged as a curious mixture of the soldier, mystic, and monk.

Spiritual Exercises, the devotional manual he wrote during his illness, not only encouraged its readers in faith, it also stressed obedience to the church. Those were to be key points in his Society of Jesus—or Jesuits. The young men Loyola gathered around him pledged to be at the command of the pope and to do all they could to expand and preserve the Catholic Church. Its tenets included an almost military, unquestioning, absolute obedience to the pope as well as the traditional vows of poverty, chastity, and obedience.

The Jesuits supported education, founding many of the finest universities in Europe. Graduates would become opinion makers—with a firmly Catholic way of thought.

Pope Paul III saw the Jesuits' potential for stemming the Protestant tide. At his instruction, they worked to return every European ruler to Catholicism. Political leadership defined the religion of a territory, and swaying kings and princes to their church meant the people followed.

In addition to returning those who strayed to the Catholic fold, the Jesuits reached out with an extensive missions program. While the Protestants focused on establishing themselves in Europe and working out their theology, the Jesuits went abroad. Strongly Catholic Spain and Portugal expanded their territories, and the Jesuits went with them to evangelize. By the time Loyola died, in 1556, they had not only touched nearly every European nation, but spread to Japan, Brazil, Ethiopia, and central Africa. Francis Xavier would expand the mission further in Japan and to India, Malaysia, and Vietnam; he died trying to bring the Gospel to China.

The Jesuits were some of the finest young men of their day. Despite the discipline and hard work entailed in devotion to the Jesuit community, they came to the order in large numbers. It is hard not to admire their willingness to sacrifice in the face of difficulties.

1545
Opening of the Council of Trent

The Council of Trent, engraved by A. Schiavonetti.

Faced with the abuses within the Catholic Church, some had fled it in protest. But many who did not agree with everything remained within the church, hoping to win over the hierarchy.

Under the pleasure-loving Leo X, who had aroused Luther, change could not occur, but Pope Paul III had an interest in reform. He appointed reform-minded cardinals and created a commission to recommend changes, paving the way for a churchwide council.

The commission gave him a painfully blunt report: The clergy had become far too worldly; many gained their offices by bribery, and monastic orders had become scandalously immoral. It pointed out the abuses in the sale of indulgences and the great number of prostitutes in the supposedly holy city of Rome.

Though the council Paul called began in 1545, it met periodically until 1563, in three main sessions that had poor attendance. Nor were political rivalries far below the surface. But the council did bring about some changes.

On the questions of morality, the Catholic Church did follow the advice of the commission. Indulgences were abolished, and clergy were exhorted to "avoid even the smallest faults."

Doctrinally, the council reaffirmed the Catholic positions. They restated that there were seven sacraments, not two, as the Protestants said; and sacraments were necessary for salvation. Denying the Reformed teachings, the church did not accept that people could know that they were justified. The bread and wine became Christ's body and blood, they reasserted, condemning the Protestant teachings on communion. Likewise the Protestant views on the importance of worship in the common languages gave way to the Latin mass.

Fearing what would happen if every plowboy could indeed read the Scriptures for himself, the council again said the church alone could adequately interpret Scripture and refused the use of the Bible in the languages of the people. The Latin Vulgate was to be used in public reading and doctrinal writings.

The reforms of the Council of Trent further separated Catholic and Protestant views. Although the Catholic Church changed what Protestants thought of as the minor issues, no alteration was made in the view that tradition and Scripture were both valid for defining the acts of the church. The doctrinal differences remained unchanged.

1549 Cranmer Produces the Book of Common Prayer

It was a Reformation church that had seen little reform.

Under Henry VIII, England had turned from the Catholic Church, but the few changes the king had made to construct the Anglican Church by no means produced a thoroughgoing Protestant church. The man who would bring England into the Reformation was Thomas Cranmer, the archbishop of Canterbury who had declared Henry's first marriage invalid. The quiet scholar who had been strongly influenced by Lutheranism was genuinely devout and well-read in the early Christian fathers. He had come to Henry's attention when he expressed his view on the king's would-be divorce.

As long as Henry remained king, Cranmer could not institute much change in the English church. But on Henry's death, his nine-year-old son, Edward VI, became king. Cranmer was one of his regents.

Supported by scholar Nicholas Ridley and preacher Hugh Latimer, Cranmer moved forward with the English Reformation. Images were removed from churches and private confessions to priests discontinued. The clergy were allowed to marry and use both bread and wine in the communion. Calvinist scholars from Europe—Martin Bucer, John à Lasco, and Peter Martyr among them—became professors at Oxford and Cambridge.

But the form of worship had yet to change. Mass was still said in Latin, and people had already begun rioting over that.

Cranmer had a superb command of English, in addition to his deep learning, and a good sense of what was appropriate in worship. In light of the volatile political and religious situation in England, the archbishop had to head a committee that could create a liturgy that was pleasing to both Protestants and Catholics. The compromise presented in the Book of Common Prayer used stately ritual but removed the Catholic elements that offended many Protestants. The Act of Uniformity, which became law in 1549, the year the book was published, required that churches use this liturgy.

The Book of Common Prayer provided the church with a literary classic and a form of worship that walked a middle line, but many complained that it was not Protestant enough. In 1552, a revised and more Protestant version would be published.

In addition, Cranmer produced the Forty-two Articles, a creed signed by the young king. Like the Book of Common Prayer, they were binding on all clergy.

When the king died, Henry's first daughter, Mary, became queen. She attempted to return England to Catholicism, in a short, harsh reign that earned her the name Bloody Mary. Under pressure, Cranmer submitted to Mary's demands that he return to the Catholic faith and signed statements revoking Protestant beliefs. But at a final trial in 1556, he publicly affirmed his beliefs and negated the signed statements. Like many other Protestant leaders—including Ridley and Latimer, who had been burned the year before—he was condemned. In the flames, Cranmer put out the hand that had signed the statements, so it might be the first part of his body to be reduced to ashes.

The book the martyr Cranmer largely wrote would return to life under Mary's sister. Elizabeth, Henry's second daughter, swung England back to the Reformation.

1559 John Knox Returns to Scotland to Lead Reform

John Knox.

The sixteenth century was a time of turmoil for the small, poor, war-torn land of Scotland. Powerful nobles supported England or France, and the internal struggles and external threats had created a political confusion that begged for change.

On the religious front, reformation had been strictly repressed. Pro-

Lutheran preacher Patrick Hamilton died at the stake in 1528. George Wishart followed him in 1548. One of Wishart's supporters, a previously obscure priest named John Knox, would take up the reform—but not for many years.

Knox was captured by the French forces sent to overcome the rebels who had responded to Wishart's death by killing Cardinal Beaton, who had ordered Wishart's death. Knox spent nineteen months as a galley slave. On his release, he went to Protestant England, where he stayed until Mary acceded to the throne. Then he fled to Europe, with other Protestants. In Geneva he became one of Calvin's most admiring disciples and soaked up Reformed theology.

While Knox was away, Scotland became more closely allied with France, through the marriage of Mary Stuart, Queen of Scots, to the heir to the French throne. Many Scots feared the rule of the Catholic French. A combination of nationalism and religious dissatisfaction arose to create a climate for reformation.

Knox returned to his country in 1559, to popular support. Battles between the queen's forces and the Protestants ended in triumph for the Protestant party. In 1560 the parliament adopted a Calvinistic profession of faith, drawn up by Knox and others. Parliament stated that the pope had no jurisdiction in Scotland and forbade the mass.

To replace the Catholic order, Knox and his followers composed the *Book of Discipline,* setting forth a modified Presbyterian church government. It also provided for comprehensive schooling, including universities. The work would become a landmark for the country, fostering hardy independence and a democratic spirit.

To guide Presbyterian worship, Knox penned the *Book of Common Order,* which shows his indebtedness to Calvin and other Swiss reformers.

John Knox and the queen were often at loggerheads. The Catholic queen's court was morally lax—an offense to the upright Knox. From his pulpit in St. Giles, in Edinburgh, he railed against her. Though the queen made no attempt to reconvert the Scots, she practiced her faith in her private chapel—something Knox could not approve.

Though Mary had much charm, she was not very wise in her political and personal dealings. After her French husband's death, she married her cousin, Lord Darnley. Following his highly suspicious death, the queen hastened to marry the earl of Bothwell. At that point even the Catholics turned against her. Scotland's nobles forced Mary to abdicate, and the way was left clear for a Protestant Scotland. Her son James, who would inherit the English throne, was no Catholic, and Knox showed his approval by preaching at the child's coronation in 1567.

1572 St. Bartholomew's Day Massacre

Just before daybreak Sunday morning, St. Bartholomew's Day.

There were hopes for peace in Paris on August 18, 1572. A royal wedding was weaving together the two warring factions of France. Henry of Navarre came from a solid Protestant family. He was marrying Marguerite of Valois, sister of young King Charles IX and daughter of the Catholic Catherine de Medici. Protestant and Catholic nobles who had fought each other for ten years turned out for this glorious affair.

Calvinism had come to France in 1555. The French Protestant Church was officially established in 1559, with seventy-two congregations in the Synod of Paris. Missionaries poured in from Strasbourg and other Calvinist cities. Soon there were 2,000 churches and as many as 400,000 adherents. The French Protestants became known as Huguenots.

Fighting had erupted in 1562, with a massacre of Huguenots at Vassy. The Protestants had developed their own military leadership and fought back, in three separate "wars of religion." The maneuverings had all the complexity of a chess game. The queen, Catherine de Medici, had sought to consolidate her own power over her young son's throne by playing off her rivals against one another.

A mix of national, dynastic, religious, and political rivalries fueled the fire. How would France relate to the nations of Spain, the Netherlands, and England? Dynastically, the queen had allied herself with the Guises, to Bourbon opposition. Politics and religion seemed to fuse, for the Huguenot nobles tended to be more republican, antiroyalist, and antipapist.

While Catherine was planning this elaborate wedding, she was also plotting the assassination of Gaspard de Coligny, the Huguenot leader. Coligny was a popular French war hero who had become a Protestant. Recently he had been gaining the ear of the teenage king; particularly he had proposed that France support the Netherlands in a struggle against Spain, a strategy Catherine bitterly opposed. On August 22, the assassination attempt failed miserably. Such a duplicitous plot, in the wake of the wedding, threatened to embarrass the royal family. Reportedly, the king remarked, "If you're going to kill Coligny, why don't you kill all the Huguenots in France, so that there will be no one left to hate me?"

That very nearly happened. In a panic, Catherine ordered a massacre of the Protestant leaders in Paris. The alert sounded at 4:00 A.M., August 24, 1572—St. Bartholomew's Day. Coligny was murdered in his room. Claude Marcel, a city official, formed mobs (including some foreign hit men) to roam the streets hunting down other Huguenot leaders. They weren't hard to find. In general, Huguenots were prosperous business people of the city. They owned their own shops. Suddenly, the resentment of the lower class was stirred against these middle-class citizens. In the name of religious purity, a horrendous massacre began.

Bodies were piled up by the hundreds. Many were thrown into the Seine. The atrocities were appalling: One bookbinder was roasted in a fire fueled by his own books—along with his seven children. Even babies were not exempt from the bloodletting.

The craze spread to the provinces in the following days and weeks. Catherine managed to quell the violence in Paris by getting Charles to sign a statement that the murder of Coligny and other Huguenots was *not* a stab at Protestant faith, but merely the quashing of a conspiracy. That may have soothed the blood-sated Parisians, but elsewhere in France the terror was just beginning. Despite royal orders to the provincial governors, approving "protection" for the Huguenots, the mobs went wild.

In Lyons, for instance, Huguenots were herded—for "protection"—into a monastery. When that became too crowded, they were moved to a prison. Yet the Catholic mob managed to storm the prison and kill them all. Everywhere, Huguenots were being shaken down, forced to pay huge ransoms for their lives, and often killed anyway.

The estimated death count ran as high as 100,000, though it was probably more like 30,000 or 40,000. Yet the massacre did not extinguish the Huguenot flame in France. Five more civil wars were waged between French Protestants and Catholics in the years that followed.

Shortly after the last of these, in 1589, Henry of Navarre—the Protestant groom at that wedding—became king. He had previously doffed his Protestant convictions for political convenience—and he did so again as king. In 1598 he tried to placate the Huguenots with the Edict of Nantes, which provided a fair amount of religious liberty—at least in Huguenot strongholds. Yet it limited Protestant incursions into Catholic territories.

The Huguenots had a brief period of prosperity, but Cardinal Richelieu rescinded some of their political privileges in 1629, and Louis XIV officially revoked the Edict of Nantes in 1685. It would be another century before Catholic control of France would be challenged again.

1608–1609
John Smyth Baptizes the First Baptists

In the first decade of the seventeenth century, two groups fled to Holland, escaping Anglican persecution. One of these became the Pilgrims. The other group became the Baptists.

It was an uncertain time in England for all Christians. Queen Elizabeth had stabilized the Anglican Reformation by taking a moderate route—the Anglican Church, she determined, would be *almost* Catholic. She had avoided the bloody civil wars that wracked the rest of Europe, but her decision bothered many of the more radical Protestants. Some of these tried to "purify" the church from within (the Puritans), but others decided to separate from the established church (the Separatists). Still it was a dangerous business to hold your own religious meetings.

When James I took the throne, in 1603, no one knew quite what to expect. The Puritans and Separatists liked the fact that he had grown up in Presbyterian Scotland. That might tilt him to their cause. The Catholics liked the fact that his mother was the ardent Roman Catholic, Mary Queen of Scots.

As it turned out, James was solidly Anglican and made things even more difficult for those who dissented from the official church.

John Smyth, a Cambridge graduate, was a preacher and lecturer within the Anglican Church at the turn of the seventeenth century. Only in his thirties, he appears to have been a seeker on the quest for religious truth. About 1606 he took the bold step of starting a Separatist church in Gainsborough, Lincolnshire. Smyth's boldness may have inspired others. Several other Separatist groups arose in the area, including one in Scrooby, at the home of William Brewster.

When opposition from the authorities grew too great, Smyth's congregation fled to Amsterdam. This was probably 1608. (The Scrooby group fled to Leyden and later sent part of their membership to America.) In Amsterdam, Smyth's church rented a meeting place from a Mennonite man. Through his contact with the Mennonites of Amsterdam, Smyth began to alter his thinking.

The Mennonites took their name from Menno Simons, the former priest who developed a substantial Anabaptist community in Holland. The Anabaptists were the radicals of the Reformation, opposing state churches of any kind and insisting on baptism of believers only.

Smyth became convinced that infant baptism was unscriptural and illogical and convinced about forty members of his congregation. He proceeded to rebaptize himself and these members.

You might consider this the start of the Baptist Church. But it almost didn't happen that way. The birth of the Baptist Church required the start of another Baptist tradition—the church split. In 1610, Smyth, doubting the legitimacy of this independent baptism he had conducted, sought to merge his congregation with the Mennonite Church. Ten church members strongly opposed the merger. They protested to Smyth, and they urged the Mennonites not to accept this group. (The Mennonites did manage to drag their feet and waited until 1615 to admit the new members—three years after Smyth died of tuberculosis.)

Meanwhile, the splinter group, led by Thomas Helwys, returned to their homeland. There, near London, they set up the first Baptist church in England. Helwys, a country gentleman who had studied law, became a vocal proponent of religious liberty, publishing a book entitled, *A Short Declaration of the Mystery of Iniquity*. He dared to send an autographed copy to King James with the inscription: "The King is a mortal man and not God, therefore hath not power over the immortal soul of his subjects to make laws and ordinances for them and to set spiritual Lords over them."

Helwys was arrested and tossed into Newgate Prison—and never heard from again.

But the Baptist movement grew. These churches became known as General Baptists, because of their view of the atonement. Smyth had borrowed an Arminian theology from the Mennonites, holding that Christ died for all humanity, rather than just the elect. A group known as Particular Baptists arose independently in 1638–1640. These were Puritans who adopted believer's baptism but retained their Calvinist theology. They also practiced baptism by immersion, which the General Baptists soon began as well. Up to this time, Smyth's followers had baptized by pouring. By 1644, there were forty-seven congregations of General Baptists in England and seven of Particular Baptists.

From the start, the two major Baptist emphases were apparent—believer's baptism and independence from the state (a conviction they shared with the Anabaptists). These have continued through the centuries. That independence has brought persecution, division, but also great individual achievement.

1611 Publication of the King James Bible

"To the most high and mighty Prince James by the Grace of God . . .": The prince was the son of Mary Queen of Scots, and the source of that quote is the dedication in the Bible that was translated at his direction.

When Queen Elizabeth, England's ruler, died childless, James VI of Scotland also became James I, king of England. At his accession the Calvinists hoped that his Presbyterian upbringing would sway him in their favor, for the English church was still a compromise. Though it had shed much of the Catholicism the reformed churches abhorred, it wasn't as Protestant as the European Lutheran and Calvinist churches. Some Anglicans with strong reformed leanings had not abandoned the state church, but they wanted to "purify" the church—thus their name, the Puritans.

James had high-handed opinions of kingship—he believed he had a "divine right" to rule, and the Anglican hierarchy and the monarch's title Defender of the Faith appealed to him. He disdained Presbyterianism, which encouraged an independence that ill accorded with a king's divine right.

Even before James reached London, the Puritans presented him with the Millenary Petition, supposedly endorsed by a thousand men. In it they asked for moderate changes in the Church of England. James had no intention of capitulating to Puritan pressures, but because they were so numerous, he could not ignore them. So in January 1604, a conference of bishops and Puritans met at Hampton Court. On the whole, the meeting, in which James threatened to "harry them out of the land," was a failure for the Puritans. Their sole victory was that they received James's approval for a new Bible translation.

The king fancied himself something of a scholar and may have thought the work worthwhile, but he also wanted to rid himself of the Geneva Bible—a popular version, published in 1560, that had a clearly Calvinistic bent. The Bishops' Bible, a 1568 version aimed at replacing the Geneva Bible, had received acceptance for church use, but the common people had never made it their own. Clearly a translation that supported the right of kings and received acceptance as a reading Bible would benefit James.

He appointed fifty-four scholars, divided into companies of seven or eight, who could work individually and in conference. To create the new Bible they referred both to the original texts and earlier translations—for example, the Tyndale Bible had a great impact on their work.

The translation went on from 1607 to 1611. Though the "Authorized Version" or King James Bible cannot be proved to have received official recognition from James, it did in time replace the Geneva Bible. It was beautifully literate, an accurate translation that has lasted centuries.

For some people it is still *the* Bible.

1620
Pilgrims Sign the Mayflower Compact

Pilgrims aboard ship sign the Mayflower Compact.

"**N**o bishop, no king," James I had proclaimed, telling the Puritans that they had a king and would certainly have the bishops of the church. But he had not reckoned with the tenacious faith of these purifiers of the church. Some wanted to stay within the church, but not all felt that reform would occur under this antagonistic king. These, the Separatists, withdrew from the Anglican congregations—and eventually from the king, too.

In response to their rejection of the Anglican church, the government imprisoned or harassed many Separatists. Even when the government didn't press them, heckling mobs interrupted Separatist meetings.

Robert Browne led some Separatists to Holland, which tolerated dissenters. But they were still strangers in the land. Dutch pluralism did not aid in their own community building, and many feared their children would become too secular.

A growing restlessness turned them toward the New World. Perhaps there they could build a pure church, untainted by the flaws of the Church of England. In a land without an established government, they could create one that reflected Calvinist ideals. Even the ruggedness of the new land could not deter them from their hopes for freedom.

Separatist leader John Robinson said, "They knew they were pilgrims." Holland hadn't been their promised land, so maybe America would be. On a ship called the *Mayflower* 102 English Separatists who had briefly returned to England set sail from Plymouth harbor.

Though they had intended to head for Virginia, a storm swept them off course, landing them in Massachusetts. One Pilgrim described the new land as "a hideous and desolate wildness."

No less than the wildness in which they had landed, however, did the Pilgrims fear the anarchy and wildness of the human nature. Their charter, which had been for Virginia, had no power here. They needed to create an orderly government under which they could establish the kingdom of God.

Huddled aboard their vessel, forty-one men signed the Mayflower Compact. In it they agreed that they undertook the new colony for the glory of God and advancement of Christianity. They committed themselves to enacting laws for the general public good and pledged to uphold group solidarity and forsake self-seeking.

The compact said in effect that the people were to govern themselves. Naturally William Bradford and the other Pilgrim fathers who signed the compact believed they did not govern apart from God—the ruler of all—but they did not provide for the rule of a human king.

James I had been shocked at their refusing the rule of bishops and would have even less sympathy with those who denied his rule. But he had enough trouble without having to deal with a small, charterless, unruly group who lived across an ocean.

1628
Comenius Driven From His Homeland

Catholics were aggressively asserting their authority in Bohemia. Protestants had already been banished, though for several years they had tried to hide. As the danger grew too great in 1628, one band crossed the mountains into Poland.

Leading them into exile was pastor-writer-teacher Jan Amos Comenius. He stopped to look back at his beloved homeland and led his people in prayer, asking that God would preserve a "hidden seed" in his people, one that would grow and bear fruit. Comenius would never see his homeland again.

The Thirty Years War consumed the center of Comenius's life. When it began, in 1618, he was a newly appointed pastor and school principal among the Unity of the Brethren (*Unitas Fratrum*), the Protestant heirs of John Hus's teaching.

Europe had become a patchwork of Catholic, Lutheran, and Calvinist territories. Bohemia, a strongly Protestant territory, was an unhappy and rebellious part of the Holy Roman Empire. On May 23, 1618, some Protestant rebels stormed the royal palace in Prague and threw their governors out the window. According to one report, the men landed in a manure pile and were not killed; but with the Defenestration of Prague, revolution was underway.

With help from Spanish forces, Emperor Ferdinand II routed the rebels at the Battle of White Mountain in 1620, and the territory was declared officially Catholic. Protestants had to leave. Comenius began a seven-year hideout. Moving furtively from farm to farm, he tried to minister to the Brethren who remained. Now, five years before John Bunyan's birth, Comenius wrote *The Labyrinth of the World,* an intricate allegory somewhat like *Pilgrim's Progress.*

Comenius and his Brethren band settled in Leszno, Poland. There he was named a bishop of the *Unitas Fratrum* and published books on the education of young children and the teaching of languages. His theories were revolutionary. All children—boys and girls, rich and poor—should be taught a broad curriculum that would give them access to various fields. Education should begin with maternal care even before birth, he said, though it should involve aspects of play and not just rote learning. He advocated a series of six-year periods comparable to preschool, elementary, junior-senior high, and university education. Above all, teachers should learn their teaching methods from nature. Learning was a matter of growth, not merely the acquisition of information.

The Thirty Years War raged on. The

Danish Protestants invaded Catholic territory but were pushed back. The Swedish king, Gustavus Adolphus, entered the fray on the Protestant side. He had some successes, but he died in 1632.

Meanwhile, Comenius continued to build his reputation as a scholar and educator. He wrote *The Way of Light,* hoping that proper education would promote peace. In 1641, the British Parliament invited him to put his theories into practice, setting up a "pansophic" college in England. Once again civil war arose, forcing Comenius to flee. He settled in Prussia for a time. From there he commuted to Sweden as an educational consultant to the prime minister, Axel Oxenstierna. He also urged the prime minister to remember the cause of the Brethren as the war drew to a close.

Curiously, France turned the tide in the war. Though a Catholic nation, France saw an opportunity to break the power of the Hapsburg dynasty and to gain some territory for itself. French forces entered the fray in 1635, and the war dragged on. In 1648 the Peace of Westphalia divided up the spoils of a war that had drained Europe. The Holy Roman Empire lay in shambles, and some estimate that Germany lost half her population in the fighting. France gained territory. The Calvinists and Lutherans gained, with the Calvinists achieving toleration.

The Brethren, however, received neither the right to return to Bohemia nor a new homeland. Comenius continued to wander for the rest of his life. For twenty-two years he traveled, ministering to the far-flung Brethren communities. When his home in Poland was raided and burned, he lost much of the encyclopedia he had been compiling. Yet thanks to a Dutch patron, he published many more books on education—including the first illustrated textbook for children, *The World in Pictures.*

Comenius was respected and honored, but he was seldom listened to. At seventy-five he appeared at an international council to plead for peace between England and Holland—but they largely ignored his counsel. He had a vision for education that would bring both spiritual wholeness and world peace, but though the first goal drew some nations, none was willing to attempt the second.

Though he could accurately be considered one of the key fathers of ecumenism, Comenius has often been ignored. The secular world appreciated him much more than the church has, and he is often hailed as the Father of Modern Education.

The "hidden seed" Comenius prayed for might have appeared much later. A group of Brethren migrated to Herrnhut, in Germany, in the early eighteenth century. There a spiritual awakening occurred that sparked a massive missions effort that reached around the world.

1646
The Westminster Confession of Faith

The Westminster Assembly.

Not everyone in England approved of the state church. From the first many had seen Anglicanism as a system that did not go far enough toward the Reformed doctrines. Queen Elizabeth I had approved the Thirty-nine Articles, in 1563, establishing an episcopal English church; from the first Puritans had pushed for a presbyterian form of government and less ritualistic services, but their demands had been largely ignored.

The Stuart kings—James I and his son, Charles I—had sought to increase the power of the episcopal system.

Charles, who wanted conformity in both Scotland and England, sought to force Anglicanism on the Presbyterian Scots. This volatile situation, clumsily dealt with, led to the English Civil War.

Charles I had a long history of battles with Parliament. In the spring of 1640, he called one that vigorously opposed him, and he swiftly dissolved it, only to call another Parliament in the fall of the same year. The primarily Puritan Long Parliament would be his downfall.

Two years later, as the same Parliament sat, the king tried to arrest some members of the House of Commons, who had opposed him. His accusation that these men had committed treason was the spark that began the war that turned England to Puritanism for a few years.

Early in 1643, Parliament abolished the episcopal system. To set up a presbyterian church in its place, they summoned an assembly at Westminster Abbey. One hundred and twenty-one ministers and thirty laypeople—some of whom were Scots—gathered to rebuild the English church.

During the six years the Westminster Assembly met, Oliver Cromwell, the leader of the Parliamentary army, led the Puritans into power. The king would be beheaded in 1649.

The Westminster Assembly created the Westminster Confession (1646), a classic in Presbyterian thought, as well as the Shorter Westminster Catechism (1647) and the Larger Catechism (1648). The beliefs they outlined were purely Calvinistic.

The confession taught the inspiration of Scripture, declaring the Bible the sole authority in Christian belief. In its original languages Scripture was "inspired by God, and . . . kept pure in all ages." However, full assurance of divine authority is "from the inward work of the Holy Spirit."

The Westminster Confession included the doctrine of predestination—a subject on which the Thirty-nine Articles had remained silent. The confession stated: "Some men and angels are predestinated unto everlasting life, and others foreordained to everlasting death." Yet "neither is God the author of sin, nor is violence offered to the will of the creatures."

Further it emphasized the relationship of God to His people through covenant. Human redemption is a kind of balance between God's sovereignty and human responsibility.

The confession provided for rule by elders, not priests and bishops, and left no room (as did the Thirty-nine Articles) for transubstantiation. Likewise it bound the believer to the sabbath, a day strictly devoted to personal and public worship.

But the Puritanism of England did not last. In 1658, with the death of Oliver Cromwell, no strong leader rose up on the Puritan side. Though Cromwell's son, Richard, had taken his father's place as Lord Protector of England, he did not have his father's leadership abilities. Richard gracefully retired, and England returned to monarchy under Charles II, Charles I's son.

In England the new king successfully restored the episcopacy. But the Scots held fast to the Westminster Confession, making it binding on the Church of Scotland. Through Scotland, *Westminster* has become a byword for "historic Calvinism."

1648
George Fox Founds the Society of Friends

Quaker founder George Fox.

The seventeenth century was an age of religious change and slowly increasing freedom. In place of the one "universal" church, many denominations grew up. The Reformation taught that the Bible alone ruled faith, but what interpretation of it should Christians accept? Differences flourished—all in the name of Scripture.

The Puritans had objected to the Church of England, which did not fall in with their understanding of Scripture, but though they disliked the Anglican priesthood, they did not do away with clergy altogether.

George Fox, who founded the Society of Friends—or Quakers—did.

Like many others, George Fox found no comfort in the formal religions of his age. Even the dissenting groups, the Presbyterians and Independents, had too much formality for Fox. He believed they had given in to government pressures—the church had become a public servant and had turned away from God.

In his search for spiritual peace, Fox turned to many advisors, but none seemed able to help him. One day, in 1647, a voice told him, "There is one, even Jesus Christ, who can speak to thy condition." It brought about a change in Fox, who henceforth dedicated himself to follow the Inner Light that God gave him—and everyone who accepted Him. All Christians—all friends of Jesus—had immediate access to God. Fox taught that through following the Light God had given, they could break Satan's power and the hold of sin.

Fox's simple but stringent teachings drew others. The Friends, as they were called, renounced oath taking, dressed simply, ate sparingly, and spoke the truth in all honesty. They opposed participation in warfare. Despite opposition from the government, they protested formalism in worship, refused to tip their hats to any man, and would not pay tithes to the state church.

Many Societies of Friends sprang up in England as the fearless George Fox preached. In the homes where they held their meetings, aristocrats and common men worshiped together. No specified clergy existed, and both men and women could speak as they felt led by the Spirit.

In a group that relied so heavily on the individual prompting of the Spirit, there were some abuses—and these turned many otherwise tolerant people against the Friends. The emphasis the Friends placed on freedom was also bound to find government opposition.

Fox spent time in jail because of his teachings. When he stood before one judge, who mocked his group's beliefs, Fox warned the man to "tremble at the Word of God."

"You are the tremblers, the quakers," the judge replied. The name stuck.

Under the rule of Oliver Cromwell, toleration became the general rule for the diverse groups that made up his army and political union. Though Cromwell admired the honesty and integrity of the Quakers, he did not extend toleration to them. Though persecution was less than under the rule of kings, such individualistic, freedom-seeking faith could not appeal to a leader of Cromwell's caliber.

Despite the persecution, the Quakers grew, for many felt the appeal of a faith that stressed that the individual must experience Christ.

1662 Rembrandt Completes the *Return of the Prodigal Son*

The flawless art of the *Return of the Prodigal Son* was created by a man who knew what it was to be a prodigal and who showed through his art how deeply the world needed salvation. Rembrandt Harmenszoon van Rijn became the greatest Protestant painter—one in whom faith and art are smoothly combined.

He was born into a deeply pious Reformed family. Though his parents had wanted him to become a scholar, quite clearly he was gifted in art. Following the custom of the day, Rembrandt apprenticed himself to established artists and learned to paint Bible stories and events from Greek and Roman history and mythology. But the art he developed as his personal style was quite different. Other Protestants confined their religious paintings to pictures depicting the Bible, and Catholic artists portrayed the saints; but Rembrandt made every painting a statement of faith. While Protestants claimed that the Bible alone was the norm for man's religion, Rembrandt showed that the Scriptures could also be the norm for religious art.

In Rembrandt's day the people in biblical paintings seemed like superheroes, differing little from the gods and demigods portrayed in mythological paintings. Not so in Rembrandt's portrayals. He showed humanity as it really was: scarred, sinful, and in need of redemption. *Real* men and women peopled his work, including his wife and son—and even street people. Dressing a rather haggard beggar in a turban, Rembrandt made him into a striking portrait of a king of Israel. A homely old Jewish man became a picture of the Apostle Paul.

Rembrandt also used himself as a model. In *The Raising of the Cross,* which portrays the sinfulness of man, he helps to crucify Christ. Even though he creates the picture, the artist cannot escape the need for personal salvation.

Masterful use of chiaroscuro—a technique in which a dark background contrasts sharply with the light striking the figures—is a hallmark of Rembrandt's work. The depth of physical darkness often clearly displays an inner spiritual light in his subject.

But Rembrandt's main goal was not to evangelize. He made his living from his painting and did both secular and spiritual works. Yet even those pieces not meaning to portray a religious scene carry with them a sense of the artist's perspective on the world and humanity. He saw beauty in God's creation of nature—and he saw both beauty and sin in the human faces before him.

Despite the seemingly firm Christian convictions of his art, Rembrandt did not have a flawless personal life. He married Saskia, a wealthy young woman, who died in 1642. Her will stated that if Rembrandt remarried, all her estate would pass to their son, Titus. Besieged by financial troubles, the artist doubtless felt he could not give up her money. Instead he kept his housekeeper, Hendrickje, as his common-law wife.

Rembrandt passed on to generations a uniquely Protestant picture of God's world. Calvin had stated: "Only those things are to be painted which the eyes are capable of seeing." Rembrandt's eyes created pictures that communicated truth. *Return of the Prodigal Son* shows Rembrandt's humanity, love for intimate detail, and keen perception of the human heart. The forgiving father, the penitent son, and the older son, dressed in seventeenth-century garb, perfectly fit the parable of Jesus. It reminds us of the timelessness and timeliness of the Scriptures.

1675
Philip Jacob Spener Publishes *Pia Desideria*

By the later part of the seventeenth century the Lutheran Church had fallen away from its emphasis on personal faith and into the desire for correct doctrine. One pastor would challenge that situation with a small book that changed Protestantism.

In his studies at the University of Strasbourg, Philip Jacob Spener had learned the biblical languages, doctrine, and history that were generally part of the course of study for the ministry. But his professors also impressed upon him the need for spiritual rebirth and Christian ethics. Spener discovered the need to apply scholarship to personal experience. Unless a person is born anew, no formal religion will be of any consequence.

As the new minister preached against laziness and immorality and sought to make his congregation practice personal Christianity, he faced controversy. The clergy of the Lutheran Church had seen themselves as the center of the church, and they felt threatened at the individualistic turn of such preaching.

Spener formed devotional meetings, known as *collegia pietatis,* which would form the basis of the movement that resulted—Pietism.

Not satisfied with preaching from his own pulpit in Frankfurt and the formation of local groups, this Lutheran pastor put his ideas for reform into writing. In 1675 he published *Pia Desideria,* "Pious Desires," which presented a six-point plan.

First, he wanted to see Christians have a deeper, more life-affecting understanding of the Scriptures. To achieve this goal, he suggested the small meetings in homes. Seventeenth-century churchmen found this a novel and possibly threatening idea.

Spener wanted the church to take the priesthood of all believers seriously, so he suggested giving responsibility within the *collegia pietatis* to lay people. Though the pastor was important, he should not carry the whole burden for spiritual nurture.

Opposing the fear of his age that individualism led to trouble, Spener advocated that the church emphasize personal experience. He perceived that correct doctrine alone led to a dead faith.

Learning from the Thirty Years War, which had proved the dangers of religious controversies, Spener sought to avoid theological conflict. If unavoidable, debates should be carried out in a spirit of charity, but he urged people to hold on to the essentials of the faith and not fuss over minor points. Better, he told them, to pray for the erring person rather than shout at him.

Not only should pastors learn their Bible and theology, they should also learn to deal with the laity, Spener said. The pastor who could not express the life of devotion could not lead his congregation in that direction.

He also encouraged pastors to give sermons that applied Scripture to life. They should inspire and inform, be understandable and uplifting. Instead of simply lecturing, pastors needed to inspire God's people.

The furor raised by Spener's ideas caused him to move from Frankfurt to Dresden and then to Berlin. In Berlin, in 1694, he and August Francke formed the University of Halle. Under Francke the university became a center for evangelism and missions. Many years after the Catholic Church had brought missions to Asia and America, Protestant missions began at Halle, with a center for studying Oriental languages and translating the Bible.

Though the clergy saw great threats in Spener's program for reform, it brought joy to laypeople. In the churches that adopted his teachings, family life improved, the moral standards were raised, and people learned that Christianity meant more than simply agreeing with a catechism. Small-group meetings encouraged a family feeling within the congregation, and the Bible came alive to believers.

Luther had emphasized the importance of congregational singing, but its use had languished. Pietism gave a great boost to hymnody, and writers like Paul Gerhardt, Joachim Neander, and Gerhardt Tersteegen produced hymns that would later be translated into the English Methodist hymnbooks.

Many churches, influenced by the warmth of Pietism, developed the Bible study, group prayer, and outreach that its founder had idealized. The practical aspects of Pietism—the emphasis on feeling and spreading Christianity—would have far-reaching effects and have been particularly influential in the development of American Christianity.

1678
John Bunyan's *The Pilgrim's Progress* Published

John Bunyan in Bedford jail, 1667. His blind child leaving him after a visit.

One of the greatest Christian classics would come, not from the halls of a great university, but from a jail cell. The man who wrote it was no scholar, but a simple preacher with a meager education.

John Bunyan was born in Elston, in Bedfordshire, in 1628. His home was a small, thatched cottage, and his father was a tinker, who spent his days pushing a cart along the roads, stopping at homes to fix metal pots.

Young John received a grammar-school education, but like most sons of his day, went to ply his father's trade. During the English Civil War, he served as a soldier—probably on the Puritan side. At nineteen he married, and his Christian wife led him to try to reform his life. But Bunyan found himself constantly slipping back into old habits. Though he lived well enough to impress his neighbors, he described himself as a "painted hypocrite."

In 1651, Bunyan began attending an Independent meeting at Bedford and was moved by the pastor's intense biblical preaching. He began to pore over the Scriptures, until the conflict within him ended in the assurance of grace. Salvation had come to John Bunyan. He joined the Bedford congregation and began to preach there, amazing people at the abilities of a mere tinker.

Though King Charles II had at first promised freedom of religion, increasingly the Anglican church had become the only accepted church. Dissent was not encouraged, and in 1661 John was sent to Bedford jail for his preaching. He remained there until 1672, when Charles issued the Declaration of Indulgence, extending leniency to non-Anglicans.

Upon his release, the Independent meetinghouse called him as their pastor. He received a license to preach and became known as Bishop Bunyan—perhaps becoming the organizing genius of Independents in the area. But the toleration was not to last.

In 1675 Bunyan again found himself in prison, and began his greatest work:

The Pilgrim's Progress. This allegory of salvation and the Christian walk has given us such colorful phrases as "Vanity Fair," "the Slough of Despond," "House Beautiful," "Muckraking," and, "Hanging is too good for him." Drawing only on his own experience and the Bible, this largely unlettered preacher created a captivating piece of literature that appeals to those who travel—or would travel—on the spiritual pilgrimage from the City of Destruction to the Celestial City.

Perhaps because so many readers experienced the same sort of pilgrimage in their lives, *The Pilgrim's Progress* became the world's best-selling Christian devotional book. Bunyan describes the most intimate states of the Christian soul. His realization of the depth of God's grace in his own life gave Bunyan an ability to speak to many people, even generations, of their own spiritual state.

Bunyan's other works, *Grace Abounding to the Chief of Sinners, The Life and Death of Mr. Badman,* and *The Holy War,* never achieved the popularity of *The Pilgrim's Progress.* Yet this one humbly written work touched thousands of lives and became a classic.

1685 The Births of Johann Sebastian Bach and George Frederic Handel

J. S. Bach.

In the same year, two German composers were born, less than a hundred miles apart. Though they would never meet, both would create timeless masterpieces of music that would be among the greatest the church has known.

With the birth of another member of the Bach family, in Eisenach, no one would have felt surprised that he would someday become a composer, for the Bach family included many musicians.

After receiving a musical education from his father and brother, in 1703 the eighteen-year-old Johann Sebastian Bach became a violinist in the Weimar royal chapel orchestra, but he soon left to take a position as a church organist. Then he married a cousin, Maria Barbara Bach, who was an accomplished singer. They had seven children, and after she died, he married again, to Anna Magdalena Wülken. Four of Bach's sons would also become noted composers.

Bach produced an amazing number of compositions. While supporting his twenty children, he also composed, played, and taught music. To Bach, composing cantatas and other service music was "all in a day's work," for to hold such a position entailed providing the music. And he produced 198 cantatas, in addition to secular music. Well known among his works are the *St. Matthew Passion, Brandenburg* Concertos, *Christmas* Oratorio, and the *Well-Tempered Clavier.*

Bach was an extremely devout Lutheran, and he inscribed all his works—secular and sacred—with phrases such as "In Praise of the Almighty's Will" and "To God Alone Be the Glory." The musician also had a temperamental spirit, which often got him into trouble with his employers, and he held his own abilities in high esteem.

Bach spent his life in various parts of Germany. Not until the nineteenth century, when Felix Mendelssohn rediscovered and popularized his works, would Bach achieve great fame in other parts of the world.

Handel was in some ways very much like his contemporary—and in some ways very different. He came from the city of Halle, where his father was a barber-surgeon. When his father forbade George to study music, legend says that at night he sneaked into the attic to practice upon the clavichord. Though his father wanted George to become a lawyer, he eventually allowed his son to study with the local organist. The court at Berlin offered to further George's musical education, and the elder Handel refused, but in the end he could not stop his son. After a year of studying law, George gave up his studies to become a violinist in a court orchestra. He also began to write operas in Italian.

Like Bach, Handel was a prolific composer, but his earliest musical works were secular. Sacred oratorios were not his greatest interest—opera and instrumental works were. To keep the opera companies happy, he had to continually provide them with new material. Audiences wanted some new entertainment each season, and the successful composer had to continually keep himself before their eyes.

How did the opera-loving instrumentalist write the *Messiah?* Invited to write an opera in London, the German composer decided to stay there. Italian opera had begun to decline. Opera companies provoked his temper, and soon Handel began to write oratorios: *Messiah,* which was first sung in 1742 in Dublin, *Israel in Egypt, Deborah, Saul, Judas Maccabaeus, Solomon, Samson,* and others.

When the ruler of the German state of Hanover became king of England, it became a bit embarrassing for Handel. How could he explain to his old employer why he had left for a foreign land? Legend has it that he wrote the *Water Music* to appease the king. It was a successful ploy.

Handel came from a German pietistic home, which impressed upon him the importance of practical Christian living as well as feeling faith. Many who have listened to the *Messiah* have experienced that faith.

1707
Publication of Isaac Watts's *Hymns and Spiritual Songs*

Isaac Watts.

Hymns do not have a long history in English-speaking churches.

Though Martin Luther, a man who enjoyed music and singing, insisted that hymns should be part of the worship of Lutherans and wrote some himself, the English were slow to use them.

The Anglicans had the Book of Common Prayer, but its liturgy did not include music. In 1562 congregations could use the collection of metrical psalms, eventually called the *Old Version,* and in 1696 Nahum Tate and Nicholas Brady provided the more singable *New Version,* but anything that was not from the Psalms was suspect. A bishop might write an occasional hymn for use in a college chapel. Poets such as John Milton and George Herbert wrote devotional pieces, but there was no provision for singing hymns. George Wither attempted to create an extensive hymnbook in 1623, but he met with little success.

While the Anglicans objected to hymns, the Baptists did not—and Independent pastor Isaac Watts decided that his people needed new songs. Though the Psalms expressed much of the faith, they did not clearly show forth specifically *Christian* elements like Christ's birth, teachings, crucifixion, and resurrection. Congregations could not sing about the Trinity, the Holy Spirit, or the church.

In 1709 Watts published *Hymns and Spiritual Songs.* Other collections came later, including *Psalms of David Imitated in the Language of the New Testament,* in which Watts said he made David "speak like a Christian." He drew strongly from the Psalms—"Jesus Shall Reign Where'er the Sun" is based on Psalm 72, and "Joy to the World" comes from Psalm 98.

Watts's more than 600 hymns—among them "When I Survey the Wondrous Cross," "O God Our Help in Ages Past," "I Sing the Mighty Power of God," and, "There Is a Land of Pure Delight"—earned him the name the Father of English Hymnody. This clergyman masterfully reflected the Christian's praise, wonder, and adoration of God. Though he may have offended the conservative churchmen of his day, his lofty hymns retain a constant awareness of eternity.

Watts's hymns had a remarkable influence on the non-Anglican churches. Nothing would match it until Charles Wesley began to write hymns, but for a long time use of Watts's works did not stretch to the Church of England. Though other churches in England, America, and elsewhere made use of Isaac Watts's hymns, no Anglican hymnbook appeared until 1861, with the publication of *Hymns Ancient and Modern,* which did include some Watts hymns.

1727
Awakening at Herrnhut Launches Moravian Brethren

It was just a confirmation service for two young girls. The Moravian Brethren who lived on the estate of Count Nicolaus von Zinzendorf were meeting as usual on August 13, 1727. But spiritual excitement had been brewing for several weeks. There had been vigils of prayer, confession of sin, earnest Bible study, and a feeling of expectancy.

It all exploded on that day. After the confirmation blessing was pronounced for the two girls, the church was swept with powerful emotion. Some wept, some sang, many prayed. There was no doubt in their minds about what was happening: They were being visited by God's Spirit. They had established a "body" here at Herrnhut, but now they were one in spirit as well.

Things had not always been so happy for the Moravians. Most of the people at Herrnhut had fled there from persecution in other areas. They were the spiritual descendants of John Hus—not Catholic, not Lutheran, not Calvinist. The world had no place for them. Even their great leader Jan Amos Comenius, renowned for his scholarship, could not find them a homeland, so they dispersed.

The regathering began in 1722, when Christian David appeared at the door of Count Zinzendorf in Dresden. Zinzendorf was a devout Lutheran from a wealthy family, and he was eager to use his resources to serve the Lord. In fact, he had thought about setting up a community that would practice principles of Christian piety. Now here was this Moravian at his door, asking if his oppressed band could settle on Zinzendorf's estate. The count granted permission.

As Zinzendorf got to know his guests, he sensed a spiritual kinship. He welcomed other Moravians to the new community and began to build a school and shops. The place would be called Herrnhut, which meant, "the Lord's watch." Were they watching for the Lord or being watched by Him? Both.

By 1725, there were ninety Moravians at Herrnhut, by the next year, 300. But with growth came problems. The refugees came from various areas and spoke different languages. Naturally, there would be economic difficulties as the new residents began to ply their trades. The community also included Lutherans as well as Moravians, so some squabbles over church liturgy took place. One teacher who settled there had been kicked out of the Lutheran Church for his heretical teaching and was very mad about that.

Naturally, his wrath fell upon the leading Lutheran of the community, Zinzendorf. The teacher marched around town announcing that the count was "the Beast" of Revelation. Eventually the man suffered a breakdown.

Concerned that the community might fall apart, Zinzendorf decided to exert some leadership. He moved from the manor house into the community itself and began visiting the members. He set up rules for community living, which all agreed to. The community selected elders to lead them. Charity work was established, and small groups were formed for spiritual growth.

During the summer of 1727, the petty differences were melting away. The community became united, focused, and the service of August 13 confirmed it.

In the flush of spiritual excitement, a twenty-four-hour-a-day prayer vigil was set up. This lasted for over a century! Other avenues of Christian service were explored. Contact was made with other Moravians throughout Europe, and they developed an involved system of fellowship and correspondence. Leaders were trained to visit these other groups and share with them what was going on at Herrnhut.

In 1732, the Moravians branched out into foreign missions, sending Leonard Dober and David Nitschmann to the West Indies. The next year, three Moravian missionaries went to Greenland. In 1734, others went to Lapland and Georgia, and 17 volunteers joined Dober in St. Thomas. By 1742, more than 70 of the Moravians had left the Herrnhut community of 600, for mission service, and the mission fields included Suriname, South Africa, Guiana, Algeria, Ceylon, and Romania.

Zinzendorf, meanwhile, was trying to establish a legal base for the Moravian church in Saxony. In his research, he had uncovered an ancient constitution for the *Unitas Fratrum,* the original Moravian church. This showed that the Moravians had at least as much historical precedent as the Lutherans and should be granted recognition. But Zinzendorf's enemies had him banished from Saxony in 1736. This sparked a period of travel for the count and other Moravian leaders. His journeys took him to America, where he established Bethlehem, Pennsylvania, as a base for mission work among the Indians. He later made London a center of Moravian activity.

By the time he died, in 1760, 226 missionaries had been sent out by the Moravians; they had baptized more than 3,000 converts. As he neared death, Zinzendorf commented to a co-worker, "What a formidable caravan from our church already stands around the Lamb!" It is even truer now.

The Brethren Church continues today, but its legacy is also seen in other denominations. John Wesley was largely influenced by Moravians and incorporated some of their concerns in the Methodist movement. William Carey, often credited with pioneering the modern Protestant missions movement, was really following the lead of Moravian missionaries. "See what these Moravians have done," he remarked on one occasion. "Can we not follow their example, and in obedience to our Heavenly Master, go out into the world and preach the Gospel to the heathen?"

1735
Great Awakening Under Jonathan Edwards

Jonathan Edwards.

In 1630, ten years after the small band of Pilgrims established their settlement in Plymouth, a great migration of Puritans began establishing a Christian commonwealth in Massachusetts. More prosperous in this world's goods than the Pilgrim fathers, these Puritans also differed in their purposes for coming to the American wilderness. They hoped to establish a society based upon the Bible, which would serve as an example for England to follow in reform and renewal. As their governor, John Winthrop, wrote, "We must consider that we shall be as a city upon a hill, the eyes of all people are upon us." As the Puritan colony grew and prospered, however, the original religious purpose of the settlement declined; the second and third generations became more concerned with the things of this world than with establishing God's kingdom in America.

The faithful watched, and some bewailed the developments. The Puritans' notion that the new land was the most likely place to develop a holy commonwealth was slow in dying. The devout had no doubt that, though England was spiritually asleep—or dead—the colonies could—or should—exhibit a deep spirituality.

Jonathan Edwards—a precocious and devout soul who had entered Yale College at thirteen—believed this. For a time, under his grandfather, the powerful and influential Solomon Stoddard, Edwards copastored a church at Northampton, Massachusetts. When Stoddard died, in 1729, Edwards remained as sole pastor.

Shortly after he had come to Northampton Jonathan had married the wise, lovely, and devout Sarah Pierpont. As Edwards fathered many children and pastored his church, he somehow found time to produce some of the world's greatest theological writing. Both his wide reading and the dramatic changes that occurred in the churches he preached in influenced his theology.

Drinking deep from the wells of Calvinism, Edwards naturally believed in election. Though he accepted that God chooses whom He will save and whom He will not, Edwards wanted everyone to be one of the elect. He knew this could not be, but he insisted that pastors must preach about the gravity of sin and the necessity of the heart turning toward God. Otherwise, he said, pastors failed in their duties, and he had only to look at some lackadaisical New England clergy to find such examples. When he preached the sermon "God Glorified in Man's Dependence," in 1731, to a Boston audience, he knew that many of his listeners snickered at his emphasis on deep-rooted sin and the necessity of inward change.

During a sixty-year ministry, Solomon Stoddard had seen five "harvests," periods of increased spiritual conviction, resulting in changed lives and increased devotion. In the 1730s Jonathan Edwards prayed for harvest. He had seen a slacking of morals and felt that an increased acceptance of Arminianism would cause an age of spiritual self-reliance. He began to preach concerning these matters.

In the winter of 1734 and through the year that followed a great change came over Northampton. Edwards said, "The Spirit of God began extraordinarily to set in." His church was thronged with listeners, many of whom sought assurance of salvation. "The town seemed to be full of the presence of God. It never was so full of love, nor so full of joy, and yet as full of distress, as it was then." Strife and gossip disappeared as nearly the whole town attended church.

Yet the man who had prayed for and preached to bring revival to his town had no flamboyant preaching techniques. His sermons centered on justification by faith alone and showed his intellectual bent. Though he may have used none of the methods that would appeal to the emotions, he received an emotional response. Critics made fun of the wailing and bodily contortions that sometimes accompanied revival preaching. Later, when he wrote about the Great Awakening, Edwards would admit that it led to some emotional excesses, but all in all, it was evidence of the Spirit of God moving in human hearts.

Edwards was not alone in preaching that led to revival. A German pastor in New Jersey, Theodore Freylinghuysen, had been working with Dutch Reformed congregations since 1720. His fervently evangelical message had brought results—and some dissension. He also aided Gilbert Tennant, a Presbyterian pastor who had come to New Jersey from his father's church and school in Pennsylvania. Gilbert and his brothers—William, Jr.; John; and Charles—all became strongly evangelical pastors in New Jersey.

The man who tied together the two revivals was George Whitefield, an Anglican minister—and friend of John Wesley—who began preaching in America in 1738. Caring little for denominational ties and all for the cause

of Christ, he tirelessly crossed the states, preaching a message of repentance. Under his influence, the entire nation began to experience revival.

1738
John Wesley's Conversion

Wesley faces the Wednesbury mob.

As a five-year-old child John Wesley had nearly lost his life in the fire that swept through his father's parsonage. He was indeed "a brand plucked from the burning," a man whom God would use to ignite faith in thousands of people.

But as John went to Oxford to study for the ministry and then helped in his father's Anglican congregation for a few years, a restlessness filled his spirit. Though he knew the doctrines of salvation, they had yet to comfort his heart.

In 1729 John returned to Oxford. His younger brother Charles and some friends had begun a "Holy Club," which John soon began to lead. Nicknamed *Methodists* by their detractors, because they used such stringent methods in their search for holiness, the young men sought salvation. But even the most stringent devotional exercises could not give John peace. Like Luther, Wesley sought to earn God's favor and found emptiness.

In 1735 John and Charles went to Georgia on a missionary journey. Crossing the Atlantic Ocean, John became impressed by some Moravians. When their vessel hit a storm, John trembled in fear of his life as the Moravians calmly sang hymns.

Charles remained in Georgia only a year, returning home because of ill health. Though John remained, the ministry did not go well, and he followed his brother back to England by 1738. He was invited to a Moravian meeting in Aldersgate Street, London, and on May 24, went "very unwillingly." At that meeting, as someone read from Luther's commentary on Romans, Wesley says, "About a quarter before nine, while he was describing the change which God works in the heart through faith in Christ, I felt my heart strangely warmed. I felt I did trust in Christ, Christ alone for salvation; and an assurance was given me that he had taken away *my* sins, even *mine,* and

saved *me* from the law of sin and death."

Wesley and his brother Charles, who had been converted three days earlier, took this new message of grace and preached it wherever they could. Another member of the Holy Club, George Whitefield, received Christ about the same time. Together they would lead England and America into revival.

When hostile Anglican churches closed their doors to the message, the young men spoke where they could: in public places or open fields. Unlike the Anglican Church, which catered to the aristocracy, their hearers were the poor of England, who hungered for hope. Crowds surrounded them when they preached.

Though John Wesley made a great income through his writings, he lived simply, giving away the extra money. He made it a point to welcome the lower classes.

Wesley tirelessly traveled 250,000 miles on horseback, preaching throughout England and Scotland. He formed the believers in each area into societies, and as the movement grew appointed other preachers, assigning each to a circuit. Societies were further broken down into fellowship classes and prayer bands. The intricate organization that again earned the label *Methodist* helped the movement last.

The Wesleys had no intention of breaking from Anglicanism. Instead they wanted to see reform within the church. The break took place slowly. When, in 1784, John provided for the continuation of Methodism after his death, Charles did not approve of the division.

Though overshadowed by his brother, Charles, too, had a great impact on Methodism. He is best known for his hymns, including, "O for a Thousand Tongues," "And Can It Be?" and "Hark the Herald Angels Sing." Unlike the Anglican Church, which remained chained to the Psalms, from the first the Methodists were a singing movement—largely due to Charles's gift with words.

Methodism gently changed British society. Even as it held to the political status quo, it encouraged a spirit of liberality that led to improved conditions in Britain: Many historians attribute to the Methodists the lack of a bloody revolution such as the one the French experienced at the end of the eighteenth century.

1780
Robert Raikes Begins Sunday Schools

Mrs. Meredith couldn't handle it. At the urging of the kind newspaper edi-tor Robert Raikes, she had welcomed a pack of street urchins into the kitchen of her home on Sooty Alley. He was even paying her a shilling each Sunday to teach these ragamuffins how to read and recite the Bible. But these kids were exceptionally difficult. Cooped up in the dank mills of Gloucester, England, for six days a week, they only had Sunday to have their fun, and on Sundays they ran wild. Farmers and shop owners dreaded their childish mischief each week. Robert Raikes hoped that this "Sunday school" might change their lives, but they brought their abominable ways into Mrs. Meredith's kitchen.

Raikes didn't let the idea die. He moved the Sunday school to Mrs. King's kitchen, where May Critchley taught the children, from ten to twelve in the morning and from one to five in the afternoon. He required that children attend with hands washed and hair combed. Before long, the children *wanted* to learn. Soon he had ninety children coming to Sunday schools each week. Slowly, they were learning to read.

This wasn't Raikes's first attempt at societal reform. As a liberal-minded editor of the *Gloucester Journal,* he was well aware of the cycle of poverty and crime. People were thrown into jail for not paying their debts, and when they got out, there was little livelihood available to them. So they resorted to crime. For years, Raikes had attempted to work with ex-prisoners, to help them break the cycle—to no avail.

"The world marches forward on the

feet of little children." That line, credited to Raikes, explains the Sunday-school brainstorm. Adults were too far gone, but children were just beginning.

The problem, he felt, was ignorance. Poor children never got the chance to attend school—they had to work to help support their families. As a result, they could never climb out of poverty. But if they could learn the basics—reading, writing, arithmetic, and biblical morals—on their one day off, they might someday change all that.

So the experiment began on Sooty Alley. In time, it grew. In 1783, confident that the experiment had succeeded, Raikes began to publicize it in his paper. In a restrained way, he reported his rationale and the results. The idea caught on.

Notable Christians supported the idea. John Wesley loved it, and Wesleyan groups began using it. Popular writer Hannah More taught religion and spinning to girls in Cheddar. A London merchant named William Fox had been developing a similar idea but decided to back Raikes's project. In 1785, Fox founded the Society for the Support and Encouragement of Sunday Schools in the Different Counties of England.

Even Queen Charlotte endorsed the Sunday schools. She summoned Raikes for a private audience and later lent her name to a fund-raising effort that Fox put together.

Fame brought opposition as well, from conservatives who feared the breaking of the Sabbath to merchants who feared loss of business on Sunday.

Some friends poked fun at Raikes, calling him "Bobby Wild Goose and His Ragged Regiment."

Still, by 1787 there were .25 million children attending Sunday schools in England. Fifty years later, there were 1.5 million worldwide—taught by 160,000 teachers. Especially heartwarming are the numbers from Manchester in 1835. That Sunday school had 120 teachers, 117 of whom had been students in the Sunday school.

Two major changes occurred through the years. At first, teachers were paid, but eventually it became a volunteer activity. At first, the curriculum was mostly "the 3 r's"—with the Bible used as a readily available text. As the Sunday schools became better funded, they were able to afford other textbooks. But then, as public education developed, Sunday schools concentrated more on Bible teaching.

The Sunday-school movement was a major phenomenon in England and America, with both religious and secular implications. It took place in the midst of a spiritual awakening that jolted the church out of lethargy and may have spared England the woes of a violent revolution. Wealthy Christians slowly became aware of their responsibility to the poor. The Sunday-school movement planted the seeds of public education and revolutionized religious education, especially as it sparked the printing of religious materials. In the late 1800s, the Sunday-school movement even provided the church with scores of new hymns.

The greatest fruits, however, are undoubtedly the countless young lives that have been touched by the simple interaction and instruction of Sunday schools.

1793
William Carey Sails for India

William Carey.

A ship hoisted its sails against the April wind and moved down the Thames River, toward the English Channel. It was headed for India, bearing William Carey, the ardent shoemaker-turned-preacher, and his fellow missionary, Dr. John Thomas.

The two men had raised money, packed their goods, and said their farewells. Now the ship poked along the coast of England before setting out on the high seas. Years of dreams, prayers, and preparation seemed to near fulfillment in Carey's life.

But rough seas and the dangers of England's war with France ended Carey's eager anticipations—the trip was off. Undeterred, Carey—who called himself a "plodder," but was actually a tireless visionary—trudged right through all sorts of opposition, all sorts of difficulties, to get the job done.

Consider his poor upbringing. His father was a weaver, who taught school to help provide for his five children. William was the eldest, and he eagerly learned to read and write, devouring adventures like *Robinson Crusoe* and *Gulliver's Travels*. His health was never strong, but he managed to apprentice himself to a shoemaker.

At the age of seventeen, he attended a dissenting church with a friend and made a commitment to Christ. He left the Anglican church of his upbringing, incurring his father's disapproval, and became more and more active with the dissenters. He married and began to preach in churches. For a time, he walked eight miles each Sunday to preach at a poor church in a neighboring town. He plunged into the study of the New Testament and the Greek language, and somehow managed to juggle three careers—cobbling, school-teaching, and pastoring.

Added to Carey's poor health were family difficulties. A baby died. His wife went through what would become a series of mental problems. They seldom had enough money for adequate food. In spite of it all, Carey became increasingly obsessed with the obligation for Christians to bring the Gospel to multitudes abroad.

At meetings of ministers in the area, Carey pled the case that Christians should spread the Gospel in distant lands. He was regularly rebuked. "If God wants to save the heathen," he was told, "he will do so, without your help or mine." He went so far as to publish a treatise, "An Enquiry into the Obligation of Christians to Use Means for the Conversion of the Heathen," stating the case for foreign missions. It was a masterful work, but not well read.

Three weeks after the treatise was published, the ministers' association meeting invited him to speak to them. Carey's text: Isaiah 54:2, 3: "Enlarge the place of thy tent. . . ." His theme: "Expect great things from God; attempt great things for God." But the ministers remained unresponsive. As the meeting drew to a close, Carey spoke up in frustration: "Is nothing again going to be done?" Why could he not find others willing to share and enact his vision?

Something *had* clicked. At the next meeting, a mission society was formed. A Christian doctor, John Thomas, volunteered to serve in India, and he needed an associate. Carey volunteered to go along.

The situation seemed absurd. Carey had a pregnant wife and three young sons. Could he himself withstand the physical pressures? But it was the culmination of his dreams. Carey plodded ahead, through a quick fund-raising tour, through the revelation that Dr. Thomas was being sought by unpaid creditors, through his wife's refusal to join him, and through the sudden interruption of the ship's voyage. That delay gave him time to return home and convince his wife, Dorothy, to accompany him.

Soon they were off again, landing in Calcutta in November, 1793. But the troubles continued: Conditions were poor; their health was bad; Thomas continued to run up debts; and there were no converts. Their youngest son died, and the two oldest ran wild.

In 1800, the Careys moved to Serampore, joining a group of Danish missionaries. There they saw their first convert to Christianity, due in part to the efforts of the oldest Carey boy, Felix, now a Christian himself. Soon a church was formed and a Bengali translation of the New Testament completed.

Three decades of mission success had just begun. By the time he died in 1834, Carey had translated the Bible into forty-four languages or dialects and had started several schools. Various mission stations actively evangelized India and neighboring Burma and Bhutan. But beyond those statistics, Carey had developed a workable philosophy of missions and put it into practice.

He was well ahead of his time. Carey had an immense respect for the Indian culture and saw the need for an indigenous Indian church. Instead of spending a lot of time condemning the Hindu religion, he affirmed the death and resurrection of Christ.

Despite his individual achievements, he was also a great team player. From experience he learned that the mission team is stronger than the individuals involved. Carey was also quick to affirm the value of women as part of these teams.

We sometimes wrongly get the idea that Carey single-handedly pulled the church into the era of missions, but he was actually one of a number of Christians in the West calling for support of foreign missions. His voice was simply one of the clearest, and he backed up his words with his life.

1807
The British Parliament Votes to Abolish the Slave Trade

William Wilberforce, Esq.

Europe in the late eighteenth century was a society gone awry; the rich got richer, while the poor starved. Debtors rotted away in dank prisons. Orphans slaved away in factories. Christianity had largely become a religion of manners for the upper classes.

In France, the frustration of the poor boiled over in the French Revolution of 1789.

Still, at the beginning of the 1800s, complacency marked the Church of England, perhaps because Britain had avoided revolution. Methodism had caught hold among the lower classes, but the upper class of society remained mostly untouched—except for a handful of notable social reformers. These Christians—William Wilberforce, Elizabeth Fry, George Mueller, Thomas Buxton, John Venn, and others—believed their dedication to Christ meant service to society, to the poor and needy.

A leading voice against slavery in the British Empire belonged to William Wilberforce, an evangelical Anglican and a member of the House of Commons. He wasn't much to look at, by all accounts, but his sharp mind and effective speech won him respect from friends and foes alike.

Wilberforce was born in 1759 and grew into a carefree young man, devoted to politics and pleasure. At the age of twenty-five, he went through a conversion of sorts, rededicating his life to the Christ he had known as a boy. The timing was inconvenient: He had just been elected to a prestigious seat in Parliament. Would this new devotion to Christ put an end to his political ambition?

Young William sought out the advice of a pastor, John Newton. The famous preacher and one-time slave trader, author of the classic hymn "Amazing Grace," urged Wilberforce to stay in politics. God needs people like you in Parliament, Newton said—perhaps we can even abolish slavery.

It became a consuming passion for Wilberforce. He brought a bill before Parliament in 1787, but opposition was stronger than anticipated. The slave traders knew how to play politics—they were challenging the abolitionists at every turn. Wilberforce expected strong support from his old college friend, William Pitt, now the prime minister. But Pitt was a moderate; he favored only gradual change, not the sudden and total abolition of the slave trade.

Wilberforce did, however, gain allies among a group of Christian activists, who became known as the Clapham Sect. They took their name from the village, south of London, where Wilberforce lived. These men became leaders in the evangelical movement within the Church of England. Several of them, including Wilberforce, were involved in the founding of the Church Missionary Society and the British and Foreign Bible Society.

In 1806, Pitt died. The abolitionists succeeded in attaching a rider onto a bill having to do with the war against France. This paved the way for the 1807 bill that stopped British slave trading. (The United States passed a similar law the same year.)

Wilberforce became a hero and used his newfound fame to push for other social reforms. He continued to work for international abolition of the slave trade and helped to establish Sierra Leone as a home for liberated slaves.

The reformer had hoped that the institution of slavery would just wither away, once slave trafficking became illegal. He was wrong. In 1823, Wilberforce set out on a final endeavor to eradicate slavery once and for all. He retired from Parliament in 1825 but continued to speak out for abolition. Thomas Buxton took up the leadership of the abolitionists in Parliament. Finally, in August of 1833, a month after Wilberforce's death, the House of Commons voted to free the slaves and abolish all slavery.

1811
The Campbells Begin the Disciples of Christ

Thomas Campbell simply welcomed people to come and worship with his church. He was pastoring a congregation in western Pennsylvania that belonged to the Seceder Presbyterian Church, a splinter denomination with Scottish roots. Upset with the petty divisions over man-made doctrines, Campbell would allow any Presbyte-

rian to come to his church and take communion, whether they were Seceders or not.

But the presbytery didn't like it. Their by-laws prohibited it. They officially investigated the matter and condemned Campbell.

In response, Campbell wrote to the synod. He explained his principles—ideas that would soon lead him to form a new denomination. The church needed unity and must break away from human theological formulations and follow the clear teachings of Scripture. He won this case. The synod overturned the presbytery's condemnation, but there remained a feeling of bitterness among Campbell's fellow pastors. He decided to branch out on his own, to start his own church.

Thomas Campbell had been a pastor for many years in northern Ireland but had moved to America for health reasons. He had left the church and school he had run in Ireland in the capable hands of his son, Alexander.

America was still the New World. Its frontier started at the Appalachians and stretched westward. Religiously, it was on the downslope of the Great Awakening. The revival started by Whitefield and Edwards on the East Coast had moved west. "Camp meeting" revivals had begun in Kentucky around 1800 and still flickered throughout the frontier.

But ironically revivals can cause division. And the Awakening in the west was quite different from the Awakening in the east. The east, for instance, had the scholarly, erudite Jonathan Edwards carefully reasoning out the wrath of God and the need for reconciliation. The west had a band of frontier preachers with minimal seminary training, who would stand on the back of a wagon to persuade sinners to get right with God. It was a difference of style, to be sure, but also of theology. The eastern revival was more Presbyterian, the western more Methodist; the east was more Calvinist, the west more Arminian; the east was more ecclesiastical, the west more individualistic.

So there were several schisms in the early 1800s: the Cumberland Presbytery, the Shakers, the New Light movement of Barton Stone, and now Thomas Campbell's group.

Campbell held meetings wherever possible—in barns, homes, and fields—and he attracted a fair number of followers. He called the group the Christian Association of Washington (for Washington County, Pennsylvania), and he wrote the "Declaration and Address," which served as a founding document for the movement. Like other church founders, he had no real desire to break away from the established church, but he was compelled by the need to move in a certain direction—and none of the churches seemed to be going that way. For Campbell, the direction was biblical and simple. His motto became: "Where the Scriptures speak, we speak; where the Scriptures are silent, we are silent."

Thomas's son, Alexander Campbell, arrived from Ireland in 1809 and immediately teamed with his father in this new enterprise. He was only twenty-three, but extremely gifted, a fine speaker, and a good debater. Together they founded the Brush Run Church in 1811 (after being denied entry by the Presbyterians). Studying Scripture, the Campbells determined that believer's baptism by immersion was correct, rather than the infant baptism they had been practicing, and so they began to rebaptize church members.

At this point they were essentially Baptist, so they affiliated with the Redstone Baptist Association in 1812. Alexander Campbell became a leading figure in the Baptist Church, speaking widely and publishing a periodical, *The Christian Baptist*. He also established a seminary at Bethany, in western Virginia. Campbell was always trying to draw the church back, back to the New Testament, back to what he judged were the biblical ways. He wrote a series of articles for his paper: "A Restoration of the Ancient Order of Things."

Not all the Baptists liked this. Campbell thought many Baptist teachings were too Calvinistic, and he regularly attacked them. He also disagreed with the Baptist understanding of baptism. Baptists saw it as an ordinance that depicted a salvation that had previously occurred. But Campbell drew from various "repent and be baptized" passages in the New Testament to argue that it was a necessary condition for forgiveness. Campbell also rejected attempts to go beyond Scripture in the explanation of the Trinity.

By the late 1820s, tensions were growing too great. The Campbellites eased out of the Baptist association and merged in 1832 with the Christian Church of Barton Stone. (Both Campbell and Stone wanted simple, biblical names for their groups, eschewing denominationalism. Thereafter, *Christians* and *Disciples of Christ* were generally used interchangeably for the merged movements.) At that point, there were 25,000 members.

The movement continued to grow, partly due to Alexander Campbell's personal prominence. Campbell served as a delegate to Virginia's constitutional convention in 1829. Fellow delegate James Madison said of him, "I regard him as the ablest and most original expounder of the Scriptures I ever heard."

The movement's growth was also due in part to the expansion of the western frontier. The Disciples had a simple Gospel for a simple time. Also Alexander Campbell was antislavery from the start, but not vehemently abolitionist. So the church was not split by the Civil War. By the turn of the twentieth century, there were over a million Disciples of Christ.

The Campbells' significance rests not only in their founding of a substantial denomination, but in their espousal of a simple, biblical faith.

Church history is filled with a tension between formal religion and simple faith. The Campbells tilted many from the oppression of formality, into a more personal faith. Spawned and nurtured in the frontiers of an emerging nation, the Disciples became a prime example of American Christianity of that age. They helped set the stage for the revivalist and fundamentalist movements.

1812
Adoniram and Ann Judson Sail for India

Adoniram Judson.

It was some honeymoon! Adoniram Judson married Ann Hasseltine on February 5, 1812, and within two weeks they were sailing for India, appointed as missionaries by the newly formed American Board of Commissioners for Foreign Missions. It seems that they spent most of their time on board skipping rope, dancing, studying the Bible, and arguing.

They were arguing about baptism. In his scriptural study, Adoniram decided that the Congregationalists were wrong about baptism, and the Baptists were right. Ann, no doubt, respected his personal decision, but reminded him that they had been sent and financed on their mission as *Congregationalists*. It would surely be more practical to think this over long and hard before making any rash decisions.

But impetuous Adoniram won this argument. Ann, too, became a Baptist, as did their fellow missionary-traveler, Luther Rice. When they reached Calcutta, the Judsons sent Rice back with a letter of resignation and an awesome task: to drum up missionary support among Baptist churches. As yet, the Baptists in America had no mission society.

Rice did his job admirably, and the Judsons were able to stay in Asia, keeping their place in history among the first foreign missionaries from the United States.

Six years earlier, no one would have guessed that either Ann or Adoniram would be headed for the mission field. Ann was a strong-willed, self-involved, fun-loving teenager. Adoniram was a moody but brilliant youth who had drifted from his religious upbringing in favor of an acting career in New York. The writings of Hannah More and John Bunyan brought Ann closer to God. For Adoniram, it was the sudden death of a college chum, the same boy who had urged him to reject Christianity. In 1808, Adoniram headed back home to the Boston area and dedicated himself to Christ.

Reading about the Asian lands of India and Burma, Adoniram felt burdened to go there as a missionary. That wouldn't be easy, because there were no mission boards in America to send him.

The Haystack Prayer Meeting changed that. A group of students from Williams College and Andover Seminary ran into a barn to escape a downpour. There, by a haystack, they began to pray for the needs of the world. Each one, including Adoniram Judson, felt drawn into missionary service. Led by Samuel J. Mills, they presented themselves to the Congregational Church for commissioning. The American Board of Commissioners for Foreign Missions was formed in 1810, but took a while to raise support for the new appointees. Impatient, Adoniram sailed for London, to try to get backing from the London Missionary Society. France was warring with England at the time, and the French captured his ship. Judson spent some unpleasant moments as a prisoner of war before he could convince his captors that he was American and not British. He arrived back in Boston safe and sound, and the board was ready to send him out, along with four others, early in 1812.

In the meantime, Adoniram had met Ann and fell in love. He promised her a life of hardship, missionary service in primitive places, hard work and few conveniences. What girl could resist? But from the start, Ann saw herself as a teammate of Adoniram's, just as fully involved in the mission enterprise. She knelt with him as they were consecrated for mission work, the day after their marriage. Then they set sail.

But more troubles awaited them in India. The British rulers of India would not let these Americans stay. William Carey suggested that they move to Burma. His son Felix was an ambassador there and could put them up for a while. There were more troubles involved in getting to Burma, but the Judsons arrived and immediately began work, learning the language, starting a school for girls, and translating the New Testament. Ann learned Burmese as well as Adoniram did and helped in the translation.

It was six years before they won their first convert. Troubles continued. Ann had health problems and had to return temporarily to the United States. Shortly after she got back to Burma, the Anglo-Burmese War broke out. Adoniram was arrested and held in prison for two years. Ann moved nearby and visited regularly. The ordeal damaged her health as much as his.

The British army liberated Adoniram, but Ann died shortly thereafter, at the age of thirty-six. Adoniram worked for twenty-four more years in Burma, and now results were more apparent. The Judsons' Burmese translation of the New Testament was published, as was a catechism written by Ann. (Ann had also produced a translation of Scripture portions into Siamese.) In all, Judson established sixty-three churches, mostly among the Karen tribe, hill people of Burma and Siam. The Karens had a tradition that foreigners would visit them and restore the knowledge of the true God, which they had lost. By now, over 100,000 of the Karen people have been baptized as Christians. The American Baptist Foreign Mission Society (a descendant of the Baptist mission society that Luther Rice formed) supported extensive work among the Karen people.

The Judsons had a hand in starting two different mission societies. These, in turn, sparked the formation of several other Christian organizations and mission boards in the United States. They pioneered a Christian ministry in Southeast Asia. And they have served as an inspiration to countless missionary couples tackling tough mission fields together.

1816 Richard Allen Founds African Methodist Episcopal Church

The Rev. Richard Allen, bishop of the first African Methodist Episcopal Church of the United States.

The incident happened in 1787 in St. George's Methodist Church, in Phila-delphia. Richard Allen, a black man, had preached there on some occasions, but on this Sunday he was seated in the gallery. For some reason, the section normally reserved for black worshipers was unavailable, and the ushers had directed blacks to another section. But apparently there was a misunderstanding, and they sat in the wrong place.

As they knelt to pray, a trustee noticed that the black worshipers were in the white section and hurried over to grab one of the black men. It was Reverend Absolom Jones, a prominent leader among the black Methodists. "You must get up," the trustee said. "You must not kneel here."

"Wait until prayer is over," Jones answered.

"No, you must get up now, or I will call for aid and force you away."

"Wait until prayer is over," Jones repeated, "and I will get up and trouble you no more."

But it could not wait. The trustee and another usher began dragging Jones and another black worshiper away. By then, prayer was finished. Allen and the other black people walked out. "They were no more plagued by us," Allen writes, adding that they had contributed generously to the furnishing of the church. They had paid for the laying of the floor on which they were kneeling.

Allen and Jones led their people to start their own services in a rented storeroom. Eventually they bought land and built a church. But they continued to struggle with white Methodists, especially those at St. George's.

Incidents like this were not uncommon in those days. But it's sadly ironic that the kneeling incident happened in a Methodist church, because the Methodists in America were actually very quick to see that slaves were people, too, and needed to know Jesus just as any white person did. Methodist missionaries were appointed and assigned the task of ministering to slaves and freedmen. And Methodist leaders soon discovered that black missionaries were the most effective among their black brethren.

Richard Allen had been born a slave, in 1760, in the home of Benjamin Chew, a prominent Philadelphia lawyer. His family was sold to a farmer near Dover, Delaware, where in adolescence Allen became a Christian. He began to meet with a Methodist group. On one occasion, he arranged for the preacher to speak at his master's home. The master, though not a Christian, was still convicted by the preacher's text ("You are weighed in the balances and found wanting"). As a result, he gave Allen and his brother an opportunity to purchase their freedom.

As a freedman, Allen worked cutting wood and laying bricks. He remained an active churchman. During the Revolution, he drove a wagon, delivering salt. He would preach to various congregations along the route. His speaking skills made him popular among both whites and blacks as he toured Delaware, New Jersey, and Pennsylvania, picking up work along the way, preaching on nights and weekends.

In 1784, the Methodist Episcopal church was officially established in the United States. John Wesley appointed Thomas Coke and Francis Asbury as his "assistants" to oversee the American church, with Richard Whatcoat and Thomas Vassey also designated leaders. Especially during the Revolutionary War, the Methodist movement in the United States had been fragmented —partly because it was still a movement within the Anglican Church, and the war strained loyalties. Wesley's actions in 1784 brought the fragments together and, for the first time, established the Methodists as a separate church.

Richard Allen came to the attention of Richard Whatcoat, who was assigned to the Baltimore circuit. Whatcoat invited Allen to travel with him as he visited the churches. Allen was later invited to join Asbury in his journeys.

When Allen landed in Philadelphia, he preached at St. George's Church on occasion, but eventually left it, as we have seen. The offended kneeler, Absolom Jones, broke away from the Methodists in 1793, forming the Colored Protestant Episcopal Church, but Allen refused. "I could not be anything else than a Methodist," he wrote, "as I was born and awakened under them, and I could go further with them."

He did indeed go further with them, starting the Bethel African Methodist Episcopal Church in Philadelphia in 1794. Francis Asbury preached the dedicatory sermon. But even then, the leaders at St. George's tried to gain control over Allen's church. Blacks had few legal rights in those days, but the Bethel Church managed to win a court case over St. George's.

Allen's star continued to rise in the Methodist denomination, even as pressure from their cross-town rival church continued to mount. Allen was ordained a deacon in 1799 and an elder in 1816—both unheard-of accomplishments for a black man. But in 1816, he decided to leave the Methodists and start a new denomination, the African Methodist Episcopal (AME) Church. Allen's church joined with several independent black churches, and Allen became bishop of the new group. Baltimore and Philadelphia were two focal points of the new denomination.

Allen provided excellent administration for the new church, fashioning it along Methodist lines. He continued to travel, preach, and plant new churches until his death in 1831. The AME church went on to experience great numerical growth in the wake of the Civil War as freed slaves sought truly free places of worship.

The new denomination was an inspiration to all oppressed Christians. For that time, it was a remarkable declaration of independence. Black believers would serve Christ gladly, but they would not be abused by their white brothers. Allen's bold leadership did much to foster a strong black spirituality in America that lives on today.

1817
Elizabeth Fry Begins Ministry to Women in Prison

It was "out of sight, out of mind" for British prisoners in the early 1800s. Prisons were dark, unsanitary, crowded, and hopeless. Offenders of many varied crimes—violent or not—could be thrown in jail, and no distinction was made between those convicted and those awaiting trial. Women whose husbands had died or run off often fell into debt and were jailed, taking their children with them.

John Howard, a Christian layman who became sheriff of Bedfordshire in 1773, had brought the squalid conditions of European prisons to people's attention. He traveled 50,000 miles and spent £30,000 of his own money hawking prison reform. Unfortunately, while people were moved, they weren't motivated to change things. Howard returned from one torturous fact-finding trip in Italy to find funds being raised for a statue in his honor. The only memorial he wanted, he told the people, was lasting prison reform. But by the early 1800s, the situation remained bleak.

The unlikely successor to John Howard was a woman, Elizabeth Fry. The daughter of a well-to-do wool merchant and banker, Elizabeth Gurney grew up in a liberal Quaker home. As a girl, she read Voltaire, Rousseau, and Thomas Paine. At age seventeen, she wrote in her diary that she had no religion.

But the next year she encountered a Quaker from America, William Savery, who instilled in her a sense of God's presence. She began to attend a stricter Quaker meeting and became more serious about her faith.

At age twenty, Elizabeth married Joseph Fry, also from a wealthy banking family. She bore eleven children. Yet her involvement with the Quaker meeting grew, and in 1811, at thirty, she was recognized as a "minister."

Three years later, she visited Newgate, a jail near London. Appalled by its conditions, she did what she could, bringing clothes for the children of the female prisoners. Despite the efforts of John Howard, Britain's penal system had worsened. Between 1800 and 1817, the number of imprisoned convicts doubled, causing tremendous overcrowding. Something had to be done, especially for the women and children, whose only crime, in many cases, was poverty.

In 1817, Fry organized a team of women to visit the female prisoners regularly, read the Bible to them, and teach them to sew. This useful occupation radically changed the nature of prison life for these inmates. London businesses began to support Fry's efforts, and she was hailed throughout Britain.

With the war against Napoleon concluded, the British people turned their attention to other problems. Prison reform was one. Fry expanded her ladies' prison-visiting committees to new areas, and in 1821 established the British Society for Promoting Reformation of Female Prisoners. Thomas Buxton, who later would help Wilberforce win the fight for abolition of slavery, published a study of Newgate prison in 1818, questioning whether the penal system actually helped or hurt society. Soon the reformers had the ear of powerful Home Secretary Robert Peel, who pushed the Prison Act of 1823 through Parliament. This radically reformed British prisons and limited (by 500) the number of offenses that called for the death penalty. Robert Peel also initiated a regular police force, whose members became known as "bobbies," from Peel's nickname.

Until her death in 1845, Fry continued to promote the improvement of prison conditions. Although other European nations followed Britain's lead, Britain itself seemed to snap back to a harsher mind-set. Yet Fry's efforts had lasting results. Along with contemporaries like William Wilberforce and George Mueller, she urged a generation of Christians to take their social responsibilities seriously. She also continued the age-old tradition of women leading the way in charitable endeavors.

1830
Charles G. Finney's Urban Revivals Begin

Charles G. Finney.

Revival had swept south and west from New England, reaching the western frontier in Tennessee and Kentucky by 1800. As it moved west, the revival became increasingly known for the emotionalism of its converts.

Like many other Calvinists, the Presbyterians doubted such highly emotional conversions, but from their own ranks came one of the most colorful and effective revivalists of the nineteenth century.

Charles Grandison Finney had been born in Connecticut in 1792. Like many people of his age, he moved west—in 1794 his parents moved to western New York. Young Finney studied in a law office in Adams, New York, and was admitted to the state bar.

Drawn to the Bible because he found many references to it in his law books, Finney began to read God's Word and attend church. After a period of intense struggle, in 1821 he had a conversion experience. He had, he said, been given "a retainer from the Lord Jesus Christ to plead His cause." Immediately he began to preach.

Finney joined the Presbyterian Church and was ordained in 1824, after studying with his pastor. Traveling on horseback, he went from village to village, drawing crowds. The tall, striking, articulate preacher spoke to them in a direct, simple fashion, as if he were still before a jury.

The camp-meeting preachers had gotten a name for encouraging too much emotionalism. Though Finney avoided theatrical mannerisms, he sought to gain his listeners' attention through excitement, for he said, "Mankind will not act until they are excited." By working together with the Holy Spirit, he sought to bring the Word to people.

In 1830, Finney led remarkably successful revivals in Rochester, New York. From that time on, revivalism became a feature of American urban life.

In 1832, Finney moved to the Second Presbyterian Church, in New York City, but he had always objected to the Presbyterian hyper-Calvinism, and in 1834 moved again to the Congregational church, the Broadway Tabernacle, built especially for him.

Finney owed some of his revival methods—called new measures—to the frontier preachers who had gained a name for emotionalism. He used an "anxious bench," a seat set out in front, where anxious sinners could come to request prayer. Finney conducted all-night prayer meetings in which sinners were prayed for by name, and women could pray publicly. Though he did not necessarily encourage them, the revivalist allowed shouting, groaning, and other evidences of emotion. These new measures became a standard part of revival work, and the churches that used them grew, despite many critic's attacks on such methods.

Before Finney visited a town, he recruited ministers and laypeople in local churches. They organized prayer meetings, and after the revival meeting, they could work with the new converts, visiting them and inviting them to church. It was a critical role, for unless local churches were willing to become involved in follow-up, Finney would not preach in that place.

In addition, the local supporters scattered handbills, posted placards, and placed advertisements in the newspapers. Promotion had become a part of evangelism.

Despite the opposition he faced, Finney's energy, determination, and intelligence—and the success of his new measures—caused the ideas to catch on. Modern revivalism had begun.

In his 1835 publication *Lectures on Revivals of Religion* Finney explained, "A revival is not a miracle, or dependent on miracle in any sense. It is the result of the right use of the constituted means."

Finney's methods were well received by a nation that had developed a high view of the value of the common man under Jacksonian democracy. The revivalist made the average person a participant in a great religious drama and appealed to the belief that every individual could make the right choice for God. By focusing on every person's ability to judge for himself, he fell in with the American idea that a clerk or farm boy has as much rationality and worth as a plantation owner.

In 1835 Finney went to Oberlin College to teach theology. Sixteen years later he would become its president. He continued to hold revivals until his death in 1875.

Circa 1830
John Nelson Darby Helps Start Plymouth Brethren

J. N. Darby.

Five men gathered for worship at a house in Dublin, on Fitzwilliam Square, in November, 1829. The host, Francis Hutchinson, presented a simple order of service and invited them to meet there regularly, at a time that would not interfere with their other church activities.

To modern minds, nothing seems especially striking about such a meeting. But at that time, it was unusual. The established Church of England dominated religious life and practice. Meeting for fellowship and worship outside the church walls was not considered proper. To celebrate communion without the proper clergy was scandalous.

John Nelson Darby was present at that meeting, but it would be wrong to consider him the founder of the Plymouth Brethren. He was one of several who provided leadership in the early days, though he became its most noteworthy spokesman.

In the first three decades of the nineteenth century, spiritual fervor was brewing in Ireland. Some Catholics converted to the Anglican Church or the dissenting churches, but an independent movement had also arisen. Groups of Christians began meeting together—apart from any established church—using only the Bible as their guide.

The Plymouth Brethren movement might go back to Anthony Norris Groves. A devout Christian dentist, he was willing to give up his practice for mission service in Persia. At first he dutifully attended Trinity College in Dublin, in 1826, to prepare for ordination. But there he came in contact with a number of independent-minded Dubliners. These friends had shaken his "high church" views. But he had already wondered, *Why do I need all these classes and exams to be a missionary?*

Ultimately he decided he did not need ordination or the official mission society, he just needed to step out in faith.

Groves gathered support from friends in Dublin and Plymouth and set out for Baghdad in 1829. Supporting Groves became a unifying factor, as groups would meet to pray for him and to collect his support funds.

Meanwhile, John Nelson Darby had been serving as a curate in County Wicklow. He had studied law at Trinity College, but soon sought ordination. He, too, was a devout churchman, but he became disillusioned by the closed-door policies of his church. His superiors seemed to care more about church membership than about Christ.

After being hurt in an accident in 1827, Darby took leave from his church to recuperate in Dublin. There he met a number of like-minded men, some from Groves's circle of supporters. The group fanned the sparks of ideas forming in Darby's mind. Shortly after this, he resigned his position, but he did not yet break with the established church. He became an outspoken proponent of church openness and unity, publishing pamphlets calling for change in church policy. He called for true spirituality among Christians and a return to Scripture. One aspect of Scripture that had been largely ignored, he contended, was prophecy. He became fascinated by theories of the end times and urged Christian leaders to look into this. A series of prophecy conferences were held in the early 1830s to consider the subject.

The prevailing view in the established church was post-millennial—that is, the church would bring about an era of peace, after which Christ would return. But Darby seized on teachings that had been set forth in the eighteenth century by the Chilean monastic Manuel de Lacunza. Lacunza suggested a premillennial return—the world would head toward destruction until Christ would come and set up His thousand-year reign. (Lacunza also proposed that Christ would appear first to remove His faithful from the worst of the tribulations, before returning fully to establish His reign.)

In 1831, the focus of the movement began to move toward Plymouth, England. The ensuing years saw some consolidation of the diverse groups. The "Brethren," as they became known, tried to strip their churches of unbiblical accoutrements. Communion was celebrated weekly; there were no ordained ministers (everyone was a minister); and people of all denominations were welcome in the name of Christ. The Brethren also believed in pacifism and, of course, the importance of prophecy.

In Bristol, a German immigrant named George Mueller founded an orphanage. Inspired by the example of A. N. Groves' heading to the mission field on faith, Mueller determined to run his orphanage on faith. He didn't ask for money, just trusted God to provide. Mueller's ministry became legendary, a testimony to the simple faith of the burgeoning Plymouth Brethren movement.

Meanwhile Darby continued to travel, speak, and write. Touring Switzerland, beginning in 1838, he started a number of Brethren churches there. A political revolution in 1845 created persecution for these churches, and Darby himself narrowly escaped.

About that time, controversies arose among the Brethren, especially regarding spiritual gifts, foot washing, the role of elders, and interpretation of prophecy. The major rift occurred between Darby and B. W. Newton, who might be considered cofounders of the movement. Newton ultimately withdrew from the church, but the conflict probably spurred a later one that drove a wedge between Darby and Mueller. The result of their disagreement was a division between Exclusive Brethren (who would not fellowship with those of unsound doctrine) and the Open Brethren (who would). Naturally, the first group's exclusivity led to several subsequent divisions, reflecting the sad irony that it is hard to hold on to both church unity and purity of doctrine.

Like the Disciples of Christ in the United States, the Plymouth Brethren injected a needed emphasis on simplicity into church life in England. The church has gained a significant following around the world, including prominent figures such as the early textual scholar Samuel Tregelles and the modern New Testament expert F. F. Bruce.

But Darby's chief claim to fame is his eschatology. His view of prophecy became known as dispensationalism, and it became a major theme in prophecy conferences of the late 1800s and the fundamentalist movement of the early 1900s.

1833
John Keble's Sermon "National Apostasy" Initiates the Oxford Movement

Cardinal John Henry Newman, a central figure in the Oxford Movement.

Methodism had sought to bring new life to the Anglican Church, but had ended by forming a separate denomination. By the late 1820s, the attendance in the Church of England had dropped drastically. While Methodism thrived, the church that had spawned it had become dry and empty.

One man who felt concern about the Anglican Church's situation was an Oxford-educated, thoroughly Anglican cleric who had an evangelical's warm heart. John Keble felt his church had lost its strength because it had turned from the rich tradition of the liturgy and writings of the church Fathers. Unless the Church of England realized its heritage of the apostolic succession, Keble believed it would lose ground to both Protestant dissenters and the Catholic Church—eventually it would die out.

Keble published a collection of devotional poetry that reflected the liturgy, with its feasts and saints' days. *The Christian Year*'s beautiful poems showed the warmth usually associated with the Methodists and other dissenters, yet it remained within the Anglican tradition.

On July 14, 1833, Keble preached at Oriel College. His sermon, "National Apostasy," attacked Parliament for reducing the number of bishops in the Church of Ireland, saying that the act was an example of the state's interference in the church. The divinely originated church should not be subject to the secular legislature.

Keble's words began the Oxford Movement (or Tractarianism), which sought renewal in the Anglican Church by returning it to the beliefs and practices of the early church. Among the adherents to the Oxford Movement were Keble's disciple Richard Froude, John Henry Newman, and Edward Pusey.

Newman began publishing *Tracts for the Times*. He, Keble, and Froude wrote ninety tracts between 1833 and 1841. The four-page leaflets, which sold for a penny each, were anonymously published, and Newman bicycled around Oxfordshire, selling them to the clergy.

Some of the tracts encouraged the Church of England to return to the Catholic fold. Although the Anglican Church was not particularly vital, it feared a return to Catholicism, especially in the wake of the 1828 repeal of laws that denied Catholics the right to hold public office—a right denied to them since the Test Act of 1673. Criticism of Tractarianism peaked in 1841, when Newman wrote a tract saying that baptism and communion were not the only sacraments. In addition he advocated belief in purgatory, Christ's real presence in the Eucharist, and invocation of the saints. The bishop of Oxford responded by ordering an end to the tract series.

Some Anglican clergy—Newman among them—did turn to Catholicism, but most of those who sympathized with the Tractarians remained in the Church of England. Though they appreciated the traditions of the church, including its vestments, genuflecting, incense, confession to a priest, frequent Communion, and even monasticism, many were in fact anti-Catholic. They wanted a religion that appealed to all five senses, but they did not particularly want a connection with the pope or his worldwide hierarchy.

After Newman departed the Oxford Movement, in 1845, it sought to hold onto the best in ritual, architecture, and music, while avoiding other aspects of Catholicism. Edward Pusey then became the movement's most eloquent spokesman.

Many evangelicals were disturbed by the practices of these Anglo-Catholics. In 1846 they formed the Evangelical Alliance. But what began as an anti-Tractarian movement became a way of drawing evangelicals into a national fellowship. Despite their objections to the ritualism of the Oxford Movement, the evangelicals could not deny that it had positive influences upon the Anglican Church. Instead of viewing themselves as English civil servants, the Anglican clergymen who supported the Oxford Movement took the apostolic tradition seriously. Instead of merely moralizing in their worship services, they began to develop a sense of reverence. As a result of the changes in perception, the old term "high church" was revived. Many Anglican clergymen and nuns began to work with the poor in the increasingly industrialized cities.

In addition, some fine hymn writers developed from the Oxford Movement. Previous hymnists had come from the ranks of the dissenters. Now Keble; Frederick W. Faber; and John Mason Neale, who translated some long-lost Greek and Latin hymns into English verse, joined them.

1854
Hudson Taylor Arrives in China

Hudson Taylor.

No one knew he was coming. Hudson Taylor got off the boat in Shanghai after a tedious voyage from England, and there was no one to welcome him. His brilliant missionary career was just beginning, but he had no place to stay. He knew no Chinese, and few of the Chinese could speak English. To top it all, there was a civil war going on—just outside the city.

Taylor asked at the British consulate for the few Western missionaries he knew. One had died, another had returned home. He finally located Dr. Walter Medhurst, of the London Missionary Society, and arranged to stay with him.

This wasn't at all the way Taylor had dreamed of it. Growing up in a Methodist home, he had heard stories of China from his preacher father. He learned of Robert Morrison, the Scottish Presbyterian who had begun ministry in Guangzhou in 1807, translating for merchants and preaching for Jesus. When young Hudson became a Christian, at age seventeen, he almost immediately sensed his calling. He studied medicine and theology and found out all he could about that great land of China.

When the Taiping Rebellion broke out in 1850, it seemed like good news at first for missionaries. The leader of the rebels had been influenced by Christian tracts. He aimed to rid China of idolatry and corruption. He even named his movement Taiping, "great peace." (He was also convinced he was the younger brother of Jesus Christ, but such eccentricities were not apparent at first.)

All England paid new attention to China. One new mission board, the China Evangelization Society, published a call for workers. Taylor, who had been put off by the London Missionary Society, offered his services. They took him right out of school. He

was twenty-two when he landed in Shanghai.

Zeal had outrun wisdom, at least as far as the mission board was concerned. Sure, they put their man on the field, but they gave no guidance, had no mission philosophy, and had done little to pave his way. They also were routinely short on funds.

Taylor had to make up his own rules. One of these had to do with dressing like the Chinese. His colleagues from England were appalled, but Taylor had his reasons. "I am fully satisfied that the native dress is an absolute prerequisite," he wrote. "Quietly settling among the people, obtaining free, familiar, and unrestrained communication with them, conciliating their prejudices, attracting their esteem and confidence, and so living as to be examples to them of what Chinese Christians should be, require the adoption not merely of this costume but also of their habits.... The foreign appearance of chapels and indeed the foreign air given to everything connected with religion have very largely hindered the rapid dissemination of the truth among the Chinese. But why need such a foreign aspect be given to Christianity? The Word of God does not require it.... It is not their denationalization but their Christianization that we seek."

Missionaries had come into this closed country on the coattails of merchants and soldiers. Ever since Morrison had translated for the East India Trading Company, the connection could be presumed. When Great Britain had conducted its shameful Opium

Wars—actually fighting to maintain the right to trade opium for Chinese silk—the one-sided treaties had even included special provisions for missionaries. The message had been clear: The ancient civilization of China was being humiliated by the modern war machines of Europe—and the Europeans brought Christianity with them. China was being turned into just another colony for the "Christian" empire of Britain.

Taylor had to contend with this history. In a way, those treaties had made it easier to be a missionary. But they made it hard to connect in any serious way with the people. He hoped he could break from the colonial mind-set by adopting local customs.

In his first six-year stint, Taylor worked in Shanghai, Swatow, and Ningpo, learning the language, translating Scripture, even running a hospital. During that time, he resigned from the mission society and went independent.

Returning to England in 1860, he began stirring enthusiasm for Chinese missions. He wrote a book about the need there and actively sought new missionaries. Taylor established the China Inland Mission—and he was determined that he would not make the mistakes of his previous mission board. CIM would not make direct solicitations for funds, would not guarantee a salary to its workers, but would share all its income evenly. It would appoint people from different nations and different denominations and would even grant both single and married women

full missionary appointment. For the time, this was radical. Taylor also insisted that CIM's missionaries follow his practice of dressing as the Chinese did.

Sixteen new missionaries went back to China with Taylor in 1866. They launched out into new areas, preaching the Gospel to those who had never heard it before. Soon CIM was the leading mission in China. By the time Taylor died, in 1905, there were 205 mission stations, 849 missionaries, and an estimated 125,000 Chinese Christians.

Hudson Taylor was not the first missionary in China. But his steady refusal to do "missions as usual" led to great success on that subcontinent.

One incident typifies the integrity and foresight that Taylor injected into his mission society. CIM, like other missions, lost people and property in the Boxer Rebellion of 1900. The British army stepped in once again, settled the crisis, and imposed huge fines on the Chinese government. This money would repay the missions for their losses. But CIM refused to accept any payment—the Chinese had lost a great deal themselves.

In the following years, CIM missionaries found that this commitment to stand with the Chinese people did more to open their hearts to Christ than any diplomatic treaty could ever have done. Hudson Taylor had known that all along.

1854
Søren Kierkegaard Publishes Attacks on Christendom

The theology of the twentieth century might be very different if it weren't for a young woman named Regina Olsen. She was the intended bride of a brilliant Dane named Søren Kierkegaard. Their engagement and breakup sent Søren into a frenzy of philosophical writing. The works he produced have done much to change the shape of modern thought.

Kierkegaard was born into an affluent family, in 1813. His father, a successful businessman, had retired early. He now enjoyed inviting professors over for dinner and sharing ideas. Søren, the youngest, was the "Joseph" of the family—his dad doted on him, admiring his quick mind.

At age seventeen, Søren was sent to the University of Copenhagen. His father wanted him to study for the priesthood, but Søren refused. This was one of several spats with his father, who continued to fund Søren's education and an increasingly spendthrift lifestyle. The younger Kierkegaard became a sort of "perpetual student." He managed to patch things up with his father shortly before the elder Kierkegaard died—and Søren went on with theological education, though he was never ordained.

Then Regina Olsen caught his fancy. She was just a teenager, but Søren decided he wanted her. The only problem was that she was seeing someone else. Søren went on the offensive, charming Regina and her family, causing Regina to break up with her other suitor, and ultimately asking for her hand in marriage.

But now he didn't want her anymore. Or maybe he considered himself unworthy of her. He seemed to have some deep, dark secret that kept him from enjoying intimacy with her. What should he do? If he broke the engagement, it would disgrace her. That would be unfair. But if *she* broke it off, it would be much better. So Søren tried to get her to break up with him. He became nasty and bitter. She put up with it for entirely too long, but she finally had her fill.

The whole episode weighed heavily on the heart of the already gloomy Kierkegaard. He was a villain and the victim of his own villainy. He began to pen a series of philosophical writings, questioning the assumptions of his day. These he published under pseudonyms. Then he would put out, under his own name, books that answered these questions.

One of the first of these—*Either/Or*—

was praised by *The Corsair,* a satirical journal that seldom applauded anything. Kierkegaard was embarrassed by the praise and asked the journal to take it back. *The Corsair* merely mocked his request and regularly began to hold Kierkegaard up to public ridicule.

This further isolated the lonely philosopher. The Regina Olsen fiasco had sullied his name in society circles, and now *The Corsair* was taunting him before the public.

But he continued to write, turning his attention to religious themes. How can one truly be a Christian in a fallen world? His answers were despairing. He had no hope in the systems or institutions of his day. Only the miracles of God, he decided, can save us.

He was not yet attempting a full-scale attack on the organized church, but his thoughts were heading in that direction. The Danish church at the time was affluent and proper, the caretaker of good Lutheran theology and ritual. But Kierkegaard saw little life in it. Perhaps fearing where his writing would lead, Kierkegaard put his pen down in 1850.

The death of his friend J. P. Mynster, bishop of Zealand, jolted him back to action. Mynster, in his own way, had been trying to breathe new life into the Danish church, with limited results. Kierkegaard took the occasion to lambaste the church for its neglect of the true teachings of Christ, for its devotion to form and philosophical systems, and for its worship of money and power. Between December, 1854, and May, 1855, he published twenty-one articles in *The Fatherland* newspaper and then in his own newsletters.

In October, 1855, Kierkegaard suffered a stroke and died a month later.

His writings influenced a few key thinkers in the nineteenth century, but his major influence did not appear until much later. Kierkegaard was hailed as the father of "existentialism," which gained prominence in the twentieth century. Philosophers and theologians developed his thought in many ways, some that might make Kierkegaard angry, others of which he'd approve.

Kierkegaard is responsible for much of the subjectivity of modern theology, but his subjectivity came out of humility. God is not an object, he maintained, which we can scientifically dissect and analyze. He is a living, acting Being who confronts us to save us.

Nor are we, as humans, just pieces in a puzzle. We are *beings,* Kierkegaard said, with wills and hopes and sorrows. Kierkegaard fought the abstract systems—whether philosophical or religious—that sought some sort of abstract Truth. Religion needs to tell us *how to live,* he insisted.

The Danish thinker also despaired about our inability as humans to reach God through reason. Our reason only takes us so far, he said, and then we must leap out into the darkness, in the faith that God will meet us there. This leap requires full commitment, a rejection of the world's values, and sometimes of the church's.

Following the heady heyday of the Enlightenment, Kierkegaard's despair was quite a surprise to the people of his day. Yet it anticipated the inhumanity of the Industrial Revolution and the rise and fall of modernism. This great Dane was a century ahead of his time.

1854 Charles Haddon Spurgeon Becomes Pastor in London

Charles Haddon Spurgeon.

It must be a mistake.

That's what Charles Spurgeon thought when he was asked to preach at New Park Street Chapel, in London. It was a prestigious church with a beautiful old building, and Spurgeon was only nineteen years old.

But it was no mistake. After Spurgeon spoke, he was invited to become the church's regular pastor. He held that post for nearly four decades.

Spurgeon was hardly the type for class-conscious London society. Born of Huguenot stock, in a rural area of Essex, he lived with his grandparents as a child because his parents were too poor to care for him. Both his grandmother and father were Congregationalist ministers, but Charles attended an agricultural school—for a few months, anyway.

Wrestling with the needs of his soul, Spurgeon determined to go to church the first Sunday of 1850. A blizzard kept him from going to the church he planned on attending, but he wound up in a nearby Primitive Methodist chapel. The speaker was ignorant, as Spurgeon recalled it, but he aimed a challenge right at young Charles. As a result, Charles Spurgeon became a Christian at the age of sixteen.

Spurgeon soon discovered that he had a gift for speaking. In 1852 he became pastor of a small Baptist church in Waterbeach. It was a coarse area, and the people were known for their drunkenness. Spurgeon developed a direct style. His hearers wouldn't stand for flowery expositions of theology—he simply told them what the Bible said. Word went out about the "boy preacher" of Waterbeach. That's when the board of New Park Street Chapel decided to give him a try.

The church had a proud history, but it had fallen on hard times. The ornate building had room for over a thousand, but lately the congregation was having trouble drawing a hundred. Eighty people attended Spurgeon's opening service. Maybe the boy preacher could make things happen.

He did. His direct style struck a chord with the Londoners. Church attendance mushroomed. Soon the seams of the old building were bursting; the church had to rent Exeter Hall, which held 4,500.

Such rapid growth caught the attention of the London press, whose reports on the upstart preacher were not always favorable. "All his discourses are redolent of bad taste, are vulgar and theatrical," wrote one paper. Another called his style "that of a vulgar colloquial, varied by rant. . . . All the most solemn mysteries of our holy religion are by him rudely, roughly and impiously handled. . . . This is the preaching that 5,000 persons hear."

Make that 10,000—and more. Exeter Hall was soon too small for the crowds who wanted to hear Spurgeon. The church rented the 12,000-seat Surrey Music Hall and packed it, with 10,000 more waiting outside. Unfortunately, the opening service there brought disaster. Some rabble-rousers shouted, "Fire!" In the ensuing panic, seven died, and twenty-eight were seriously injured. The incident did nothing to endear Spurgeon to the London press.

But there was a new evangelical excitement in England in the 1860s, and Spurgeon was in the middle of it. Historians have called it the Second Evangelical Revival. Other preachers, such as Alexander Maclaren, in Manchester, and John Clifford, in London, were also drawing crowds. By 1861, the New Park Street Chapel had built a new facility, the Metropolitan Tabernacle, which held 6,000. Spurgeon's ministry was just beginning. He published his sermons, plus commentaries and devotional books—140 books in all, during his lifetime. He founded a pastor's college and the Stockwell Orphanage, which cared for 500 children. He became president of a Bible-distribution society. He preached wherever and whenever he could.

Spurgeon's style may have been simple and direct, but he was no theological slouch. He was a Calvinistic Baptist. In a way, this merging of traditions helped both—bringing the structure of Calvinism to lower-class religion and offering the sincerity of Baptist faith to the upper-class churches.

His gift was communication. Reading his works today, one finds a modern power in them. Remember that he lived in an age of style: *What* you said was often not nearly as important as *how you said it*. But Spurgeon didn't have time for polite circumlocution. He employed strong images and choice verbs to get his point across. In so doing, he set an example for preachers to come. The written works of this "prince of preachers" continue to sell widely even today.

1855
Dwight L. Moody's Conversion

D. L. Moody.

The seventeen-year-old was trying to make it in the big city of Boston. After pounding the pavements for weeks, he landed a job as a shoe salesman in his uncle's shop. He lived upstairs. "I have a room up in the third story," he wrote, "and I can open my winder and there is

3 grat buildings full of girls the handsomest there is in the city—they will swar like parrets [sic]."

One of nine children raised by a young widow in rural Northfield, Massachusetts, Dwight Lyman Moody hadn't received much education, but he had dreams and determination. Yet Boston wasn't kind to him. "If a man wants to feel that he is alone in the world," Moody wrote once, "he don't want to go off in the wilderness where he can have himself for company, but let him go into some of these large cities, and let him pass down the streets where he can meet thousands and have no one know him or recognize him.

"I remember when I went off in that city and tried to get work and failed. It seemed as if there was room for everyone else in the world but . . . me. For about two days I had that awful feeling that no one wanted me."

Moody listened to abolitionists ranting at nearby Faneuil Hall. He joined the YMCA, an organization recently imported from Britain, and he began attending Mt. Vernon Congregational Church to hear the preaching of the famous Edward Norris Kirk.

He found the preaching powerful and overwhelming—so overwhelming that it sometimes put him to sleep. "A young student from Harvard . . . gave me a punch with his elbow and I rubbed my eyes and woke up. I looked at the minister, and lo and behold, I thought he was preaching directly at me. I said to myself, 'Who has been telling Dr. Kirk about me?' . . . At the conclusion . . . I pulled my coat-collar up and got out as quick as I could."

His Sunday-school teacher, Edward Kimball, kept track of young Moody, urging him to return when his attendance lapsed. He also challenged Moody to read the Bible regularly; Moody tried but couldn't understand it. "I have seen few persons whose minds were spiritually darker than was his when he came into my class," Kimball wrote later.

On April 21, 1855, Kimball felt it was time to ask Moody for a commitment to Christ. He headed for the shoe store, had second thoughts and walked past it, then dashed inside. He found Moody wrapping and shelving shoes. The young man was ready to listen. That day, D. L. Moody became a Christian.

It was a while before Moody understood the implications of his faith. In fact, he was denied church membership at first because he failed the entrance exam—he could not explain what Christ had done for him. But his heart had changed. He was not ashamed to be a Christian and kept learning more about his faith.

He soon tired of Boston and took his dreams west to Chicago. His brash ways were much more acceptable there, and he succeeded in shoe selling. He also became involved in evangelistic efforts. Once he wandered into a mission on North Wells Street and asked if he could teach a Sunday-school class. He was told that the mission had plenty of teachers, but not enough students. If he could drum up the students, he could teach them. This was no problem for one with Moody's sales skills. He was soon teaching crowds of young urchins.

By 1861 he was working full time in ministry, both with his Sunday school and the YMCA. He gained support from local businessmen such as John Farwell and Cyrus McCormick. In 1864 his mission became a church.

By 1871 Moody's ministry in Chicago was comfortable, secure, and thriving. He had thought of traveling as an evangelist, but why leave such a healthy situation? The Great Chicago Fire changed his mind. His church, his home, the YMCA were all in ashes, and so were the businesses of his best supporters. It proved difficult to raise money in other cities to rebuild the Chicago ministry, so Moody took to the road.

In 1873 he set out for England. His evangelistic meetings took the British Isles by storm. After two years, he returned to the United States as an international celebrity. He was invited to preach in many American cities.

Building on the revivalist tradition established by Charles Finney, Moody brought evangelism into the industrial age. He preached a simple Gospel, free of denominational divisions. That broadened his appeal—and support. He made strong alliances with business leaders. *These* were the leaders of the new generation, not the preachers. He pressed them to put their wealth into good causes, such as caring for the urban poor. Moody brought business techniques to his evangelistic planning. Music, counseling, and follow-up were all parts of an organized approach toward getting at people's hearts.

In 1879, Moody turned his attention toward education, establishing the Northfield Seminary for girls, then the Mount Hermon School for boys. He started summer Bible conferences and a Bible institute now named for him. At first, he was afraid of competing with seminaries, but he saw more and more need for practical training in ministry. His problem was not so much with the liberal trend in American seminaries, but their isolation from the common people. He aimed to train communicators who could carry God's simple truth to the masses who needed it.

That practical edge has continued in the empire that bears his name. The Moody Bible Institute, for instance, continues to train pastors, missionaries, and other church workers. But Moody's influence has stretched far beyond that. He was a forerunner for evangelists such as Billy Sunday and Billy Graham, and the social aspect of his evangelism helped inspire a deep-running commitment to social ministry among evangelicals.

1857
David Livingstone Publishes *Missionary Travels*

David Livingstone.

All his life, David Livingstone tried to reconcile scientific pursuits with Christianity. As a teenager, he refused to read the Christian books his father gave him, preferring works on science and travel. The book that finally brought about his conversion was one that tried to fit together faith and science.

The next year, Livingstone read a pamphlet calling for missionary doctors in China. He knew what he had to do. He enrolled in a medical school in Glasgow and eventually applied to the London Missionary Society. Because he lacked theological credentials, the LMS did not fully accept him at first. By the time they did, the Opium War had broken out in China, and it was inadvisable to send missionaries there.

Though it must have seemed terribly unfortunate at the time, these turns of events were decisive for Livingstone, his future exploits, and for the continent of Africa. Shortly afterward, Livingstone met Robert Moffat, who had pioneered a mission work in southern Africa. Livingstone set his sights on that continent and joined Moffat's team in 1841.

The mission station was 600 miles inland, but Livingstone was restless. There was so much more of the continent to reach; he could not be happy as a medical missionary at an established outpost. He needed to explore. He joined another missionary in setting up a new station and later journeyed even farther inland.

This ministry was exceptionally difficult. Livingstone labored for ten years among the Tswana people and only saw one convert. At one point, he was attacked by a lion and severely injured. Moffat's daughter, Mary, nursed Livingstone back to health. In 1845 Livingstone married her. All in all, it would not be a happy marriage. Mary found David's wanderlust unsettling.

Livingstone bucked at the LMS's "conservative" missions policies. The pattern was to go to one area at a time, gain converts, build a church there with the missionary in charge, and move on only when that church was well established. It was a slow process. Livingstone saw that conditions were bad for evangelism in Africa. Ignorance of African culture combined with the Africans' sour experiences with white slave traders to create great resistance. Why not infiltrate the inland in positive ways, help the Africans develop their own trade, and learn about their ways? This might not build churches in the short term, but it might create conditions that would be more favorable to evangelism in the next generation.

At the end of 1852, with his family safely packed away to England, Livingstone set out on a cross-country expedition. He had already discovered the Zambezi River. It had to come from somewhere. Maybe he could find an inland river route across the continent from the Indian Ocean to the Atlantic. This would open up trade opportunities for the indigenous peoples and, in the process, strike a blow against the slave traders.

The trip west was difficult, fraught with disease, drought, and attacks from animals and hostile tribes. He finally reached the Atlantic in 1854 and could have sailed from there to England. But there was more exploring to do. Could the Zambezi be followed all the way to the Indian Ocean? He ventured eastward again, reaching the coast in 1856.

From there he sailed for Britain, arriving to a hero's welcome. Exploration of uncharted territory was highly acclaimed in those days. An explorer like Livingstone would be hailed as we might honor the first astronaut to land on Mars. Not only was Livingstone pounding out new geography, he was doing so for several noble reasons: missionary work, commerce, and the eradication of slavery. The account of his journeys, *Missionary Travels,* penned in 1857, was a best-seller.

When Livingstone returned to Africa the following year, it was not with the London Missionary Society. Though he claimed he was still primarily a missionary, he went as an agent of the British government. But this expedition was disastrous. It turned out that the rapids of the Zambezi River could not be navigated by ship. Alternate routes could not be found. The hopes for an inland passage across Africa were dashed. Meanwhile, Mary Livingstone had become an embarrassment. David's fame and her insecurity had driven her to drink. Once he had left for Africa, she was not treated well. She frantically sailed to meet him, but died shortly after their rendezvous.

With his expedition recalled, Livingstone returned to England in 1864. This time he was a failure, yesterday's news, given only the polite honor of a relic. He set out on his own one last time to his beloved continent. This time he sought the source of the Nile. In the process he discovered several inland lakes.

Years passed with no news from him. A few expeditions went out to find him. The most famous of these involved Henry M. Stanley, reporter for the New York *Herald,* in 1871. Finding Livingstone at last at Ujiji, on Lake Tanganyika, he uttered that great understatement, "Dr. Livingstone, I presume." But he could not convince him to come home. (Stanley later became a missionary to Africa himself.)

Livingstone died in 1873. He was found on his knees in a primitive hut. His heart was buried in his adopted homeland, and his body was returned to England. There this great missionary was honored with a burial in Westminster Abbey.

Like many of the major movers in Christian history, David Livingstone was a maverick. He challenged the prevailing ideas of missions in his day, always pushing outward. He had a vision for the combined economic-spiritual well-being of the African people yet seemed to avoid most of the colonialist mentality of his contemporaries. And the fact is Livingstone's work did create conditions for the growth of Christianity. A century after his death, the African church was spreading rapidly.

1865 William Booth Founds the Salvation Army

As industry grew, so did abuses against the working class.

England was moving away from an agricultural way of life into a factory-oriented one, and the slums of London were growing. Thousands poured into London, from the countryside, seeking work, and often they lived and worked in the worst of conditions.

The church should have been the first to alleviate the suffering, but it remained at a loss. Like all of England, London had been divided up into parishes, the lines of which had not changed for centuries. Despite the increased population of the city, the Church of England had no provisions for extra clergy or churches. Creating a new parish took an act of Parliament, which was a long, slow process.

Nor had Methodism, which had largely become a middle-class religion, been able to effectively reach the working class. Methodists had made efforts to reach those lost to the Church of England, but still the new back-alley poor remained untouched by the Gospel.

Concerned about the plight of the

poor, in 1865 William Booth and his wife, Catherine, established a mission to the poor in the East End of London. From their beginnings in a humble tent came the ministry of the Salvation Army.

Around the evangelizing couple were overcrowded homes filled with family violence, drunkenness, prostitution, and unemployment. The prosperity that was a hallmark of the Victorian middle class did not extend to the East End.

No efforts at legislation seemed to solve the problem, and William believed it would only alter when hearts were changed. Once people knew Christ, their behavior and conditions could improve.

That didn't mean the Booths ignored the problems around them. They set up "Food for the Million" shops, offering cheap meals. Once a man had a full stomach, he was more likely to listen to their message of Christ's salvation.

Though Booth followed many of the organizational ideas of the Methodism he had left behind him, he went one step further, eventually creating an organization that followed military lines. One of his followers had advertised a meeting as "The Halleujah Army Fighting for God." Booth's strict control of his organization led to some people calling him general. By 1878, the group had taken the name the Salvation Army, and their general had consciously organized it with uniforms, officers, marching brass bands, and a magazine named *The War Cry*.

Some Christians were offended by the Army. After all, the marching bands didn't have the dignity of the Anglican music. Was the devil using the Salvation Army to make Christianity look ridiculous? But the Army had success. The bands could be heard on city streets, and they played popular secular tunes, with Christian words put to them. "Why should the devil have all the best tunes?" Booth asked.

In addition, family life improved under the Salvation Army's influence. They effectively addressed the problems of the hungry and the homeless, and the Gospel was preached to many who never set foot inside a church.

But if Christians objected to the Salvation Army, some non-Christians had even stronger reactions. As the working class converted to Christ, they took on the Salvation Army's policy of teetotalism. That hurt the brewers' business, and they became especially hostile to the Army. During the last two decades of the nineteenth century, Army officers were assaulted and their buildings damaged.

But even the greatest scoffers had to admit that the Army had done a good work as they transformed drunken child beaters into stable fathers and good workers.

Catherine, William's wife, ably supported him in his efforts, and their mission was carried on by their large brood of children. The Salvation Army spread not only throughout Britain, but into every corner of the world.

Through his life William traveled 5 million miles, preached nearly 60,000 sermons, and drew about 16,000 officers into service with him. His best-selling book *In Darkest England and the Way Out* showed many Victorians that they did not need to go to foreign missions to discover "poor heathens" who needed Christ. Booth established agencies that cared for the physical and social needs of people and preached the Gospel. Through his career, he honed techniques of communicating to the masses and sharing Christ. When he died, in 1912, 40,000 attended his funeral.

As the Salvation Army carried its message to the poor of England, it emulated the work of the One who had ministered to fishermen, harlots, and lepers.

1870
Pope Pius IX Proclaims the Doctrine of Papal Infallibility

Pius IX.

Would Italy be an area on the map or a unified nation?

Who would rule the new nation?

In the middle of the nineteenth century, these were questions waiting for an answer. Europe had seen a lot of changes in 1848, as a tide of nationalism swept the continent. In France, Italy, and a dozen other nations, people began to assert their rights to have their own countries, based on language and geography, instead of being ruled by other nations. Sicily sought to free itself from the Bourbon monarchy, and the northern Italian lands sought to put off the restraints of Austrian rule.

The new pope, Pius IX, supported the *risorgimento,* "resurgence," which wanted to create an Italian-speaking state. When he gave the Papal States a constitution, the pope pleased Italian liberals. It did not last long. When revolutionaries assassinated the new prime minister, the pope fled the Papal States for a while. He returned with the aid of the French military; now he saw the threat in the liberals and wanted to encourage the old absolutist rule.

In 1869, the beleaguered pope called the First Vatican Council. The liberal philosophies and increased nationalism had encouraged freer thinking in the church. Many priests and bishops had begun to question the pope's power. In a world that was no longer uniformly Catholic, the papacy had also lost political influence. The church needed to address itself to the challenges of liberal thought and the undermining of the importance of tradition in the church.

In 1854, Pius had pronounced that the Virgin Mary was conceived without sin—the doctrine of the Immaculate Conception. Though many Catholics had accepted that for years, now it became a firm doctrine of the church.

Nine years later the pope had followed that with the Syllabus of Errors. In an effort to stem the tide of liberalism, he had listed things no Catholic was allowed to believe in, including: modern thought such as rationalism or socialism; civil marriages; and many forms of religious toleration.

The Vatican Council addressed the issue of the role the pope played in the church. Pius sought to establish two things: that the pope, the Vicar of Christ, has full, direct power over the entire church and its hierarchy; and that when he speaks *ex cathedra* ("from the chair," in his capacity as pope), he is infallible. In spite of the liberalism in the church, the pope won the day at the First Vatican Council. Both were made doctrines of the church.

Though the liberals disapproved, to many people such absolutism was welcome. They lived in an age of confusion; so much had changed politically and philosophically. Many Catholics needed assurance that some things—like the pope and the teachings of the church—remained firm.

The pope would not keep his political authority, for about two months after the First Vatican Council, Victor Immanuel captured Rome, and its inhabitants voted for the formation of the kingdom of Italy. Though the pope had lost temporal power, he gained in spiritual effectiveness. From the Vatican he exerted more authority than even the most powerful prelates of the Middle Ages.

The Catholic Church would remain largely unchanged until Vatican II.

1886 Student Volunteer Movement Begins

It was one of Dwight L. Moody's summer conferences. The great revivalist invited college students to the Mt. Hermon conference grounds at Northfield, Massachusetts, for a month of Bible study and fellowship. In July 1886, 151 students attended.

For the first two weeks, it was a pretty ordinary conference. Nothing was said about missions. Bible study was the order of each day. But one student from Princeton had been praying about the needs of the world. He felt that God would use this gathering to spark a movement of missionaries. That student was right.

He collected twenty-one like-minded students to pray with him. They prayed that a spirit of missions would pervade the conference. On July 16, speaker A. T. Pierson delivered a rousing missionary challenge: "all should go and go to all." The spirit became even more intense July 24, with "the meeting of the ten nations." Representatives of ten different countries and nationalities spoke briefly, reporting on the needs in their lands. In the remaining week of the conference, many students decided to devote their lives for mission service. By the end, one hundred of them had made such a commitment.

On the last day of the conference, the students considered ways to keep this spirit alive and to spread it. They appointed Robert P. Wilder to travel to various colleges throughout the year, talking about what had happened at Mt. Hermon and starting groups of students committed to missions. In the next year, Wilder and an associate visited 167 institutions, and 2,200 students pledged themselves to the mission field.

But by 1888, the spirit was fading. The movement needed leadership and organization. Meeting at Mt. Hermon, a core group of fifty people decided to appoint a triumvirate of leaders: Wilder, representing the Inter-Seminary Missionary Alliance; Nettie Dunn, from the YWCA; and John R. Mott, from the YMCA. Mott would prove to be a powerhouse, turning this student movement into a worldwide juggernaut of ecumenical and evangelistic activity.

Mott had just graduated from Cornell University, where he was active in the YMCA leadership. He had a zeal for winning souls, so he took his role in the newly formed Student Volunteer Movement very seriously. Communication, publicity, and organization—Mott excelled in these areas. He made sure that mission societies knew that SVM was not competing with them, but rather supplying them. Mission-minded students at various schools were grouped into "bands" and met regularly for prayer and encouragement. Student Volunteer conventions would be held every four years. Mott and other leaders traveled widely in their continuing effort to find, train, and send new missionaries.

The motto, broadcast loud and clear, was: "The evangelization of the world in this generation." Mott wrote a book with that title. By 1914, SVM had been responsible for sending an estimated 5,000 missionaries to the mission field.

But beyond those numbers, the movement was responsible for a new missionary excitement in the world. Other organizations spun off from it. In 1895, Mott launched the World's Student Christian Federation and became its first general secretary. The Laymen's Missionary Movement was born at an SVM conference in 1906, rallying support for missions among the laity. Mott was also a major figure in the International Missionary Conference at Edinburgh in 1910. This led to the later formation of the World Council of Churches.

Mott became widely known and exerted great influence. President Wilson offered to make him ambassador to China; he refused. Princeton considered making him college president; he refused. Mott even had a chance to be Secretary of State; he refused. He was a man with a mission, and that mission was missions.

Missions enthusiasm died down in the United States after World War I. But the SVM-inspired missionaries, of course, served for many years. The Student Volunteer Movement had done what William Carey had done a century earlier—sparked interest in missions at a crucial time.

1906
Azusa Street Revival Launches Pentecostalism

"**B**reathing strange utterances and mouthing a creed which it would seem no sane mortal could understand, the newest religious sect has started in Los Angeles."

That's what the Wednesday, April 18, 1906, *Los Angeles Times* said. "Meetings are held in a tumble-down shack on Azusa Street, and the devotees of the weird doctrines practice the most fanatical rites, preach the wildest theories, and work themselves into a state of mad excitement in their particular zeal."

Such negative publicity actually helped to bring in the crowds. Something supernatural was going on in this old building. William J. Seymour, a black Baptist holiness preacher, recently arrived from Houston, was calling believers to go an extra step. Two extra steps, actually: He wanted them to be "sanctified" and to be "baptized in the Holy Spirit." The baptism, he said, would be accompanied by speaking in tongues.

There had been a few other outbursts of tongues speaking around the country and in Europe in previous years, but Azusa Street was a major eruption. The meetings went on in that "tumbledown shack" for several years. Many people traveled there just to see what was going on.

The world was ripe for revival. The late 1800s saw a massive Industrial Revolution. People were becoming cogs in society's machinery. The gap was widening between rich and poor. Unfortunately, the church often leaned toward the rich. Even the traditionally "common" groups like the Baptists and Methodists were emphasizing propriety more than spiritual energy. Thanks to past revivalists like Finney and Moody, the churches were full. But many who professed Christianity were still lacking something.

The "holiness" movement had been a first step toward renewal. These stirrings—mostly within the Methodist Church—sought a "second blessing" from God, in which believers would be "sanctified" to live a holy Christian life. Keswick teaching also had its impact, both in Europe and America. Incubated in the annual Keswick Conventions in

Great Britain, Keswick teachers urged Christians: "Walk in the power of Christ's resurrection," "let Christ reign within your soul." Nothing too radical occurred here, just a drive for more fullness in the Christian experience, using language that Pentecostals would later borrow.

Another stream of thought that added urgency to the incipient Pentecostal movement was premillennialism, popularized by J. N. Darby and the Plymouth Brethren. The turn of the century brought both pre- and postmillennialism to the fore. Many touted the onset of a "Christian century" in which the church (and technology) would usher in God's kingdom. But the premillennialists claimed that the end times were near, featuring, as prophesied, an upsurge of spiritual activity.

For background to the Pentecostal movement you might want to go back to 1896. William F. Bryant led a revival in Cherokee County, North Carolina, that included tongues speaking. As these manifestations continued, people were put out of churches, church buildings were torched, and Bryant himself was shot. Tongues speaking was not popular in Cherokee County.

Certainly the Welsh revival of 1904–1906 had an impact on the religious climate of the time. Evan Roberts, a former miner, traveled throughout Wales and later the world, proclaiming the Spirit's enlivening ministry. Tongues speaking was not specifically emphasized, but spiritual power was. A couple of Los Angeles–area pastors had visited Wales and tried to bring this revival back to their churches, with limited success. Yet the seeds of restoration were being sown in Los Angeles.

Or you might want to look at the turn-of-the-century Restorationist Movement, which called for a return to the gifts and practice of the apostolic church, especially healing. John Alexander Dowie claimed he was Elijah the Restorer and set up a Christian community (which later became Zion, Illinois). In Maine, Frank Sandford also claimed to be Elijah the Restorer, setting up a community in Shiloh.

In 1900, Charles Fox Parham spent about six weeks in Shiloh. A Methodist holiness preacher from Kansas, he was searching for the "apostolic faith." He and his wife had started a "healing home" in Topeka, where people could stay for free as they prayed for healing. In Shiloh, Parham was impressed by Sandford's "the Holy Ghost and Us" Bible school. It was decidedly antiacademic. The Bible was the only text, the Spirit the only teacher. Parham founded a similar school when he got home. About forty students enrolled.

That December, Parham asked his students to search the Scriptures to see if there was any sign that was supposed to indicate the Spirit's baptism. As they came together for their New Year's Eve watch-night service, they had the answer: tongues. Agnes Ozman prayed to receive the Holy Spirit, and "glory fell upon her," as Parham tells it, "a halo seemed to surround her head and face and she began speaking in the Chinese language, and was unable to speak English for three days." Over the next month, most of the students had similar experiences.

Parham's efforts to spread this revival in Kansas City and Lawrence failed. Churches opposed it; the newspapers mocked. In 1903, a woman from Texas was healed after Parham prayed for her, and she invited him to conduct a revival in Galena, Texas. It was very successful. By 1905, such "Pentecostal" or "Full Gospel" meetings were being held in Missouri, Kansas, and Texas, with an estimated 25,000 adherents.

After a Houston campaign in 1905, Parham established another Bible school there. One of the more promising students was William J. Seymour. A woman from Los Angeles visited the Houston school and had an experience of Spirit baptism. Returning home, she urged her Nazarene mission church to call Seymour as an associate pastor.

Ironically, the church that brought the Pentecostal revival to Los Angeles wanted nothing to do with it. Seymour's emphasis on tongues speaking offended some church members, and he was denied further access to the church. Eventually he conducted services in the home of some friends. These services went on for three days and nights, drawing many more than the house could hold. The people arranged to move to a building on Azusa Street, formerly a Methodist church. There, sitting (and standing!) on pews of planks, amid building supplies, the people continued their Spirit-filled worship. The church was christened the Apostolic Faith Gospel Mission.

All the lines of spiritual renewal

seemed to converge in this building. It was the Pentecostal Mecca. For years, it served as the focal point for a growing Pentecostal movement. People visited and sought to take back with them whatever it was they found there.

Despite this geographical focus, the Pentecostal movement was extremely diverse. There were a number of charismatic leaders, including Seymour and Parham, who gathered followers and bickered with one another. The movement was also intentionally antiorganizational and antidenominational—just move as the Spirit leads. This may explain the plethora of small Pentecostal denominations that exist today.

The Assemblies of God, now the largest Pentecostal denomination, started as an attempt to gain some cohesion—and some regulation—in the movement. There were charges of financial and sexual misconduct on the part of leading preachers. There were also numerous doctrinal disputes.

A group of southern Pentecostals, led by Eudorus N. Bell, called themselves the Apostolic Faith and began seeking unity in the movement. As others joined, the name changed to the Church of God in Christ. By 1913, it included 352 ministers in a loose association, with no binding authority. In April, 1914, the group summoned Pentecostals to a meeting in Hot Springs, Arkansas. The purposes: unity, stability, chartering of the movement, and establishment of a missions program and a Bible school. Thus the Assemblies of God denomination was born.

While Pentecostal issues have been divisive for many non-Pentecostal churches, Pentecostalism probably has been the most energetic arm of Christianity in the twentieth century. Its emphasis on missions and evangelism has resulted in phenomenal growth for the movement, both in the United States and around the world.

1910–1915 Publication of *The Fundamentals* Launches Fundamentalist Movement

Cover of volume 1, *The Fundamentals*.

Lyman Stewart had a dream. He also had a lot of money. President of the Union Oil Company, Stewart was concerned about the rising tide of modernism in American churches. Something should be done about this; people should be alerted; the common Christian has to be made aware of the threat to our traditional faith. Perhaps a book, a series of books, a massive informational effort. But Stewart knew he was no scholar.

Sitting in church one day, he heard a message from A. C. Dixon, pastor of Chicago's Moody Church. This was the man he needed. After the service, Stewart talked with Dixon about his ideas. "It is of the Lord," said Dixon. "Let us pray."

That was the beginning of a publishing effort that gave the fundamentalist movement its name and perhaps its focus. Dixon pulled together an impressive board of Christian leaders, forming the Testimony Publishing Company. Lyman Stewart got financial help from his brother, Milton. Together they put $300,000 into the project. Leading Bible teachers of the day were sought to write articles for this series of 125-page booklets. The articles covered basic doctrinal subjects as well as issues of the day—socialism, evolution, and money. Dixon edited the first five, then moved to London. Louis Meyer edited the next five before he passed away. R. A. Torrey edited the final two. The Stewart brothers were unnamed in the twelve booklets, calling themselves only "Two Christian Laymen."

In all, there were nearly 3 million copies published over the next six years, for distribution to "every pastor, evangelist, missionary, theological student, Sunday school superintendent, YMCA or YWCA secretary" they could find. A third of these booklets were sent abroad, most of them going to England.

It is unclear what impact the booklets had. Like the apologies of the early church fathers, *The Fundamentals* probably did more to unite and educate those who already agreed with them, rather than convince and convert their intended readers. It was Curtis Lee Laws, a Baptist editor, who coined the term *fundamentalist* in 1920, referring to Baptist conservatives who held to the "fundamentals" of the faith.

In retrospect, it appears that the fundamentalist movement synthesized some earlier trends in the American church and strongly opposed several trends in society and liberal scholarship. It is hard to get a handle on. The movement was social and theological, alarmist, and evangelistic, triumphalist, and despairing.

Start with the *revivalist* tradition, most clearly exemplified by Dwight L. Moody. It taught that the fine points of theology were unimportant, compared with the conversion of souls for God's kingdom.

Add the *holiness* tradition, with strong roots in the Methodist camp, advanced in the late 1800s by the Keswick Conferences. Personal righteousness was seen as an essential outgrowth of a life lived close to Jesus.

Stir in a mushrooming *millenarian* sentiment. As the twentieth century approached, there was more of a sense that the world might be ending soon. The rapid pace of the Industrial Revolution left many wondering where it would all end. Prophecy conferences abounded in the late 1800s. Some Christians, looking at the bright side of human achievement, predicted that the 1900s would be a "Christian century." Post-millennialists held that Christians would bring about an era of righteousness and peace. But the social upheaval of the day also fostered a pre-millennialism, especially seen in the dispensationalism of J. N. Darby. Many adopted the view that the world would just get worse until Christ came to end it all.

The Industrial Revolution may have shaken these ingredients together, but the real catalyst was "modernism." Its key component was the evolutionary theory of Charles Darwin. Throughout the history of science (at least since the Inquisition), there had been a sort of gentleman's agreement between the church and the laboratory: It was assumed that scientific truth would be compatible with religious truth. Now, suddenly, Darwin had published descriptions about the evolution of species and, ultimately, the origin of humanity that did not agree with the church's teachings. What's more, these ideas were gaining acceptance in the academic world.

Meanwhile, among philosophers and theologians (in Germany, primarily) some new ideas about God and the

Bible were brewing. These theories undercut the absolutism that the church had assumed for centuries. They questioned the authority of the Bible and the accepted identity of Christ. What's more, these ideas were being embraced in an alarming number of seminaries.

Common people were being told by these academics and clerics that it was silly to believe the Bible, that it was respectable to believe in evolution. Conservative Christians fought back. In 1895, the Niagara Bible Conference affirmed five "essentials" of Christian faith: (1) inerrancy of Scripture; (2) virgin birth and deity of Christ; (3) substitutionary atonement; (4) physical resurrection of Christ; (5) bodily return of Christ. These were widely accepted in conservative churches.

But there was still little cohesion to fundamentalism. You could rally around opposition to Darwin's theory, but when you started ranting about Immanuel Kant and Friedrich Schleiermacher, you lost some people. Some figured these theories would just go away; others thought it was best to concentrate on evangelism and missions (the church was still in the midst of a heyday of missions awareness).

It took World War I to jolt the fundamentalists into action. Before America entered the war, most Christians (like most Americans) were opposed to it. In fact, in its early stages, conservative Christians were assailed by liberal Christians for being unpatriotic and not supporting the war effort. (Some of these conservatives' opposi-

tion to the war came from a biblical pacifism, some from a desire to be "separate" from the world.)

But as the atrocities of the Germans were publicized (and probably overhyped), fundamentalist preachers seized on an obvious connection: Germany was the birthplace of modernist philosophy! So this is where it leads—brutality, barbarism, and destruction.

Suddenly, the world's future was at stake. The fundamentalist movement really began to move after the war. The World's Christian Fundamentals Association, led by William B. Riley, was formed in 1919, warning about how dangerous modernism was *to American society*. Preachers such as Billy Sunday and John Roach Straton began to decry the social ills that were on the rise in post-war society. Working as revivalists, they turned the holiness tradition outward. This great nation would slide into barbarism, they claimed, unless it turned back to God's truth.

For the next five years or so, fundamentalists gained ground. In major Protestant denominations, especially among the Northern Baptists and northern Presbyterians, fundamentalist forces tried to push back to the basics. Creeds, doctrinal statements, requirements for missionaries, and investigations of seminaries were all on the agenda. They had minimal success. In most cases, the end result was a denominational split.

The epic battle occurred not at a church convention, but in a courtroom in Dayton, Tennessee, at the famous

Scopes trial. The eyes of the nation were on the celebrity lawyers—William Jennings Bryan for the fundamentalists, Clarence Darrow for the evolutionist schoolteacher. Bryan won the battle but lost the war. Scopes was found guilty (the verdict was later overturned), but Darrow made Bryan look bad. Public opinion may have already been turning against the fundamentalists, but this sealed it. They became known and mocked as backwoods, ignorant zealots.

After 1925, fundamentalism retreated into itself, separate from the world, awaiting Christ's return, and studying God's inerrant Word. It remained an insulated subculture, giving rise to the evangelical movement of the 1940s and thereafter, and spawning a neofundamentalist resurgence around 1980.

1919
Karl Barth's *Commentary on Romans* Is Published

Dr. Karl Barth, relaxing between sessions of the First Assembly of the World Council of Churches, and Dr. Emil Brunner.

In the nineteenth century, liberalism had emphasized the progress of man and reform in the world.

But if man was so advanced, why did he become involved in a world war? If his discoveries in technology and science were so effective, why had he trained them on others?

People had become enamored with their own possibilities. The strides that were being made in science seemed to make the world a less mysterious place. Instead of seeking a supernatural God, many looked to create a paradise on earth.

Darwin and other scientists questioned the supernatural elements of the Bible. Was man really a special creation? Could miracles really happen? When we can control nature ourselves, why do we need God? The liberal theology of the age portrayed a God without wrath, a Christ made up of ethics, and a kingdom of this world.

But the First World War brought all that into question. With the progress of Christian Europe called into doubt, many saw the bankrupt nature of liberal thought. One of those men was a pastor, Karl Barth. Faced with the atrocities of the war, the liberal pastor turned to the Letter to the Romans. What he found there changed his faith and created an upheaval in theology reminiscent of Augustine, Luther, and Wesley.

His *Commentary on Romans,* which has been called "a bombshell on the liberal theologians' playground," described God as sovereign and transcendent. The fall of man, shown in Genesis 3, is real, said Barth. There man's whole being was marred by sin, and he can no longer discover God's truth on his own. God must disclose Himself to man, and He does it through Jesus Christ.

Barth's restatement of doctrine, using classically Protestant terms,

caused much discussion. By 1930 the pastor had become a professor of theology in Germany.

Along with others in the Confessing Church, Barth opposed the Nazis, and he penned large parts of the "Barmen Declaration," which called Christians to oppose the deceptions Hitler had used against the church. A year later, in 1935, Barth was expelled from Germany and went to Basel, Switzerland, to teach theology. During his time there he wrote prodigiously, including his major work, the thirteen-volume *Church Dogmatics,* a Protestant masterpiece.

Barth's ideas became the basis for *neo-orthodoxy.* This twentieth-century theology is antiliberal in its emphasis on study of the Scriptures, sin, and its serious attitude toward God's sovereignty, but it takes an ambivalent attitude toward the historicity of the Bible, especially the Old Testament. While affirming most biblical teachings, it does not necessarily accept that every event in the Bible occurred in space and time. Its critics have said neo-orthodoxy seeks to "have its cake and eat it, too" by affirming traditional doctrines while giving in to the skeptics who doubt the historic nature of Christianity.

Theologians such as Emil Brunner, Gustaf Aulen, Reinhold and Richard Niebuhr, and Friedrich Gogarten shared most of Barth's beliefs about God's sovereignty and man's sin and emphasized that faith means more than saying yes to a few theological propositions. Because neo-orthodoxy posits the need for a "leap of faith" over seemingly difficult or contradictory truths, it has been called *crisis theology*.

In a world that faced two massive wars, Barth's ideas returned a wandering church to the themes of sin and God's sovereignty. Many Christians find his voluminous writings both stimulating and frustrating. Barth flirted with universalism, the idea that God will eventually save everyone, though he never confronted the question head-on. In his Christ-centered theology, he often read Christ into the Old Testament in unlikely places. And he did not accept the infallibility or inerrancy of Scripture.

On the positive side, Barth encouraged serious Bible study, emphasized dynamic preaching, and returned man to an understanding of his need for an Almighty God. In a time when many had turned to the world for hope, he called them to look to Christ.

1921
First Christian Radio Broadcast

Pioneer Christian Radio broadcaster Paul Rader.

Radio was just two months old. The Westinghouse Company had started it all in Pittsburgh, announcing results of the 1920 election on a station using call letters KDKA. The first listeners used homemade contraptions, but now Westinghouse was rapidly selling pre-made radio sets—and these buyers needed programs to listen to. In the scramble for programming, the station decided to put a church service on the air.

One engineer at Westinghouse was a choir member at Calvary Episcopal Church in Pittsburgh. So arrangements were made to broadcast a service from there on the first Sunday evening of 1921. The skeptical senior minister let his associate, Lewis B. Whittemore, take the service. Two KDKA engineers—one Catholic, one Jewish—ran the equipment. They donned choir robes so their presence on the platform wouldn't distract the congregation. The response to the broadcast was so positive that the service became a regular feature on KDKA.

In the Chicago area, preacher Paul Rader took a brass quartet up to a rooftop "studio," consisting of a pinboard box with a hole in one side. "You just get ready and point your instruments at the hole there," said a technician. "When I say play, you play."

He thrust an old telephone microphone through the hole and said, "Play." The quartet played. Rader preached. The favorable response led Rader to seek other Chicago-area stations. Noticing that Chicago's WBBM closed down each Sunday, he arranged to use its studios. For fourteen hours every Sunday, Rader ran his own once-a-week station—WJBT, "Where Jesus Blesses Thousands."

As with other technological advances, many evangelical Christians feared the introduction of radio. After all, wasn't Satan the "prince of the power of the air"? Most pioneer radio preachers faced more opposition from the church than from secular society.

In Omaha, Nebraska, WOAW (later WOW) began to broadcast in April, 1923. The station was turned down by several preachers before they asked R. R. Brown, a Christian and Missionary Alliance minister who was new in town. Brown sought the advice of a friend, who said he had been praying that God would "gain an advantage" over this new (and potentially worldly) radio station. Might Brown be that advantage?

Brown agreed to do the first program only, but as he left the studio after the broadcast, a man met him, claiming that he had been convicted by the Spirit and converted through that broadcast. Brown shouted, "Hallelujah! Unction can be transmitted!"

In Chicago, WGES was preparing a remote broadcast from the Illinois Products Exposition in 1925. They were about to go on, but their musicians hadn't arrived. By chance a station official heard two students playing cornets at the Moody Bible Institute booth and ran over to "borrow" their services. A few days later, the station invited Moody Bible Institute to put on a one-hour program each Sunday. This eventually led to Moody's own station, WMBI.

In 1928, Donald Grey Barnhouse became the first radio preacher to buy time on a national network, airing on CBS from Philadelphia's Tenth Presbyterian Church. In 1930, Clarence Jones and Reuben Larson launched the first missionary radio station, HCJB in Quito, Ecuador—the first radio station in that country.

In the radio craze of the mid-1920s, many churches and ministries started broadcasting. By 1928 there were sixty religious radio stations. Then the Federal Radio Commission instituted new rules, standardizing frequencies and eliminating much confusion. The regulations killed the smaller stations but aided the more established ones. By 1932, only thirty religious stations remained. But in the next half century, Christian media strength grew. Leaders like Billy Graham, Rex Humbard, Oral Roberts, and Pat Robertson, not to mention Bishop Fulton Sheen, blazed the trail into television in the 1950s and 1960s. Radio and TV played a major role in the resurgence of fundamentalism in the late 1970s.

The original move into Christian radio, back in the twenties, revealed a bit of the schizophrenia of American fundamentalism. *Separation* had been the byword. Fundamentalist preachers such as Billy Sunday urged hearers to avoid "worldliness" in all its forms. But fundamentalists were also the caretakers of an outgoing Gospel. To be true to it, they had to get the word out. That necessitated using every means available—even the airwaves—to preach about Jesus. Thus the emergence of Christian radio is a precursor of the evangelical movement of the 1930s and 1940s, where the drive for evangelism began to soften the hard line of the separatists.

As Christian television expanded out of Christian radio, religious broadcasting became big business. The mystique of television had captured the general public in America so much so that it became the major source of leisure time activity, or inactivity, for most people. Christians, too, were caught up in its mystique. Entrepreneurial preachers built vast organizations and institutions (leisure parks, universities, crystal cathedrals) on the base of their television ministries. They sought to carve out a strong political presence in the eighties with one of their number, Pat Robertson, even entering the race for president.

The religious television ministries have reached only a small fraction of the North American public. The secular broadcasting audience ratings analysts always knew that and never saw religious programming as a strong threat to win away their audiences. But Christians were enamored to think they at least had a presence in the powerful world of television and were subsidizing religious broadcasting at a level of $2 billion per year in America by the end of the 1980s.

Sadly, moral scandals involving two of the biggest ministries garnered far more "gross rating points" in audience counts than religious television programming had ever achieved. Just as television changed the way America elected politicians through the seventies and eighties, so television religion has no doubt decisively affected the public perception of the nature and meaning of Christianity. It is too soon to really know how religious television has affected the church during this period, but it will be important to find out.

1934 Cameron Townsend Begins Summer Institute of Linguistics

Cameron Townsend singing with Tzeltal Indians in Mexico.

Cameron Townsend got an early lesson in the relation between linguistics and evangelism. As a young mission-ary in Guatemala, he worked up the nerve to approach people on the street and ask about their relationship with Christ. He memorized his introductory question in Spanish: "Do you know the Lord Jesus?"

He didn't realize that *Jesus* was a common first name in Spanish, and that his word for "Lord"—*Senor*—also meant "Mister." He expected a response that might lead him to talk about spiritual things. But all he got was a matter-of-fact, "Sorry, don't know him. I'm a stranger here myself."

It was 1917. Most American young men of his age were in Europe fighting a world war. Perhaps it was Townsend's frail appearance that made the recruiter offer him an exemption to sell Bibles in Guatemala.

At first it must have seemed that Townsend was in over his head. But he eventually learned Spanish and began to work among groups of Indian believers. Burdened for the Cakchiquel Indians of the highlands, Townsend realized that few of them even knew Spanish. To have an impact on them, he would have to learn their language.

This wasn't easy. His wife, Elvira, wrote in a prayer letter, "Do pray that we may quickly learn this awful language. With no grammar or books of any kind from which to study, it is indeed hard. We have a little book of our own in which we mark down different words and phrases which the Indians tell us when we visit them. However, some of these words have such awful sounds that it is almost impossible to write them down. But surely the language of the Cakchiquels is the Lord's just as much as English or Spanish or Swedish, and we know that he will give us this Indian language that we may soon be able to explain the gospel to them in their own tongue."

The prayer was answered. By 1931, the Townsends had produced a complete New Testament in the Cakchiquel language. Shortly afterward, ill health forced them both back to the United States. Cam was hoping to move to a ministry in South America after they recuperated. L. L. Legters, a colleague and supporter of Townsend's work in Guatemala, urged him to work in Mexico, closer to home. Together, Townsend and Legters developed a new idea.

"I suggested that we found a summer institute where pioneer missionaries could be taught how to reduce a language to writing and to translate the Scriptures," Townsend wrote later. Since only two United States universities offered courses in descriptive linguistics, and these four-year programs would be too time consuming for missionaries to take, something special was needed. Legters and Townsend proceeded on two tracks. They decided to set up a linguistics school for missionaries in the United States, and they planned to ask the Mexican government to allow them to send Bible translators to learn the unwritten languages of the Indians.

In 1934, the Summer Institute of Linguistics began on a farm in Sulphur Springs, Arkansas, with an impressive curriculum. When the best professors couldn't come to the institute, the in-stitute went to the professors (there were only two students the first year, a few more the second).

At first, these translators got little cooperation from the Mexican government. But Townsend had some top-notch scholars on his side. He was one of very few front-line experimenters in this emerging science of linguistics. Eventually, the Mexican leaders saw the value of learning the Indians' languages and granted enthusiastic support for Townsend's work.

Townsend was never one for organizations. It was the missionaries who did mission work, not the offices back home. But by the early 1940s this translation work was getting too big to handle on a free-lance basis. The Summer Institute had moved to the University of Oklahoma, and there were 130 students. There were 44 translators working in Mexico already, and Townsend was calling for 50 more. Some sort of support organization was needed. So in 1942, the Wycliffe Bible Translators was officially formed, named for the great medieval British translator. The Summer Institute of Linguistics would continue to interact with foreign governments, but Wycliffe Bible Translators would organize support in the United States.

The translation work expanded broadly from there: Guatemala, Peru, Colombia, and Ecuador. A flight corps, the Jungle Aviation and Radio Service, was established to get the missionary translators safely in and out of remote regions.

By now, these three organizations have over 6,000 workers in over 50 countries. They have produced portions of Scripture in more than 300 languages and are working on more than 800 others.

The work of the Wycliffe translators has opened up hundreds of people groups to the Gospel. It has been a major step forward in the modern missions' drive to reach unreached people—those with little or no access to Christianity.

But Townsend's organization also represents a subtle shift in American Protestantism. In the 1930s and 1940s, fundamentalism was breaking out of its shell. Stringent separatism was giving way to aggressive evangelism. While maintaining its doctrinal integrity, the Wycliffe organization was unashamed to ally itself with secular universities, linguists, governments, or anthropologists in order to get the job done. The "evangelical" movement saw numerous missions and Christian-education organizations arise, willing to try new methods to get the Gospel across.

1945
Dietrich Bonhoeffer Executed by Nazis

Dietrich Bonhoeffer in Tegel Prison, Berlin, 1943.

Christians may disagree with his theology, but few can fail to admire Dietrich Bonhoeffer's firm stand against the Third Reich—even to the point of giving his own life.

Bonhoeffer, a student of Karl Barth, received a doctorate in theology from the University of Berlin when he was only twenty-one. He was a Lutheran chaplain and lecturer there when Hitler came to power in 1933.

Aware of its influence over people, Hitler had wooed and deceived the church, gaining much support from Lutheran and Catholic clergy. The idea of a distinctly German church appealed to these "German Christians." The Nazi ideas had begun to infiltrate the church.

But others feared and suspected Hitler and his ideas about Aryan superiority. About one-third of the Protestant clergy, who led what was called the Confessing Church, stood against the German leader. They ascribed to the Barmen Declaration, written mostly by Karl Barth, which pointed out the doctrinal errors of the German Christians.

In 1935 Bonhoeffer became head of a Confessing Church seminary. But it was closed in 1937, and Bonhoeffer was forbidden to publish or speak publicly. Two years later, when offered the possibility of moving to a teaching position in America, Bonhoeffer rejected it in favor of the goal of serving his fellow Germans.

His brother-in-law drew him into the resistance movement, and Bonhoeffer became part of a plot to kill Hitler. He and others felt that the German leader was the Antichrist. So the clergyman became a double agent in the German military intelligence office. First he unsuccessfully tried to gain support of the plot from the British, but passed on messages to them, from the plotters. The plot failed.

When Bonhoeffer was arrested, in 1943, it was not for his work as a double agent, but for helping to smuggle fourteen Jews into Switzerland. In prison, Bonhoeffer wrote pieces that would be published posthumously under the title *Letters and Papers From Prison*.

Had Bonhoeffer lived longer, perhaps he would have further explained some of the challenging but puzzling ideas he set forth during his imprisonment. Theologians have argued over his phrase "religionless Christianity"; the "death of God" theologians believe it means one thing, while evangelicals view it in another way. When he claimed "the world has come of age," what did Bonhoeffer mean? Did he seek to secularize the Gospel, or did he see—as many do today—that people simply no longer understand the traditional concepts of Christianity?

"How can we speak in a 'secular' way about God?" Bonhoeffer asked. We know that he disagreed with other theologians, like Rudolf Bultmann and Paul Tillich, who wanted to "demythologize" the Gospel, but he never set forth a program of his own.

Though many questions concerning him remain, Bonhoeffer left no doubts on one key element of his beliefs: Faith is costly. His book *The Cost of Discipleship* calls Christians to a stringent, self-denying faith. Too many, said Bonhoeffer, had accepted a Christianity of "cheap grace," which encouraged an easy faith. Instead of treating the ethical parts of the New Testament as an impossible ideal, Christians should strive for them. Real religion means more than having the right ideas about God; it means following Him—to the death, if necessary.

Bonhoeffer followed his own counsel. While in prison he sought to serve others. On April 9, 1945, as the Allied armies made their final advance on Germany, he was hanged on a charge of treason. Though Christians frequently have ethical problems with Bonhoeffer's involvement in the plot to assassinate Hitler, his stand against Hitler's attempts to make the church part of the Nazi regime and his willingness to die for Christ may provide every generation with a challenge to sacrificial faith.

1948
World Council of Churches Is Formed

Dr. John R. Mott (right) greets Dr. W. A. Visser 'T Hooft, General Secretary of the World Council of Churches, at the World Council of Churches first General Assembly in Amsterdam, Holland. Both were key figures in the World Council formation.

Whenever people have been encouraged to think for themselves, there has been church division. Where two or three are gathered together, you're likely to have four or five opinions.

The Bible speaks of the oneness of believers, but it also speaks of the need to hold on to truth. Many reformers, as we have seen, have grabbed for truth—and as a result broke away from churches they considered false. Others, such as Alexander Campbell and John Nelson Darby, stood up against petty church divisions in the name of church unity. But unfortunately, their ideas of truth were challenged, too, and the unity they sought was never realized. "Speaking the truth in love" is never easy to do.

But John R. Mott and his associates realized that effective mission work required cooperation and church unity—and perhaps church unity required mission work. A flock of geese stays together as long as all are moving in the same direction. If Christians merely sit around thinking, they'll never agree on the fine points of theology. But if you put them to work spreading the Gospel of Christ, maybe then we can be the unified body Christ wants.

The Student Volunteer Movement, led by Mott, resulted in a whirlwind of missions activity. It operated across denominational lines. Other organizations spread the activity beyond colleges, to older laity. In 1910, the International Missionary Conference met in Edinburgh, to plan strategies for world evangelization. This is generally regarded as the beginning of the ecumenical movement. With John R. Mott as a major mover, the thousand delegates set in motion two organizations—the Faith and Order Movement (for doctrinal issues), and the Life and Work Movement (for missions and ministry).

Progress was generally slow—and interrupted by world wars. Every ten years or so, these "movements" would meet to discuss world needs and the status of the churches. The Life and Work Movement met in Stockholm in 1925 to discuss the relation of Christianity to society, politics, and economics. Two years later, the Faith and Order Movement convened in Lausanne to attempt the difficult task of hammering out some doctrinal unity.

In 1937, meeting separately in Oxford and Edinburgh, the two organizations voted to merge. Church leaders met in Utrecht, in 1938, to draw up a constitution. But World War II kept the churches from going any further with these plans.

After the war, however, there was an even greater sense of unity as churches worldwide sought to pick up the pieces. A meeting in Amsterdam in 1948 finally merged the two previous bodies into a World Council of Churches. There were 135 church bodies represented, from 40 different nations. After a lifetime of ecumenical effort, Mott, now in his eighties, was elected honorary president.

Describing itself as "a fellowship of Churches which accept Jesus Christ our Lord as God and Saviour," the WCC called churches to work together, study together, fellowship together, worship together, and to meet together in special conferences from time to time. It denied any plans to form a new "world church." It would not have any centralized power. It merely aimed to give churches around the world the opportunity and resources to cooperate with each other.

From the start, a few major United States Protestant groups have refused to join—most notably the Southern Baptists and Missouri Synod Lutherans. The Roman Catholic Church views itself as a unity and thus would not join, though Vatican II opened some doors to discussion. Yet the WCC remains an active and influential worldwide organization. Kenneth Scott Latourette calls it "the most inclusive body that Christianity has ever possessed."

Many conservatives have attacked the WCC's "revolutionary" mind-set. It is now apparent that organizational church union will not be achieved in this millennium—and maybe never. New ways of cooperation and uniting together as Christians are being discovered and implemented. But Jesus' prayer that "they may be one" (John 17:21) is yet to be fully answered.

1949
Billy Graham's Los Angeles Crusade

The tent in Los Angeles where Billy Graham's 1949 crusade was held.

"You would have been thrilled if you could have seen the great tent packed yesterday afternoon with 6,100 people and several hundred turned away, and seen the scores of people walking down the aisles from every direction accepting Christ as personal savior when the invitation was given."

A thirty-year-old preacher was writing from Los Angeles to the staff of the small Bible college in Minneapolis, where he was president. He called it "by far the largest evangelistic campaign of my entire ministry." But it was only the beginning for Billy Graham.

Crowds flocked to the huge tent set up at Washington Boulevard and Hill Street—"the Canvas Cathedral." The scheduled three-week campaign stretched to eight as people kept coming. Celebrities were publicly converted as Graham presented his simple Gospel. It is said that newspaperman William Randolph Hearst decided to "puff" Graham—giving him unusual publicity. Whatever the case, the Los Angeles meetings were the talk of the nation, catapulting Graham to fame.

It must have been a surprise for the fair-haired boy from North Carolina. The eldest child of a Christian dairy farmer, Graham had been converted at a rally led by southern revivalist Mordecai Ham. His passion turned from baseball to saving souls. By the age of twenty-two, he was already ordained as a Southern Baptist minister.

In 1943, he graduated from Wheaton College and married Ruth Bell, daughter of a noted medical missionary to China. He took a pastorate in the Chicago area, but soon got involved with Torrey Johnson, first speaking on Johnson's "Songs in the Night" radio broadcast and later serving as full-time evangelist for Johnson's new ministry, Youth for Christ. In this capacity, he held several citywide campaigns in the late 1940s, including a tour of Great Britain in 1946–1947.

From the start, he had a style of cooperative evangelism. That is, the campaign would not be limited to a particular church. All Christian leaders in a community would be invited to help plan the campaigns. This decision has drawn flak from many conservatives, but it has contributed greatly to Graham's broad appeal.

In the early 1950s, Graham followed the Los Angeles success with noteworthy campaigns in Boston and elsewhere. In 1954, a preaching trip to London made him an international celebrity. He befriended President Eisenhower and numerous other well-known world figures.

Graham quickly mastered the mass media. He wrote the bestseller *Peace With God* in the 1950s and several others since. His "Hour of Decision" radio broadcast has continued for decades. With his father-in-law he cofounded *Christianity Today* magazine to help Christian leaders stay theologically alert. Later his organization launched *Decision* magazine for the masses. Graham's crusades have been regularly televised nationally, and World Wide Pictures, an outgrowth of the Billy Graham Evangelistic Association, has produced dozens of feature films.

Also a major player in world missions, Graham sponsored the 1974 Lausanne Congress, which revolutionized evangelical missions policy by moving toward more indigenized work. In 1983 and 1986, his organization brought itinerant evangelists from all over the world to Amsterdam for massive meetings of education and encouragement. The Billy Graham Center at Wheaton College provides training in communications and ministry, as well as archives and a museum of twentieth-century evangelism.

In recent years, Graham gained access to Communist countries, despite their officially atheistic policies. Some criticized him for not using his stature to protest the persecution of believers in these countries, but Graham has generally focused on evangelism, not social comment.

This tall, good-looking baseball player from North Carolina has become the major religious figure of the last half of the twentieth century. His staff estimates that 2 million have "come forward" in his meetings, signifying conversion. Over 100 million have heard him in person, with countless millions touched by his media ministries. He has done all this by sticking to what he does best—preaching a simple Gospel.

1960 Beginnings of the Modern Charismatic Renewal

The vicar of a nearby church called on Dennis Bennett, rector of St. Mark's Episcopal Church in Van Nuys, California, for help. The vicar had a couple of friends who had "received the baptism of the Holy Spirit" and were speaking in tongues.

Though Bennett didn't know much about the issue, he agreed to meet with the couple. Then he, too, experienced the baptism.

The baptism spread through the area, and the couple's church began a prayer group. Their meetings were enthusiastic but orderly and often lasted until 1:30 A.M. By April 3, 1960, about seventy members of Bennett's church had been "baptized with the Spirit."

Though charismatic activity was not permitted in Bennett's formal worship services, news of it got around, and many people had questions. Eventually it led to a split. Bennett resigned from the church, and it was uncertain how many members would remain with the church.

Unlike many who split from a church as the result of disagreement, Bennett decided to remain within the Episcopal priesthood. He moved to Seattle, and the struggling church he pastored there took on a new life. The charismatic movement spread, and Bennett became a national figure.

The center of the movement remained in Van Nuys. Jean Stone, a member of St. Mark's, founded the Blessed Trinity Society in 1961, to provide fellowship and information for the burgeoning charismatic movement. In 1962 the society launched its "Christian Advance" seminars. These were designed for the traditional denominations, to acquaint them with the ministry and gifts of the Holy Spirit. For though the charismatics were sometimes reviled or misunderstood, they generally found a place as a minority group within noncharismatic churches —where they sometimes grew to majority status.

Quickly the movement spread throughout the Los Angeles area, and as the national press focused on it, it spread nationwide. Late in 1966 a group of Catholic scholars at Duquesne University, in Pittsburgh, began to look at the charismatic experience. Early the next year several of them experienced that. After a weekend retreat, there were about thirty more adherents, both students and professors, and a charismatic community was born.

For the most part, the charismatic movement began in the upper and middle classes. It started in quite affluent Californian churches and affected the traditionally higher class Episcopal and Presbyterian denominations. Within the Catholic Church, it began not on the parish level, but in the universities. However, from this beginning, it spread to all levels of society.

Oddly enough, the charismatics had little obvious connection with the established Pentecostal churches. Their movement had not been established as an outreach of a Pentecostal church and took place within traditionally non-Pentecostal denominations. But there was a connection. The original couple whom Bennett counseled had received the baptism because of the influence of Pentecostal friends. That pattern was continued elsewhere.

Why did the charismatic movement achieve such rapid popularity? Scholars point to several reasons.

In the wake of a 1951 Oral Roberts campaign, dairyman Demos Shakarian formed the Full Gospel Business Men's Fellowship International, which pulled together Pentecostal laymen in fellowship. The organization immediately gave Pentecostalism some respect in the non-Pentecostal world.

The decline of the "healing movement" in the late 1950s allowed Pentecostals to return to a focus on evangelism, and in 1968 the popular Pentecostal preacher Oral Roberts became a Methodist. But longtime Pentecostal leader David du Plessis probably influenced the introduction of the charismatics into the mainline churches more than these. For many years he worked as a sort of unofficial ambassador for the Pentecostal movement, speaking to scholars and non-Pentecostal leaders—including some in the World Council of Churches—about his beliefs. Du Plessis's warm spirit and personal dignity did much to gain him a hearing.

The way had been prepared for the charismatic movement, and once people in the mainline denominations lost their fears about the charismatics, they readily responded to their teachings.

The charismatics have become one of the most dynamic expressions of Christianity in the twentieth century, effectively reaching out to those not touched by more traditional churches. They have enthusiastic expressions of worship, combined with an optimism that they are in the place God's Spirit has placed them. Openness to new methods of evangelism, added to these other assets, has made them a worldwide phenomenon, one that has had outstanding success in Third World countries.

1962
Second Vatican Council Begins

In an effort to hold back the liberal thought that had swayed many within

its communion, the Catholic Church had drawn a sharp line against such ideas in the First Vatican Council. But by the middle of the twentieth century, some important issues remained unaddressed. Though the church had held tightly to tradition, wasn't it time to make some changes?

The archbishop of Venice, Angelo Roncalli, was elected pope in 1958 and took the name John XXIII. Within three months of his election, he called an ecumenical Catholic council. The new pope could see that the world had changed, and the Catholic response needed to address those changes. The council's aim was *aggiornamento,* "bringing the church up to date."

The new emphasis the pope wished to create was one on pastoral care. Instead of focusing on politics or learning, John XXIII wanted to care for the flock.

In October 1962, more than 2,000 cardinals, bishops, and abbots arrived in Rome—making it the church's largest council. They included 230 Americans, over 200 Africans, and more than 300 Asians.

The pope addressed the clergy in St. Peter's Basilica. He pointed out the growth of materialism and atheism and commented that in a world in spiritual crisis, the church must not respond by withdrawing or condemning others. It must "rule with the medicine of mercy rather than severity."

Unlike some previous popes, John did not attempt to dictate to the Second Vatican Council. Yet many sweeping reforms in the pastoral role of the church took place.

For centuries all Catholics had worshiped in Latin, but few understood the language of the mass. Though the dignity and mystery may have appealed to some, many did not comprehend it. Vatican II made native tongues the languages of the mass.

Although the hierarchy was not changed, some attitudes toward it altered in Vatican II. Both clergy and laypeople were accepted as the people of God, and all could share in ministerial functions. All Christians—not just priests, monks, and nuns—have a Christian calling, said the council, and laypeople live theirs out within their vocations.

Though Vatican I had seen the pope as the successor to the apostles, Vatican II extended that to the whole body of bishops. Together with the pope they shared apostolic authority.

The council document "On Divine Revelation" emphasized that Scripture —not tradition—was the primary basis of divine truth. Though it did not throw aside the long-held traditions of previous years, the council gave the Bible more importance and encouraged all Catholics—laypeople and scholars—to study the Bible.

In the decree "On Ecumenism," dramatic change took place concerning attitudes toward non-Catholics. Those in other denominations were stated to be Christians, "separated brethren," ending the idea that *Christian* equated with *Catholic*. Other believers did not need to "return" to Rome.

In its last session, in 1965, the Second Vatican Council struggled with questions of politics. Though the church had a long tradition there, it now renounced power over the political realm.

Response to Vatican II was mixed. Some in the hierarchy objected to the changes and debated them hotly. Some conservative Catholics objected to the new course of the church, but many more Catholics—and many non-Catholics—experienced great hope for the church. Vatican II opened some doors between denominations and encouraged serious Bible study in an unprecedented way.

The Catholic hierarchical system did not change, and the way was not laid for excessive individualism in the Catholic Church, but the Second Vatican Council did bring about an increased openness and a consideration for the layman that has powerfully affected the world's largest church body.

1963
Martin Luther King, Jr., Leads March on Washington

"**I** have a dream. . . ."

The man who had it would spend his life seeking it and give his life for that dream.

His name was Martin Luther King, Jr., and his dream was ". . . that my four little children will one day live in a nation where they will not be judged by the color of their skin but by the content of their character. . . ." Those words would shake America.

The young minister had been born into a family of Baptist clergymen and had been educated at Morehouse College and Crozer Theological Seminary. He earned a Ph.D. from Boston University. In 1954 he became pastor of Dexter Avenue Baptist Church, in Montgomery, Alabama.

One year later, a black woman, Mrs. Rosa Parks, took a step that changed King's life. Though blacks were required to ride in the rear of the public buses, she sat in the front—the seats in the back were filled, and she took the first available seat in the front. She was arrested for breaking the segregation law.

Martin Luther King, Jr., supported her by leading a boycott of the Montgomery bus system. After all, blacks formed most of the ridership of the bus system, and they were being treated unfairly. So blacks refused to ride the buses as long as the discrimination lasted. They felt it was "more honorable to walk the streets in dignity than to ride the buses in humiliation."

Their boycott lasted over a year, but the blacks won in the end, and with that victory Martin Luther King, Jr., was pushed into the American struggle for civil rights.

Influenced by the nonviolent methods of Ghandi, King and others protested. "We shall match your capacity to inflict suffering. . . . Do to us what you will and we shall continue to love you," King responded to his attackers. Following in Jesus' footsteps, he proclaimed, "Jesus eloquently affirmed from the cross a higher law. He knew that the old eye-for-an-eye philosophy would leave everyone blind. He did not seek to overcome evil with evil. He overcame evil with good. Although crucified by hate, he responded with aggressive love."

With the organization of the Southern Christian Leadership Conference, which he headed, King campaigned in the cities of the south: Jackson, Selma, Meridian, and Birmingham; but his influence also extended beyond that as he led attacks on the social injustices of the northern cities.

A close circle of black Protestant

ministers, including Jesse Jackson, supported King, but whites, Catholics, and Jews soon joined his ranks. Their nonviolent methods met with the attack of hoses, clubs, dogs, and beatings. And though many Christians supported him, some of King's most vocal opponents also claimed the name of Christ. In the spring of 1963, King was arrested for having led a protest march in Birmingham, Alabama. Pastors in Atlanta had criticized him for leaving his home church in Montgomery. What right did he have to get involved where he did not belong? they asked.

In "Letter From a Birmingham Jail," King responded that "injustice anywhere threatens justice everywhere." To those who stood outside "the stinging darts of segregation" and counseled him to wait, he answered: ". . . When you are harried by day and haunted by night by the fact that you are a Negro, living constantly at tiptoe stance, never quite knowing what to expect next, and are plagued with inner fears and outer resentments; when you are forever fighting a degenerating sense of 'nobodyness'—then you will understand why we find it difficult to wait."

The March on Washington, in 1963, would become one of the most critical events in civil-rights history, for its influence is credited with the passage of the 1964 Civil Rights Act and the 1965 Voting Rights Act. At that march, Martin Luther King, Jr., set forth his dream:

"I have a dream that my four little children will one day live in a nation where they will not be judged by the color of their skin but by the content of their character. . . . With this faith we will be able to hew out of the mountain of despair a stone of hope. With this faith we will be able to transform the jangling discords of our nation into a beautiful symphony of brotherhood. With this faith we will be able to work together, to pray together . . . knowing that we will be free one day."

In 1964, King received the Nobel Peace Prize, a partial recognition of the validity of that dream.

King went to Memphis, Tennessee, in support of a garbage-workers' strike in 1968. On April 4, as he stood on the second-floor walkway at his motel on Mulberry Street, talking with associates, he was gunned down by an assassin. Though the bullet took his life, it did not end the ongoing dream.

In response to the courage and determined witness of this clergyman, the third Monday in January was named Martin Luther King Day. He is the only American clergyman to have a day named in his honor.

1966–1976
Chinese Church Grows Despite Cultural Revolution

Over a thousand people filled the church, most of them elderly, but there were some young couples and of course teenagers in the balcony. Some lovely Gothic windows had been smashed by rocks, but no one seemed to care. They were singing hymns, accompanied by an old upright piano. A Methodist minister welcomed the worshipers, a Presbyterian read Scripture, a Baptist preached.

The date was September 2, 1979. The site was the Mo En Church, in Shanghai (formerly the Moore Methodist Church). This was the first public Chinese worship service in thirteen years that was open to the Chinese people.

The Cultural Revolution that started in 1966 had closed down churches and persecuted Christians. Anything foreign was reviled—and Christianity, as the product of foreign missions, was especially hated. The church had to go underground for more than a decade. When it resurfaced, amazingly, it was stronger than before.

Christianity made its first inroads into China in A.D. 635, with the Nestorian Christians, but it failed to take root among the people. The work of Franciscan missionaries in the thirteenth and fourteenth centuries and of Jesuits in the sixteenth and seventeenth similarly failed to produce widespread lasting results. China was a closed civilization, resistant to foreign ideas.

Trade wedged China open, and Protestant missionaries in the 1800s came hand-in-hand with merchants. Hudson Taylor did the most to break out of the colonial mission patterns, adopting Chinese clothes and customs, and venturing out to needy areas. But the 1800s were rough times for China. The Manchu dynasty weathered several rebellions. And the rest of the world, especially Great Britain, was trying to pull sleepy China into modern times, though China didn't want to go. As a result, the Chinese suffered great indignities from foreigners.

Things changed rapidly in the 1900s. Sun Yat-sen led a successful rebellion and set up a republic, though it was dominated by regional warlords. Chiang Kai-shek united the country in the 1920s and 1930s, but he was overthrown by Mao Zedong in 1949. Mao set up a Communist government that was officially atheistic. Churches were tolerated and controlled. Mao determined that foreigners would not humiliate China again, so the Communists forced churches to take an antiforeign stand (the "Christian Manifesto" of 1950), and foreign missionaries were forced out.

The Three-Self Reform Movement (later called the Three-Self Patriotic Movement) sought to bring churches into line with Communist goals—self-government, self-support, and self-propagation. Still, the church bore up under such pressure. The removal of missionaries weakened it, to some extent, but also forced the Chinese church to fend for itself, which it did quite well.

Things got worse in 1966. Mao, the aging revolutionary, may have felt his revolution slipping away. His Great Leap Forward program of 1958–1960 had failed, and modernists in his party were restless. He launched a savage Cultural Revolution, stirring up hysteria, especially among young people, against any vestige of foreign influence. Even Communist leaders were not exempt from denunciation or arrest. There was massive rioting. Artistic and academic pursuits were severely curtailed. Of course, church activities were, too. All places of worship were closed and Christian meetings forbidden. Mao himself was practically deified. The "little red book" of Mao's sayings was read and memorized while Bibles were burned.

Though the rioting soon waned, the policies remained in effect until 1976. Both Mao and his right-hand man, Zhou Enlai, died that year. Deng Xiaoping, a moderate who had been ousted, returned to power and began introducing modernizations. Most notably, the "Gang of Four" who led the Cultural Revolution were arrested and tried.

China still opposed Christianity, but the hysteria had subsided. By 1979, churches were allowed to reopen. (Actually, two churches in Beijing had been opened in 1972, at the request of Christian diplomats from Africa and Indonesia, but these were attended mostly by foreigners.) Also in 1979, the Three-Self Patriotic Movement was reopened, with a gifted spokesman, Bishop K. H. Ting, urging the reunion of all Protestant churches. The government expressed official toleration of the churches that unite with this movement, but many of the house churches remain fearful of government control.

Yet, as tensions eased, many Christians began to talk about their ordeals. When the churches closed, they had to meet in small groups, in private homes. Rather than discouraging growth, this fostered it. Christian families found strength from such fellowship and influenced those around them. There was no national organization, but one house-church might meet occasionally with a neighboring one. Teachers, including many women, would travel discreetly from gathering to gathering. There was persecution and arrest, but there were also times when local officials winked at Christian meetings— because they knew the Christians were hard workers and valuable citizens.

Not since the early fourth century had such a substantial house-church movement been seen. The circumstances—government oppression— were similar, and so were the results. The numbers are astounding: one county had 4,000 Christians before the Communist takeover; now it has

90,000. In one major city, only 1 percent of the people were Christians in 1949, now it's 10 percent; one village had 10 believers in 1945, now it has 250.

What has caused this growth? Experts have been studying it. Simplicity, they say. Hardship has resulted in purity of faith, a spirit of caring, strong lay leadership, devotion to prayer, and trust in Christ's lordship. As hateful as the measures of the Cultural Revolution were, they have resulted in a Christian faith that is stripped of the accoutrements of Western culture. The Chinese have developed a truly indigenous church.

No one knows the number of Christians in China. Estimates vary widely. All agree, however, that the multiplication of Christians under the communist governments has been astounding. It may indeed represent one of the most dramatic expansions of the faith in the history of the church.

Illustration Sources

Date	Person or Event	Source
64	*Fire in Rome*	The Mansell Collection
70	*Titus*	Italian Government Travel Office
C. 156	*Polycarp*	BGC Museum
196	*Tertullian*	Canton Baptist Temple Company, Canton, OH
C 205	*Origen*	Willet Studios, Philadelphia, PA
270	*Anthony*	National Gallery of Art, Washington, Samuel H. Kress Collection
325	*Council of Nicea*	North Wind Picture Archives
385	*Bishop Ambrose*	The Mansell Collection
405	*Jerome*	National Gallery of Art, Washington, Samuel H. Kress Collection
432	*Patrick*	The Mansell Collection
563	*Columba*	The Mansell Collection
590	*Gregory I*	The Mansell Collection
664	*Synod of Whitby*	The Mansell Collection
716	*Boniface*	The Mansell Collection
731	*Bede*	The Mansell Collection
732	*Battle of Tours*	North Wind Picture Archives
1095	*Crusades*	North Wind Picture Archives
1115	*Bernard*	Tony Lane
1215	*Innocent III*	The Mansell Collection
1273	*Thomas Aquinas*	Datafoto
1378	*Catherine of Siena*	Lombardi—Sienne
C. 1380	*Wycliffe*	Painting, *The Dawn of the Reformation,* by W. F. Yeames
1456	*Gutenberg*	Religious News Service Photo
1478	*Spanish Inquisition*	North Wind Picture Archives
1498	*Savonarola*	Canton Baptist Temple Company
1512	*Sistine Chapel*	Italian Government Travel Office
1534	*Henry VIII*	From the portrait by Holbein
1545	*Council of Trent*	The Mansell Collection
1572	*St Bartholomew's Day*	North Wind Picture Archives
1620	*The Mayflower Compact*	North Wind Picture Archives
1678	*Bunyan*	American Baptist Historical Society

1707	*Watts*	BGC Museum
1735	*Great Awakening*	BGC Museum
1738	*John Wesley*	Ken Bloom Gateway Films
1793	*Carey*	Board of International Ministries, American Baptist Churches
1812	*Judsons*	BGC Museum
1830	*N J Darby*	BGC Museum
1830	*Finney*	Oberlin College Archives
1854	*Hudson Taylor*	Canton Baptist Temple Company, Canton, OH
1857	*Livingstone*	BGC Museum
1910	*Fundamentals*	BGC Museum
1919	*Barth*	Religious News Service/World Council of Churches
1921	*First Christian radio broadcast*	BGC Museum
1945	*Bonhoeffer*	Trinity Films
1948	*World Council of Churches*	Religious News Service Photo
1949	*Billy Graham*	BGC Museum

Other illustrations courtesy of Christian History Institute.

Index

The following entries are designed to help readers cross-reference major events and people. Those entries already included in pages 7–9 have not been reproduced here.